Contents

3 Editorial: Human Beings Thinking Like God in and for 'these last days'

7 *Jeannine K. Brown,* Interpreting Gentile Women in Matthew: Misrepresentation, Misappropriation, and a Missed Chance

25 *Alan H. Cadwallader,* Orality and Gospel Research: Revisiting Mark's Gospel

49 *Keith Dyer,* Making a Mark: Biography, Gospel, Apocalypse?

65 *Chris Seglenieks,* The Divine Identity of Jesus in John 4

81 *Marie McInnes,* David in the Gospels and Acts

93 *Mary J. Marshall,* The Rise and Rise of James the Just in Luke–Acts

109 *Christoph Stenschke,* '… at the same time he hoped that money would be given to him by Paul': Corruption in the Book of Acts and its Implications

Book Reviews

125 *Robyn Faith Walsh.* The Origins of Early Christian Literature: Contextualizing the New Testament within Greco-Roman Literary Culture (Cambridge: Cambridge University Press, 2021)

128 *Benjamin L. Gladd.* Handbook on the Gospels (Grand Rapids: Baker Academic, 2021)

130 *Eric Eve.* Relating the Gospels: Memory, Imitation and the Farrer Hypothesis (LNTS 592. London: T&T Clark, 2021)
Eric Eve. Solving the Synoptic Puzzle: Introducing the Case for the Farrer Hypothesis (Eugene, OR: Cascade Books, 2021)

135 *Daniel Daley.* God's Will and Testament: Inheritance in the Gospel of Matthew and Jewish Tradition (Waco: Baylor University Press, 2021)

137 *Bernardo K. Cho.* Royal Messianism and the Jerusalem Priesthood in the Gospel of Mark (LNTS 607. London: T&T Clark, 2019)

139 *Brittany E. Wilson.* The Embodied God: Seeing the Divine in Luke-Acts and the Early Church (New York: Oxford University Press, 2022)

141 *Kylie Crabbe.* Luke/Acts and the End of History (BZNW 238. Berlin/Boston: Walter de Gruyter, 2019)

144 *Nickolas A. Fox.* The Hermeneutics of Social Identity in Luke-Acts (Eugene, OR: Pickwick Publications, 2021)

146 *J. D. Atkins.* The Doubt of the Apostles and the Resurrection Faith of the Early Church: The Post-Resurrection Appearance Stories of the Gospels in Ancient Reception and Modern Debate (WUNT 2.495. Tübingen: Mohr Siebeck, 2019)

149 *David R. Bauer.* The Book of Acts as Story: A Narrative-Critical Study (Grand Rapids: Baker Academic, 2021)

151 *Arco den Heijer.* Portraits of Paul's Performance in the Book of Acts: Luke's Apologetic Strategy in the Depiction of Paul as Messenger of God (WUNT 2.556. Tübingen: Mohr-Siebeck, 2021)

153 *Eckhard J. Schnabel.* Jesus in Jerusalem: The Last Days (Grand Rapids: Eerdmans, 2018)

Human Beings Thinking Like God in and for 'these last days'

According to the Biblical account, the temptation to *be* like God, by usurping his position as the determiner of what is good and what is evil, is as old as Eve and Adam (Gen 3:5). It became a characteristic of 'the present evil age', from which we need rescuing (Gal 1:4). However, the call to *think* like the God we are not, instead of like the human beings that we are, came from Jesus of Nazareth (Mark 8:33). For Jesus, this was to become a characteristic of 'these last days' before the arrival of the new age, for which he rescues us (Luke 19:10). Jesus called for thinking in the light of the kingdom of God that will shape the future, in such a way that it already begins to shape the present. 'Thy kingdom come'.

Human thoughts are ideological thoughts, so often serving some cause of world domination driven by the thoughts of a few, but always to be inflicted upon the many. Human thoughts construct a view of the world as (a certain segment of) humanity sees it. Such human thoughts may have a pedigree, respectable or otherwise. They operate within the framework of certain assumptions and presuppositions which, once accepted, generate a pathway for thought which largely determines the conclusions that may or must be drawn from that thinking process. They might be intensely personal or predictably collective. They may unite some, or they might polarise many. They may be acceptable to society as currently constituted, or they might be cancelled by the noisy classes seeking to control how society ought to be. But whatever their character, they remain human thoughts. Perhaps with rhetorical extremity Jesus not only pitted such thinking against that of God, but firmly associated it with the one he called 'the enemy', who, in biblical thought, goes way back to humanity's original failed temptation. 'Get behind me Satan'.

If the last two issues of *JGAR*, launched in the pandemic, required some comment upon the plague itself, perhaps the feature that requires comment in this *JGAR*, in these latter days of the pandemic, is the polarisation that has been caused by pandemic responses advocated by big government, big money, and big media. Ideologically driven, this human thinking has brought another plague on all our houses. Despite the ideological bloodshed of the twentieth century, the lessons of that century have apparently still not been learned—as if the same human thinking can be applied in a different century with a different outcome? So far, that doesn't seem to be going so well. And the ideological bloodshed seems to be spattering many different floors. Even theological and biblical conferences now feel more like ideologically divided political arenas, rather than being characterised by a common endeavour at listening to our ancient texts, in order to bring their different voice into our divided world with a perspective that looks to God's greater program of the restoration of all things—his ends, through his means. In dismissing human thinking as being associated with the root of all evil, Jesus proposed a prophetic, visionary, even apocalyptic alternative. Seek God's kingdom and his righteousness. Deliver us from this time of testing. Rescue us from our flawed human projects. 'Thy will be done on earth as it is in heaven'.

As a small offering to our global problems the 2023 Centre for Gospels and Acts Research biennial conference will convene on 28–29 September 2023, under the banner:

God Beyond Ideology. Rediscovering Theology through Narrative.

Keynote addresses from Greg Forbes and Denise Powell will tease out aspects of the move from the Human Narrative towards the Divine Narrative that promises Transformation of human life. Parallel papers will explore further aspects of this most significant issue. How can Gospels and Acts Research get beyond simply further propagating or parodying the various ideological positions that so deeply divide our contemporary world? Do these stories centring upon Jesus of Nazareth speak to this world about God? Do they speak with God? Do they speak for God? How do contemporary readers hear these ancient texts anew? Do these texts from the past bring any message for the present that might shape the future? If so, how can it be told afresh, and how can it be heard? Can Jesus of Nazareth find a voice and gain a hearing once again through these stories about him?

As one positive result of the pandemic, the necessary experiments in socially-distanced conferences have left their legacy. As the Call for Papers now goes out, it announces that the conference will cater for both face-to-face AND online attendance and presentation. Pre-recording of papers will also be possible to allow for asynchronous presentation. One advantage that immediately presents itself is that those who may have been precluded from attending, due to the tyranny of distance, may now participate in the proceedings in one form or another. For the Call for Papers and registration details, see the SCD website www.scd.edu.au.

Perhaps the offerings of this present issue of *JGAR* might also be described in terms of Jesus' polarity between thoughts human and thoughts divine.

Although God made us 'male and female', human thinking continues to struggle to think like God about this most fundamental aspect of human life. Revisiting the women in Matthew's Gospel—so often misrepresented, misappropriated, or simply missed—**Jeannine K. Brown** seeks to recover their impact upon the Gospel and their past and present theological significance.

Jesus reiterated his program in the same terms as the prophet Isaiah, to speak the word of God to those who see but don't see; who hear but don't hear or understand. Human thinking takes place in a world experienced through our senses, but without the turning of the heart those senses do not bring the forgiveness and healing of God (Mark 4:10; Matt 13:13–15). But nevertheless the gospel of God comes to us through those same senses, and the promise of proper hearing is that the world will be seen and understood with the eyes and mind of God. In the light of Jesus' sense-mingling challenge to 'see how you hear' (Mark 4:24), **Alan H. Cadwallader**'s delightful discussion of the oral dimension of the gospel brings an innovative invitation to attenuate attention on the oral/aural aura of the Gospels. For, as **Keith Dyer** also reminds us, our texts do not bring us a word written on tablets of stone, but on human hearts through human ears. Despite the many attempts to classify the genre of the Gospels according to categories derived from comparison between other written texts, Keith asks whether this is an exercise in the application of 'high culture' that threatens to ossify the impact of Jesus on the masses which nevertheless keeps bubbling up from below? Or, to put the question in another way, perhaps we can ask whether this human thinking about genre allows the Gospel reader to hear and see afresh, so that they can think God's thoughts after him?

Examining Jesus' encounter with the Samaritan woman (John 4), **Chris Seglenieks** probes beyond the merely human perception of the Messiah to uncover features pointing towards his divine identity. In a follow-up to her previous article in *JGAR* 4, **Marie McInnes** explores what the readers of the Gospels and Acts might hear in the frequent references to David, and what these might evoke for their perceptions of Jesus. As they hear, what will they see about him, what will they understand about his role in God's wider purposes?

But although he clearly set himself at the centre of the purposes of God, what was the human context in which Jesus of Nazareth was operating? **Mary J. Marshall** teases out a hypothesis concerning the historical roots of the rise of his brother James to prominence in the early church, assembling plausible evidence for placing Jesus and James in the context of a family with connections to the Essenes. Perhaps this influence contributed to the division within earliest Christianity between Jewish and Gentile believers? (Ah, division—another familiar product of human thinking?)

Thinking human thoughts rather than divine may also lie behind the theme of human corruption exposed in the book of Acts by **Christoph Stenschke**. This book that traces the development of the Jesus movement from Judea to Rome portrays instances of corruption, sometimes on the surface of the narrative and sometimes just below it. The gospel of the Nazarene went into a world characterised by the misuse of power and by greed, both of which go hand-in-hand with corruption. And so it does today.

Just as in the first century, so too in the twentyfirst. As the gospel spreads with its call to think like God, it passes through a world that is populated by human thinking with all its negative consequences for human life. The struggle to live as created, male and female, united by our common humanity. Divided by other arbitrary divisions. Corrupted by inner greed and outer power games. What a world it was. What a world it is.

But this is the world into which the gospel of God went, and into which it still goes. Women have theological significance. Christianity is a grass roots movement with its own way of expressing itself, perhaps defying imposed high-culture classification. The gospel about the Christ is a message that comes through the senses and especially through hearing, with all the delights in the beauty of words and sounds, rhythmicalising together. It has deep roots in Israel's ancient past, with David the king forming a paradigm for prophetic fulfilment in Jesus of Nazareth. For all his connections with the human movements of his time, and with real human family, a thoroughly human king, but for those with eyes to see, perhaps a king that is more than human? Rejecting human thinking in favour of thinking like God about the world arises from firstly thinking like God about the descendant of David who was acclaimed as Son of God. The one who taught us to pray 'Our Father in heaven'.

In the midst of the greed, abuse of power, divisions, struggles between the sexes, political posturing and generalised corruption, there is something in the Gospels and Acts that still needs to be said to a world that still needs to hear it. Never has there been a better time to engage in research in these fundamental documents of the Christian movement, and never has there been a better time to communicate clearly the results of this research. In these last days, these documents continue to invite us into a different kind of world, not through thinking human thoughts, but by thinking like God. Hearing, seeing, turning, healing. Not in order to *be* like God, but in order to *think* like God for the sake of this world in these last days.

Peter G. Bolt
Executive Editor

Interpreting Gentile Women in Matthew
Misrepresentation, Misappropriation, and a Missed Chance

JEANNINE K. BROWN

Abstract

Although not many women appear in Matthew's storyline, the evangelist includes at least six Gentiles in his mix of female characters. As women and as Gentiles (of various ethnicities), they sit doubly outside of the centres of power and access in Matthew's storyline. We could also note that they have not always fared well at the hands of male interpreters of Matthew. Their portrayal has often been characterised by misrepresentation (especially in the case of the four women in the genealogy), misappropriation (the Canaanite woman), and what I call 'a missed chance' for significance (Pilate's wife). The goal of this paper is to take another look at these women to see what we might learn about their impact on Matthew's story as well as their theological significance for the evangelist and for contemporary Christian interpretation.[1]

I have spent my career studying Matthew's Gospel, from my dissertation, to three commentaries, to a dozen or so articles and essays focused on Matthew, fully or substantially.[2] I was not drawn to Matthew because of his portrayal of women. In fact, I focused initially, in my dissertation, on the Matthean portrayal of the twelve disciples—all men.[3] Matthew is not renowned for his attention to women, whether female characters or female interests. Luke is typically the Gospel commended for most attention to female disciple-types.[4]

Yet, as I have studied Matthew over the years, I have increasingly spent time with the women of Matthew and found much to appreciate in them. One distinctive feature of this small but illustrious group is that almost a third of the women in Matthew (counted as characters or those women named by Matthew in his narrative commentary) are Gentiles. There are the four Gentiles that Matthew highlights at the front of Jesus' genealogy (Matt. 1:3,5,6), the Canaanite woman and

---

1 This article was originally a presented paper for the joint session of the Matthew and Christian Theology program units, Annual Meeting of the Society of Biblical Literature (virtual meeting), December 8, 2020.
2 For a selection of my Matthean work, see bibliography.
3 Brown, *Disciples*.
4 Although even here the precise role and value of women in Luke-Acts is a matter of debate.

her daughter from Jesus' Galilean ministry (15:21–28), and Pilate's wife who appears on the scene ever so briefly during Jesus' trial (27:19).[5]

Certainly, these women fit Matthew's interest in the motif of Gentile inclusion. Considering this distinctive (Matthew's sizable percentage of *Gentile* women), I suggest we might learn more from this small band of Gentile women scattered across Matthew. The goal of this article is to take a closer look, against the backdrop of the tendencies in male-dominated scholarship to skew at times our reading of these seven women by misrepresentation, misappropriation, and, in the case, of Pilate's wife, what I refer to as a missed chance. In the final turn, I explore some implications for theologising with Matthew for Christian reflection.

1. Four Gentile Women in Matthew's Genealogy: A Tendency Toward Misrepresentation

Almost as soon as Matthew begins his Gospel, he introduces the reader to four women from Israel's history: Tamar (1:3), Rahab, Ruth (1:5), and 'the wife of Uriah' (Bathsheba; 1:6).[6] These four are woven into the otherwise patrilineal genealogy of Jesus—a genealogy that concludes with a fifth woman, Mary ('Jesus…was conceived by Mary'; 1:16). A key interpretive issue is whether the four women at the front of the genealogy are meant to be connected integrally and thematically with Mary at its conclusion. Before moving to interpretive questions, however, it is instructive to hear something from the history of interpretation.

Any number of early church writers (the 'church fathers,' i.e. male interpreters for the most part) read these women as the 'sinners' in Jesus' genealogy. Jerome wrote,

> In the Savior's genealogy it is remarkable that there is no mention of holy women, but only those whom Scripture reprehends, so that [we can understand that] he who had come for the sake of sinners, since he was born from sinful women, blots out the sins of everyone (Commentary on Matthew, 1.3).[7]

In a sermon, Severus (fifth–sixth century) offers this interpretation, which resembles Jerome's sentiment:

> These were women with whom they [i.e., Judah and David] became united by fornication and adultery. By this means the genealogy revealed that it is our very sinful nature that Christ himself came to heal (Severus, Cathedral Sermons, Homily 94).[8]

Another early sermon by an anonymous church father read Rahab and Bathsheba typologically. This choice produced a more positive reading of Rahab (she is a more noble figure in the end) and helps him to connect her typologically to the church. 'Rahab the harlot was a figure of the church […] For although the church was once a worshiper of idols, she became the companion of angels, the bride of Christ and the daughter of God' (Anonymous, Incomplete Work of Matthew, Homily 1).[9]

---

5   We could note an eighth female Gentile (mentioned rather than sketched as a character), this one referenced by Jesus in 12:42: 'the queen of the South'.
6   All translations of the biblical text, unless otherwise noted, are my own, with most drawn from my commentary translation in Brown and Roberts, Matthew.
7   Jerome and Scheck, *Commentary on Matthew*, 59. As Levine, 'Gospel of Matthew', 467, rightly interjects, 'were "sin" the genealogy's concern, then many of the men listed would be better candidates'.
8   Simonetti, *Matthew 1–13*, 6.
9   Simonetti, *Matthew 1–13*, 7.

With this author's pairing of David and Bathsheba, however, David comes off much better in the analogy.

> Even in his worst sin lay the mystery of Christ and the church. David, taking delight on his high roof, saw the very beautiful Bathsheba bathing, desired her and beckoned her, though she was married to a Hittite man. There is a prefiguring even here, though it may seem unlikely. Christ, while in his high heaven and still joyful in his divinity, saw in advance the very attractive church of his people displeasing him with sordid behavior and weakened in good works, when it was still the devil's bride. He laid eyes on her, loved her and drew her to himself (Anonymous, Incomplete Work of Matthew, Homily 1).[10]

But we don't need to go back a thousand years and more to hear the propensity of male interpreters to read these four women in scandalous terms. A figure as influential and thoughtful as Raymond Brown leans toward scandalous associations in his analysis of the Matthean genealogy.

> These women were held up as examples of how God used the unexpected to triumph over human obstacles and intervenes on behalf of His planned Messiah. It is the combination of *the scandalous or irregular union* and of divine intervention through the women that explains best Matthew's choice in the genealogy.[11]

This is a common view in contemporary scholarship, especially when the four women are read as integrally connected to Mary at the conclusion of the genealogy, since the birth of Jesus suggests an irregular union—and uniquely so for Matthew. Nonetheless, this reading is problematic in that it jumps too quickly to a negative and wholly sexual assessment of these four women, something male-dominated readings are prone to do. Yet the conclusion of the story of Tamar and Judah in Genesis 38 highlights her vindication, when Judah grants that Tamar has shown herself to be more 'righteous' [צְדָקָה] than he was in her actions (38:26). And Rahab and Ruth both turn from their own gods to acknowledge and commit to Yahweh and are implicitly commended by their respective narrators for doing so (Josh. 2:11; Ruth 1:16–17). Additionally, interpretation of the story of David and Bathsheba has been rife with conjecture that has spread culpability evenly between the two, with little textual support for this reading. More to the point for understanding Matthew's intentions, Jewish reflection on these four women (including what we hear elsewhere in the New Testament; e.g. James 2) was typically positive, for example, Philo's evaluation of Tamar as virtuous (*Deus Imm.* 136–137) and rabbinic portraits of Bathsheba as without fault in her interactions with King David (*b. San.* 107a–b).[12]

These few examples demonstrate that misrepresentations of these four women are commonplace in the history of interpretation up the present. Particularly persistent is the tendency to reduce these women to the sexual encounters that resulted in their offspring. One might push back to note that this is a genealogy, which by form and structure places emphasis on the act of conception for each person mentioned. Yet I'd suggest that this is not how we tend to read the men in the genealogy. Do we, for example, immediately and necessarily recall when reading 'Abraham begot Isaac' (NKJV) Abraham's long-standing infertility with Sarah (or in contrast his success in having a child with Hagar)? And if Matthew had omitted reference to these four women, would the audience

---

10 Simonetti, *Matthew 1–13*, 8.
11 Brown, *Birth of the Messiah*, 73–74 (emphasis mine). While Brown presses against Jerome's view to some extent, he still refers to Tamar as 'a seductress' and Uriah's wife as 'an adulteress' (72); and he suggests that Sarah, Rebekah, and Rachel are unmentioned 'because there was nothing scandalous about their union' (74).
12 See other rabbinic references in Davies and Allison, *Matthew*, 1:170.

have read into 'David begot Solomon' the rape of Bathsheba by David as the sum total of his role in Jesus' genealogy? I would suggest we think more broadly about the person mentioned than just the conception attributed to them. So why limit these women to the situation surrounding the conception of their children? Why hyper-sexualise them?[13] As Anna Case-Winters notes, 'Much has been made of issues around sexuality for these women [...] However, this really does not distinguish them from the men in the list (!)'.[14]

The most compelling reading of the four women in Matthew 1:3–6—the one that fits the Matthean evidence best—identifies them as Gentiles in Jesus' genealogy. Tamar seems to be a Canaanite (38:2; Philo, *Virt.* 220–22),[15] as is Rahab, a resident of Jericho (Josh. 2:1). The narrator of Ruth emphasises multiple times across the story her identity as a Moabite (1:4,22; 2:2,6,21; 4:5,10). Bathsheba has typically been understood to be an Israelite, since she is referred to as the daughter of Eliam (2 Sam. 11:3), who is often assumed to be Eliam, son of Ahithophel the Gilonite, one of David's counselors (15:12; 23:24–39). Yet these two men are not necessarily the same person simply because they share the same name. Bathsheba could be a Hittite, for example, as she married a Hittite.[16] In fact, Matthew's inclusion of her as 'the wife of Uriah' (τῆς τοῦ Οὐρίου; Matt. 1:6) presses the astute reader (one who knows the Jewish Scriptures) to hear a Gentile association, regardless of her known or unknown ethnicity. The longer attribution, 'Uriah the Hittite', occurs in over a third of Old Testament references to Uriah.[17]

This reading is not absent from the history of interpretation, although it is not dominant. We hear it in Isho'dad of Merv, a ninth-century Syriac commentator, who wrote:

> But again, because the Apostles were commanded to go forth and preach to all nations, they wished to teach us by the mention of these women, that even the Gentiles had partnership in the descent of the tribe from which the Messiah arose, and that if they repent, there is nothing to prevent them from the full remission of sins, that they may also become the Israel of God.[18]

While it is possible to highlight the non-Jewish identity of these four women in a generic way, a better way forward is to give attention to the specific ethnicities of these and other Gentile women in Matthew. Tamar and Rahab are Canaanites (as are the two women of Matt. 15:21–28); Ruth is a Moabite; Bathsheba may by Hittite or may represent the Hittites via her marriage to Uriah. Later in the article, Pilate's wife—a Roman—will be addressed. Following the lead of Love Sechrest, it can be helpful to attend to 'the particular identities' of Gentile characters in Matthew.[19] Doing so helps the interpreter of Matthew to avoid constructing a simple binary between Jews

---

13 On the tendency to sexualise women in their roles in biblical narrative, see Levine, 'Discharging Responsibility' on the woman of Matt. 9:20–22. She writes, 'In the same way that biblical commentators usually assert that Luke's "Woman who was a sinner" must have been a prostitute (as if women could commit no sin other than one involving the body in general and sexuality in particular), so too do they usually insist that if a woman has a medical problem, the problem must have something to do with "female troubles"' (381).

14 Case-Winters, *Matthew*, 24.

15 While this cannot be fully demonstrated from the text of Genesis, she certainly wouldn't have been an Israelite (an anachronism for any of the wives of the patriarchs, in any event). Bauckham has an extensive discussion of this issue and highlights Philo's perspective for an understanding of Matthew 1 (*Gospel Women*, 33). Philo identifies her as 'from Palestine Syria' (i.e. a Canaanite) and as a 'foreigner' (Philo, *Virt.* 221–22).

16 Bauckham, *Gospel Women*, 22.

17 See Brown and Roberts, *Matthew*, 25–26, 413–414.

18 Gibson, *Isho'dad of Merv*, 8. Cited in Boxall, 81.

19 With Sechrest, 'Enemies', 95–96, focusing her exploration on the Roman centurion (8:5-13) and the Canaanite woman of 15:21-28, as she describes how they represent two different kinds of enemies in Matthew.

and non-Jews, an insight drawn from Wongi Park's ethnoracial reading of Matthew.[20] Instead, by noticing the variety of ethnicities represented in Matthew, we can avoid viewing 'Gentile' as a non-ethnoracial category, in other words, as a universal category that then can be contrasted with the particularism of Jewish identity.[21]

Mary's presence at the conclusion of the genealogy is the central obstacle raised to interpreting these four women as signaling inclusion of a variety of ethnoracial identities in the lineage of Jesus. Mary, the fifth woman of the genealogy, is not Gentile but Jewish. If we move through the genealogy with the assumption that all five women function together for Matthew, the Gentile (or ethnoracial) explanation falters. Yet, as Richard Bauckham has helpfully argued, 1:16 shifts significantly from the formulaic pattern of verses 2–15: 'A begot B' and so on. A break occurs in verse 16 because Joseph does not beget Jesus. This is the 'conundrum' of the genealogy, which Matthew goes about solving in 1:18–25, via Joseph's formal adoption of Jesus into his family and so into his lineage.[22] As this break occurs, Matthew introduces Mary, 'of whom [ἧς, feminine] Jesus was begotten'. As Bauckham argues,

> Mary appears in the genealogy because Matthew cannot otherwise explain Joseph's relationship to Jesus. This most fundamental reason why Mary appears in the genealogy has no precedent in the other four women, and so it is not at all obvious why their function in the genealogy should have to be related to Mary.[23]

Anders Runesson concurs that Mary's role in the genealogy is exceptional rather than integrally connected to the four women who appear earlier in it.[24]

If Matthew includes Tamar, Rahab, Ruth, and 'the wife of Uriah' in Jesus' genealogy because of their identity as Gentiles, then the reader can also hear an emphasis on their 'righteous or loyal behaviour'. They outshine their male counterparts in the Scriptural stories about them, as Amy-Jill Levine argues.[25] If so, Matthew is accenting *'ethnic origin in combination with their good deeds toward Israel and the Jewish people.'*[26] And as we pull back to look across Matthew, 'these women are connected [...] to a handful of Gentiles who appear in Matthew's narrative to signal God's inclusion of Gentiles in the restored kingdom',[27] including the Canaanite woman and her daughter, and Pilate's wife. In this way, Tamar, Rahab, Ruth, and Bathsheba guide the reader toward an ethnically diverse and inclusive vision for the salvation God is enacting through Jesus.[28]

---

20 Park, *Race and Ethnicity*.
21 Park, *Race and Ethnicity*, 64. Park incisively addresses decided tendencies in mainstream scholarship to 'deracialise' Matthew's Gospel, for example, by defining the Matthean community as a 'non-ethnoracial entity that exists independently of first-century Judaism'. My delineation of the variety of ethnicities within the Matthean category of 'Gentile' is an attempt to mitigate such 'deracialisation'.
22 Brown and Roberts, *Matthew*, 29.
23 Bauckham, *Gospel Women*, 21–22.
24 As Runesson, 'Giving Birth', 313, suggests, 'These women were in different ways part of the preconditions necessary for the Davidic line to be kept intact [...], but Mary's position is exceptional, which is indicated also by the virginal conception that follows'.
25 Levine, 'Gospel of Matthew', 467.
26 Runesson, 'Giving Birth', 313 (italics original).
27 Brown, *Matthew*, 12.
28 As I discuss below, attention to this inclusive vision should not come at the expense of the realities of Jewish particularism, which Matthew and Matthew's Jesus assume and affirm. As Levine, 'Anti-Judaism', 413, proposes, 'The point is not Jewish exclusivism; it is rather history, and salvation history' (which is grounded in Jewish temporal priority).

2. A Canaanite Woman and Her Daughter: A Tendency Toward Misappropriation

The next Gentile women we encounter in Matthew are unnamed—a Canaanite woman and her daughter (15:21–28). The woman pleads with Jesus for her daughter's healing, whom she describes as 'tormented by a demon' (15:22). She is first ignored by Jesus and then told he has been sent 'only to the lost sheep of the house of Israel' (15:24). As she continues to plead with him, Jesus demurs one more time: 'It is not good to take the children's bread and toss it to the house dogs' (15:26). Her reply that even the dogs receive crumbs from the table, amazes Jesus, who immediately heals her daughter (15:27–28).

A couple of tendencies are evident in the history of interpretation that continue to impact the current interpretive milieu. First, not surprisingly, readings of this encounter tend toward a desire to get Jesus 'off the hook' for what seems a decided lack of mercy, verging on rudeness toward this woman, who was later called Justa.[29] A key facet of this strategy involves proposing that Jesus responds as he does the first three times to test the woman to show either her faith or her humility. We hear this interpretive strain already in John Chrysostom and Augustine (late fourth–early fifth centuries), as well as in contemporary scholarship.

Chrysostom interprets Jesus' hesitation as a test when he writes, 'So we might surmise that this is the reason he put her off, that he might proclaim aloud this saying ['great is your faith,' v.28] and that he might crown the woman: "Be it done for you as you desire"' (The Gospel of Matthew, Homily 52.3).[30] Augustine proposes that 'she was ignored, not that mercy might be denied but that desire might be enkindled [and] that humility might be praised' (Sermon 77.1).[31]

At first glance, Luther, in a sermon on the faith of the Canaanite woman, moves away from this testing framework by acknowledging the potentially problematic nature of Jesus' words. He writes, 'Christ is nowhere pictured as pitiless as in this gospel [in this passage]'.[32] He continues, 'Faith takes Christ captive in His word, when He's angriest, and makes out of His cruel words a comforting inversion'.[33] Yet Luther concludes by revealing his agreement with the view that Jesus was all along intending to test Justa:

> We see here why the Lord presented Himself so unyielding and refused to hear her, not because He wanted to present an unfriendly image as not wanting to help her, but rather that her faith might be so evident, that the Jews who were the children and heirs of the kingdom might learn from the gentile, who was not among the children and had no inheritance, how they were to believe in Christ and place all confidence in Him.[34]

Luther's negative assessment of 'the Jews' is also apparent in this sermon, especially when we note that the only characters in the episode in Matthew are Jesus, his disciples, and the woman and her daughter (15:21–28).[35]

Much contemporary Gospels scholarship continues to foster the tendency to portray Jesus as testing Justa to draw out her faith, and as a result to exonerate Jesus from rudeness and/or

---

29 Although she is left unnamed by Matthew, in the history of interpretation she has been referred to as Justa, so I have used that name in my discussion of her interpretive history.
30 Simonetti, *Matthew 14–28*, 30.
31 Simonetti, *Matthew 14–28*, 27.
32 Luther, in his *Reminiscere* Sunday sermon (1534); Thornton and Varenne, *Faith and Freedom*, 127.
33 Thornton and Varenne, *Faith and Freedom*, 128.
34 Thornton and Varenne, *Faith and Freedom*, 128–129.
35 Jesus leaves Jewish leaders, present in 15:1–20, to travel to the vicinity of Tyre and Sidon (15:21).

ethnocentrism. David Turner is characteristic in his suggestion that Jesus 'is evidently testing her faith'.[36] Michael Wilkins writes, 'In a sense, Jesus is testing her'.[37] Even when scholars are hesitant to embrace this idea fully, they often raise the possibility, with the result that Jesus is protected from the full force of his words.[38] Yet as Case-Winters offers, 'Perhaps it is better to face the text head on'.[39] If Jesus is not testing this Canaanite woman's faith and is truly hesitant to minister to this woman, his words at 15:24 provide a clear reason for his hesitancy: 'I have been sent only to the lost sheep of the house of Israel'. We see a similar moment of reluctance at 8:7, where Jesus asks of a (Roman) centurion requesting healing for a servant: 'Should I come and heal him?' The grammar of 8:7 suggests that these words are a question; the use of an explicit subject (ἐγώ) is redundant except for emphasis and therefore suggests Jesus wonders why the centurion is approaching him. 'In this rendering, the oddity of a gentile asking a Jewish healer for help is emphasized'.[40]

In this reading, Jesus stays true to his divinely guided mission to Israel (10:5–6; 15:24) during his earthly ministry, apart from exceptional cases where a Gentile supplicant shows remarkable faith exhibited in their 'striking perseverance'.[41] Jesus diverges from the immediate focus and scope of his ministry when he encounters such extraordinary situations. In such a scenario, we can affirm that Jesus learns something from the woman (Case-Winters) and is 'shown a better way' (Gnadt),[42] even as he continues to live out his ministry to Israel until after his death and resurrection when his presence will accompany his followers on a mission to all nations (cf. 28:19).[43]

A second tendency in the history of interpretation centres on the way this text about the Canaanite woman has been appropriated for use in Christian discourse. It has been easy (and not necessary always inappropriate) to view Justa as a model for the church: believers are to emulate her bold and determined faith. We can see an interesting pattern of representation and appropriation happening quite early in the text's interpretive history.

For example, Augustine reads this Canaanite woman as a 'figure of the church' and her humility as a contrast to the Jewish people who were 'puffed up with pride' and 'unwilling to respond to Christ the author of humility' (Sermon, 77.11–12).[44] Others follow a more complicated path but with similar implications. Epiphanius the Latin (late fifth, early sixth century), for instance, highlights a difference in the representative roles of the woman and her daughter. 'This woman is the mother of Gentiles, and she knew Christ through faith. Thus on behalf of her daughter (the Gentile people) she entreated the Lord. The daughter had been led astray by idolatry and sin and was severely possessed by a demon' (Interpretation of the Gospels 58).[45] Similarly,

---

36 Turner, *Matthew*, 387.
37 Wilkins, *Matthew*, 540.
38 Keener, *Matthew*, 417; France, *Matthew*, 594; Davies and Allison, *Matthew*, 2:549. Beare, *Matthew*, 342, provides a counterpoint: 'These suggestions are so many tokens of the embarrassment of commentators in their desperate attempts to get away from the incredible insolence of the saying'.
39 Case-Winters, *Matthew*, 201.
40 Brown and Roberts, *Matthew*, 85. These two accounts (8:5–13; 15:21–28) have a number of features in common, including a moment of hesitation on Jesus' part in the face of a Gentile supplicant, the requests for healing on behalf of another person, and the affirmation of their abundant faith (8:10; 15:28). Reading Jesus' initial response as a question also fits with the centurion's subsequent acknowledgment of his own unworthiness for Jesus to visit his home and of faith in Jesus' authority (8:8); Levine, 'Matthew's Advice', 30.
41 Hagner, *Matthew*, 440.
42 Case-Winters, *Matthew*, 202; Gnadt, 'Gospel of Matthew', 622.
43 Feminist scholars also contend that this woman corrects Jesus with her more inclusive vision; e.g. Wainwright, *Shall We Look*, 88; Gnadt, 'Gospel of Matthew', 622.
44 Simonetti, *Matthew 14–28*, 31.
45 Simonetti, *Matthew 14–28*, 27.

Hilary of Poitiers considers it likely that the woman is a proselyte (e.g. showing her knowledge of the law by calling Jesus 'son of David'), with her daughter being 'a type for all the Gentile people' (who are 'in the grips of unclean spirits') (On Matthew 15.3).[46] In these portraits, the Canaanite woman, as proselyte or near-proselyte, tends to be preserved from the taint of Gentile idolatry and even the demonic (represented by her daughter), and yet she is still able to be 'the mother of Gentiles' (Epiphanius) and so a type of the Gentile church.[47]

The clear losers in this analogy are the Jewish people. As Louise Lawrence sums up such early interpretive tendencies,

> Whether as representative mother of the Jerusalem above, of the idol-worshipping Gentiles who are in need of conversion, or of the entire Gentile church, these selected fathers view this Canaanite 'mother' positively in salvation-historical terms, and frequently use her as a foil to the obtuseness and non-receptivity of the Jewish 'children'.[48]

Justa, as a stand-in for the church in her positive portrayal, leaves little room for Jews—whether Jewish believers in Jesus, such as Jesus' disciples (15:23), or even the potential for positive portraits of the Jewish people more generally (e.g. 21:9,11). As Luz notes about Jerome, 'Frequently repeated is an inventive and sharp formulation of Jerome to the effect that formerly the Jews were children and the Gentiles were dogs; now it is the other way around'.[49] Epiphanius the Latin follows suit in his suggestion that 'the unreceptive Jews were made loathsome dogs out of children' (Interpretation of the Gospels 57).[50]

Reading the Canaanite woman as Gentile representative is not, on its own, an unhelpful or inappropriate reading. Matthew may very well have intended this woman to function representatively, at least in part. As we can see from a wide-angle view of Jesus' Galilean ministry in Matthew, the evangelist portrays and highlights two Gentiles—a centurion (8:5–13) and this Canaanite woman—within a ministry in Galilee focused specifically on Israel (see 10:5–6; 15:24). He does so to accent the theme of Gentile inclusion, which has already been presaged by the women of Jesus' genealogy and the magi in the birth narrative (2:1–23; cf. 4:12–16). Yet the impact of this motif in Matthew's original context would have been significantly different from the impact of affirming this Canaanite as Gentile representative in later Matthean interpretation, especially when coupled with a denigration of Jewish people.

In Matthew's social world, the effect of this theme would be to provide a more inclusive vision of the people of God. Matthew seems to be written, in part, to encourage primarily or possibly exclusively Jewish churches in Matthew's audience toward embracing a Gentile mission. In this context, there could be no question of a replacement theology. And although the Jewish leaders (from 15:1–20) provide something of a foil for this Canaanite woman for the Matthean reader, the Galilean ministry being narrated is filled with *Jewish* people—who exhibit a wide variety of responses to Jesus and his ministry, from faith (e.g. 9:2,22,29) to curiosity (e.g. 12:22) to rejection (especially by Jewish leadership; e.g. 12:14,24). In the pericope in view, Jesus' Jewish disciples, who have been guided to go in ministry only to 'the lost sheep of the house of Israel' (cf. 10:5–6),

---

46 Simonetti, *Matthew 14–28*, 28.
47 Although Hillary, in discussing 15:24, also identifies the daughter as 'a type of the church' (On Matthew 15.4); Simonetti, *Matthew 14–28*, 28.
48 Lawrence, 'Canaanite Woman', 264–265. In her prior discussion, Lawrence has cited from Origen, Hilary (Poitiers), Epiphanius the Latin, and Theodore of Mopsuestia.
49 Luz, *Matthew 8–20*, 337.
50 Simonetti, *Matthew 14–28*, 29.

are acting on Jesus' words as they ask Jesus to send her away (15:23). And, while Jesus grants the woman's argument that dogs can eat the dropped crumbs that belong to the master's children, he does not dismiss the children's right to eat in the process.[51] A certain amount of Jewish particularity remains crucial in this passage and for Matthew's portrayal of Jesus and of his people.[52]

On the other hand, once the church has become primarily or almost exclusively Gentile in composition, emphasising the Canaanite woman as Gentile representative sets up her portrayal to define the Gentile church positively (as humble and full of faith), with Judaism becoming the foil (as proud and legalistic). As Chrysostom writes, 'Then compare her humility with the proud language of the Jews: "We are Abraham's seed and were never in bondage to any man." "We are born of God." But not so this woman' (The Gospel of Matthew, Homily 52.3).[53] In this later ecclesial context,[54] the Gentile emphasis in this text 'no longer demonstrated the power of God's love that bursts the borders of Israel; it almost exclusively justified the legitimacy of the church's status quo in history. It no longer opened new doors; it merely injured the Jews who were not present in the church'.[55]

That the Gentile church appropriated Justa by making her in their own image has a certain amount of irony, since Matthew shapes the disciples' portrayal as a foil to her characterisation. Jesus' inner circle—his most loyal followers—fall short of this Canaanite woman's courage and faith. Matthew's ideal reader, already prone to find themselves akin to the disciples in some important ways, will rightly feel some sense of distance from them here.[56] Nevertheless, while recognising this woman as an exemplar of faith (as Matthew intends), the ideal reader should be cautious of appropriating this person on the margins as a mirror of their own faith. 'Facile identification with the Canaanite woman is akin to privileged people identifying themselves unreflectively with the "hero" stories of the less advantaged'.[57] Instead, the Canaanite's 'otherness' can provide the reader with a vision of the wide embrace of the kingdom and a critique of 'narrow views of who is "worthy" of the kingdom'.[58]

3. The Wife of Pilate: A Missed Chance

The final Gentile woman to appear in Matthew is the wife of Pilate, who is mentioned briefly during Jesus' Roman trial (27:19). She warns her husband of Jesus' innocence, a truth she attributes to a dream she has had. There is little historical reference to Pilate contemporaneous to Matthew. In addition to the Gospels, Philo and Josephus refer to him quite briefly, and Tacitus mentions only his sentencing of 'Christus' (*Annals* 15.44). Some coins minted by Pilate (29–31 C.E.) and a stone inscription also attest to him.[59] About Pilate's wife we have no corroborating testimony

---

51 Levine, *Matthean Salvation History*, 152.
52 Nolland, *Matthew*, 635; Levine, 'Matthew's Advice', 474.
53 Chrystostom draws here from John's Gospel for words he ascribes to 'the Jews' (Simonetti, *Matthew 14–28*, 30).
54 In other words, 'In a situation in which the gentile church was solidly established and Jewish Christianity had practically disappeared'; Luz, *Matthew 8–20*, 341. See also Levine, 'Matthew's Advice', 39–40.
55 Luz, *Matthew 8–20*, 341.
56 Brown and Robert, *Matthew*, 422. For ways the evangelist shapes the reader through negative as well as positive portraits of discipleship, see 334–336.
57 Brown and Robert, *Matthew*, 421.
58 Brown and Robert, *Matthew*, 422.
59 Carter, *Pontius Pilate*, 12; see also McGing, 'Pontius Pilate', 416–438.

at all.[60] Yet this one who is called *Procla* in the fourth-century Gospel of Nicodemus ('The Acts of Pilate') has had a fascinating 'afterlife'.[61]

There are two prominent features of Procla's portrayal in the church's ongoing interpretation that are relevant for this discussion. First, she is portrayed fairly positively by early church fathers, like Origen, Hilary, and Asterius. Origen (second–third centuries) calls her 'blessed' because her potential future suffering was alleviated by what she suffering in her dream; and he also raises the possibility that God desired to convert her through her dream (Commentary on the Gospel of Matthew, 122).[62] Hilary (fourth century) sees her as a prototype of Gentile faith. As van der Bergh summarises Hilary's view, 'She, already "faithful" (*iam fidelis*), calls the unbelieving people—and her husband—to faith in Christ (*ad Christi fidem advocat*)'.[63] In such readings, she 'becomes a symbol of the church',[64] similar to the Canaanite woman of Matthew 15.[65] From this perspective, it is fitting and unsurprising that Procla has become revered as a saint in the Greek and Coptic churches (*Hagia Prokla*).

A second relevant facet of Procla's portrayal is her role *vis à vis* her husband—early church fathers seem more interested in how she informs Pilate's guilt or innocence rather than in her unalloyed characterisation.[66] As has often been the case for women in male-dominated history writing, she becomes most compelling to various authors as she provides evidence for her husband's portrait and ultimate fate. In this way, traditions about her have missed a chance to explore her for her own sake and on her own terms.[67]

For Chrysostom and Ambrose, because Pilate ignored his wife's warning, he is guilty of Jesus' death. Chrysostom (fourth century) notes that the suffering that Pilate's wife experiences should have made her husband more sympathetic toward her and so heed her warning (The Gospel of Matthew, Homily 86.1).[68] Chrysostom directly indicates Pilate's culpability in another sermon (on John), when he characterises Pilate by fear and a lack of wisdom. Chrysostom goes on to write that the dream his wife experienced should have been enough to 'terrify' Pilate (*In Joannem*, 85.1).[69] Ambrose (fourth century) places culpability with Pilate when he writes that, in spite of the divine origin of his wife's dream, he 'did not abstain from such a sacrilegious judgement' (*Expositio evangelii secundum Lucam*, 10.100–101).[70]

---

60 Regarding the historicity and possible sources for Matthew's brief reference to Pilate's wife, Gillman proposes the evangelist draws from legendary material about Pilate's wife (as Dibelius had earlier suggested) and identifies a possible Caesarean provenance for this interest and material based a few factors: (1) Pilate (with his wife) being a resident of Caesarea; (2) the connection of Caesarea with an interest in wives of ruling elite in Acts (Bernice in Acts 25:13—26:32 and Drusilla in Acts 24:24–26); and the discontinuance of a regulation that had forbidden provincial governors from bringing wives with them to their assignments, which likely only piqued interest in and produced legends about such women (Gillman, 'Wife of Pilate', 163–164). Compare the story of Julius Caesar's wife, Calpurnia, and her dream (Dio Cassius 44.17.1; Gillman, 'Wife of Pilate', 164).

61 Alternatively, Kany, 'Frau des Pilatus', argues that this moniker was not assigned to Pilate's wife until the early seventeenth century.

62 Origen and Heine, *Commentary of Origen*, 2:736.

63 Van der Bergh, 'Reception', 73, drawing from Hilary's commentary on Matthew (33.1).

64 Van der Bergh, 'Reception', 80.

65 The Gospel of Nicodemus portrays her as already a God-fearer or a convert to Judaism prior to her dream (2.1).

66 These writers (e.g. Origen, Chrysostom, Athanasius), also show a keen interest in how 27:19 contributes to Christology and specifically emphasis on the divinity of Christ; Van der Bergh, 'Reception', 80.

67 Referring to her as 'Mrs. Pilate', *Pontius Pilate*, 93, Carter illustrates the kind of derivative role she has held. For the most part, I have used the language Matthew provides to refer to her when exegeting the text itself. I've also used Procla to refer to her by a name when discussing the history of interpretation.

68 Simonetti, *Matthew 14-28*, 280.

69 Van der Bergh, 'Reception', 78.

70 Van der Bergh, 'Reception', 79.

Some early church fathers have a more positive characterisation of Pilate *vis á vis* his wife's warning. For these writers, Pilate—because he heeds her warning—is able to effectively wash his hands of guilt. Origen, for example, suggests that 'it was not so much Pilate that condemned him [Jesus] [...] as it was the Jewish people' (*Contra Celsum* 2.34).[71] Hilary understands Pilate's wife, because of her suffering in her dream, to have 'invited [Pilate] into the same glory of future hope'. Hilary goes on, 'Then Pilate washed his hands and to the Jewish nation declared himself innocent of the blood of the Lord' (*Commentarius in evangelium Matthaei*, 33.1).[72] While both Christian interpreters read Pilate's characterisation more positively, they do so at the expense of 'the Jews'.[73]

What is telling in each of these readings is that Procla's characterisation is routinely passed over, apart from the effect she has on her husband's portrait (or on Jesus' portrayal). Yet this tendency toward a utilitarian view of this female character amounts to a missed opportunity. There is evidence in her brief portrait that Pilate's wife not only functions as a corrective to Pilate's choice to have Jesus executed, but also offers something substantive on her own terms for understanding Matthew's purposes—Christological and ecclesial. Although brief, virtually her entire portrayal comes from her own words, other than Matthew's indication that she is Pilate's wife and has sent him a message: ἀπέστειλεν πρὸς αὐτὸν ἡ γυνὴ αὐτοῦ λέγουσα. And her own voice—though she is only given fourteen Greek words—is quite rich in Matthean vocabulary and significance: μηδὲν σοὶ καὶ τῷ δικαίῳ ἐκείνῳ· πολλὰ γὰρ ἔπαθον σήμερον κατ' ὄναρ δι' αὐτόν. At least three motifs from the first Gospel coincide with her warning to Pilate and suggest that her presence in Matthew matters.

First, she notes that in the course of the night[74] she has had a dream (κατ' ὄναρ), a motif that connects her to Joseph and the magi in the first two chapters of Matthew's Gospel where the same idiom occurs five times. There, God has worked through dreams to warn the Gentile Magi (2:12) and to warn Joseph multiple times (1:20; 2:13, 19, 22). In Matthew 27:19, the phrase κατ' ὄναρ leads the reader to hear God behind the dream of Pilate's wife and to suspect that this third recipient of such a divine message has responded positively to it (as Joseph and the Magi have).[75] This connection serves to emphasise Pilate's negative response to his wife's report. Given that he does not change course in spite of her dream, his culpability is highlighted by this brief interlude. As Dorothy Jean Weaver proposes,

> Pilate's wife [...] responds immediately and faithfully to the dream that she has had. And this prompt and faithful response sets the actions of Pilate's wife in sharp and positive contrast to those of her husband, who neglects the divine warning and takes action instead to save himself rather than his 'righteous' prisoner.[76]

---

71 My translation. Origen includes a reference to Matt. 27:18 in the ellipsis indicated in the translation.
72 Van der Bergh, 'Reception', 73. Hilary goes on to apply Jewish culpability (and Gentile faith and absolution) to his own context (73).
73 And even Ambrose portrays Pilate as more tolerable than the Jews *(Iudaeos)*; Van der Bergh, 'Reception', 79. In this regard, we can hear a similar refrain to ecclesial reflection on the Canaanite woman. These Gentile women were used by Christian interpreters to provide a positive, representative portrait of the church, with the Jewish people receiving the brunt of castigation and blame.
74 The use of σήμερον in this instance appears to signal the nocturnal portion of the 24-hour period in view, with the Jewish accounting of a full day beginning at sundown (BDAG, 921). This is Chrysostom's view as well: 'The time of the dream also is significant, for it happened on that very night' (The Gospel of Matthew, Homily 86.1; Simonetti, *Matthew 14–28*, 280).
75 For (primarily) later ecclesial views that Procla's dream comes not from God but from the devil, see sources cited in Luz, *Matthew 21–28*, 499, n.61.
76 Weaver, *Irony of Power*, 58.

Gillman notes that this is the only place in Matthew—in fact, in the entire New Testament—where the message of a dream is disobeyed.[77]

If the first Matthean motif highlights that Pilate's wife has been the recipient of divine revelation, the second appears to tie her to Jesus in suffering. Pilate's wife expresses that she has 'suffered a great deal' (πολλὰ...ἔπαθον) in the dream she has received. This same language is used at 16:21 (πολλὰ ἔπαθον), the first time in the Gospel where Jesus' impending suffering is referenced. The evangelist may be using this intra-textual echo to align Pilate's wife with Jesus' experience and so shape her portrayal even more positively. Earlier in the passion narrative, a (Jewish) woman has identified with Jesus and his coming execution by preparing him for burial (26:6–13). This Roman woman identifies with Jesus' suffering in some way in the experience of her dream: she has 'suffered a great deal [...] because of him'.

Finally, the way Pilate's wife describes Jesus fits a significant motif in the passion narrative, that of Jesus' innocence. She warns Pilate to have nothing to do with 'this innocent [or righteous] one' (τῷ δικαίῳ ἐκείνῳ).[78] Jesus' innocence has already been affirmed by Judas, who laments he has betrayed 'innocent blood' (αἷμα ἀθῷον). At 27:24, Pilate will unsuccessfully attempt to remove his culpability by washing his hands and claiming he is 'innocent of [Jesus'] blood' (ἀθῷός εἰμι ἀπὸ τοῦ αἵματος τούτου). As Bond notes, Pilate 'attempts to show his innocence [but] is already too deeply implicated and cannot abdicate his responsibilities'.[79] Additionally, the crowd that has been assembled by the Jewish leaders (see 26:47; cf. 27:20) calls for Jesus' blood to be on them and on their children (26:25).[80] Distinguished from all of these figures or groups, Jesus, for Matthew, remains the only innocent one.

Given the significant thematic alignment between the words of Pilate's wife and Matthew's own interests, it seems extremely likely that she is portrayed positively by Matthew. This alignment helps to inform her rather ambiguous open words, 'Nothing to you and to that innocent person' (a wooden rendering of what is a Hebrew idiom taken over into Greek).[81] We should most likely hear an implied imperative in this clause (rather than an indicative; e.g. 'There is nothing in common between you and that innocent person'), especially following the pattern of the other dreams in Matthew, which provide warnings meant to result in tangible actions. If it functions as a warning, the sense would be that Pilate should have nothing to do with Jesus (as in most English versions).[82] Most commentators, rightly in my estimation, take her words as a defense of Jesus, especially given the context and her description of Jesus as 'innocent' or 'righteous'. Additionally, Pilate has no choice but to render a judgement. Given Roman absolute power to condemn or exonerate such prisoners, Pilate has no option to opt out of making the decision that will determine Jesus' fate.

---

77 Gillman, 'Wife of Pilate', 162.
78 For Matthew, these terms, δίκαιος and ἀθῷος, are synonyms or near equivalents (cf. Ps. 93:21; LXX). The textual variant δίκαιον at Matt. 27:4 for ἀθῷον suggests that scribes understood the two terms as at least sometimes synonymous.
79 Bond, *Pontius Pilate*, 136.
80 As Brown and Roberts, *Matthew*, 248, suggest, 'Matthew connects language of "blood" (αἷμα, *haima*; 27:4, 6, 8, 24, 25) and "innocence" (ἀθῷος, *athōios*, or δίκαιος, *dikaios*) across this chapter to juxtapose Jesus's innocence with the culpability of others (27:4, 19, 24–25)' (cf. 23:35). For a thoroughgoing discussion of who in Matthew is culpable for Jesus' death, see Brown and Roberts, *Matthew*, 516–521.
81 For the related Hebrew idiom, see examples in Judg. 11:12; 2 Sam. 16:10; 19:23 (Eng: 19:22); 1 Kgs 17:18; and 2 Kgs 3:13. In these contexts (with the question signaled at front; e.g. מַה־לִּי וָלָכֶם), it has to do with a purported relationship (or non-relationship) between the two parties. None of these has an initial negative particle, as is the case with the Greek of Matt. 27:19.
82 Even here, the sentiment remains potentially ambiguous, as in Nolland's interpretation: 'The statement is made in terms of the interests of Pilate and his wife and not in terms of the interests of Jesus [...] Pilate is being advised to play no role in this process'; Nolland, *Matthew*, 1172; see also Carter, *Pilate*, 94.

In her warning to Pilate and her concern for 'this innocent one', Matthew portrays Pilate's wife as another positive Gentile woman in line with the four women of Jesus' genealogy and with the Canaanite woman and her daughter.[83]

4. Theological Significance

Reflection on the theological import of these characterisations of Gentile women in Matthew, and for Christian theology particularly, raises at least two areas for potential appropriation, the first focused on ethnicity and the second centred on gender.

4.1 Matthew's Gentile Women and Ethnicity

As the church across the centuries became increasingly Gentile in composition, the church found it relatively easy to view Gentiles in Matthew as representing themselves and as exemplars (in the case of the Canaanite woman and Pilate's wife) or at least as redeemed foremothers through their inclusion in the line of the Messiah (i.e. the four women in the genealogy). Yet their commendation and especially their appropriation have often been accompanied by a disparaging of the Jewish people, as many interpreters of the church displayed 'the Jews' as a foil for the faith and understanding of these Gentiles.[84] In light of this history, we should be careful in the comparisons we make. First, in Matthew's narrative, it is not the Jewish people who are compared negatively with the Canaanite woman or Pilate's wife. In the first case, it is the disciples (and even Jesus!) who provide a foil to this Canaanite's exemplary faith (cf. 15:28 with the 'little faith' of the disciples at 14:31; 16:8).[85] And during Jesus' trial, it is the Jewish leadership specifically (27:12,20) and Pilate himself (27:24,26) who provide the negative contrast to his wife's positive portrait. Even at the conclusion of the trial, when the Jewish crowd (whipped up by the Jewish leadership; see 26:47; 27:20) is willing to take responsibility for Jesus' death (27:25), Pilate is the one who determines Jesus' fate, and so is the one who provides the most vivid contrast to his wife in this scene.[86] Second, ecclesial interpreters of Matthew often fused the Jewish people of their own context with the most negative portrayals of Jews (i.e. certain Jewish leaders) in the narrative. This misalignment has wreaked havoc for Jewish communities across history. As we consider how to appropriate (or avoid appropriating) the Gentile women in Matthew for Christian theology, we should be ever cognisant of the damage we might do to our Jewish brothers and sisters by glibly ignoring historical considerations of Matthew and of Christian historical practices of harm done toward Jewish people.

One strategy that may help to mitigate anti-Jewish interpretation and use of Matthew is a recognition of the variety of ethnicities represented in the Gospel. In the exploration of Matthew's

---

83 In an intriguing interpretation of Pilate's wife by a female interpreter in the ecclesial history, Aemilia Lanyer (1569–1645) casts Pilate's wife as the narrator of a poem about Jesus' passion, who asserts that she represents all women in withholding approval for Jesus' condemnation and crucifixion (*Salve Deus Rex Judaeorum*, 833–834; Woods, 'Lanyer', 318).

84 Including the Gentile men in Matthew who are portrayed positively, such as the Magi and two centurions (8:5–13; 27:54), though not Pilate or his soldiers.

85 Literally, the Jewish leadership, and specifically some Pharisees and scribes from Jerusalem, who are highlighted in the previous passage (15:1–20), also provide something of a foil to this Canaanite. Yet, in narrative terms, they are not a part of the same scene.

86 For the final word on the Jewish people (λαός) in Matthew, Carter, *Matthew*, 528, insightfully points out that the Jewish leaders at 27:64 are concerned that the people (λαός) 'might hear and welcome the resurrection message'.

Gentile women in this article, we have glimpsed a landscape that complexifies a simple binary between Jews and Gentiles—a binary implying that 'Gentile' is a monolithic and universal category. Instead, we hear of Old Testament women of Canaanite descent, Moabite descent, and with ties to Hittites in the opening genealogy, and, in later chapters, two Canaanite women and a Roman woman are introduced into the story. As Park has critiqued, dominant readings of Matthew have tended to see the narrative moving (in binary form) from Jewish particularity to a Gentile universality, whereby a 'universal non-ethnoracial Christianity swallows up a particular ethnoracial Judaism'.[87]

4.2 Matthew's Gentile Women and Gender

Another angle for theological consideration is the question of gender in Matthew's Gospel. While women—including Jewish women—flank the Gospel (namely, the four women and Mary in the opening genealogy, and the women at Jesus' tomb who witness to his resurrection; 28:1–10), men 'outflank' them. Matthew opens with reference to Jesus, David, and Abraham; and the large number of men in the genealogy eclipses by sheer volume the five women included. In the final verses of the Gospel, eleven male disciples and Jesus close out the story (28:16–20). This is not surprising given the androcentric lens of the Gospel, and of first-century texts generally. Yet it might seem disappointing from the perspective of Christian theologising.

We should not, however, take the paucity of central female characters in Matthew and its androcentric viewpoint as the whole story in this Gospel. Important for consideration is the Matthean motif of the 'surprising equality in God's reign' that emerges in chapters 18—20 and 23.[88] We hear of this theme first in a call for disciples to renounce preoccupation with status to pursue humble service across Matthew 18—20. Positive exhortations include taking on the humble social position of a child (18:2–3) and embracing the status of servants and slaves instead of pursuing greatness and being first in rank (20:25–28).[89] These exhortations interweave with narrative episodes that highlight Jesus' attention to those who have more limited status in the Graeco-Roman world, including women (19:4–9), eunuchs (19:10–12), and children (19:13–15; cf. 18:2).[90] Matthew also adds a parable in these chapters that emphasises the potentially surprising equality of the kingdom (20:1–15; esp. v.12). In Matthew 23:8–12, Jesus calls his followers to humble positions over against the exalted status categories of rabbi, teacher, and father. Regarding that latter title, Elisabeth Schüssler Fiorenza refers to Jesus' prohibition of its use a 'critical subversion' of patriarchy.[91] As Bauckham summarises this important theme,

> If the kingdom of God belongs to slaves, the destitute, and the children, then others can enter the kingdom only by accepting the same lack of status. The kingdom of God makes all equal by requiring all to come down to the level of the lowest. In this way Jesus envisages and implements an egalitarianism in radical opposition to the hierarchical structures of his contemporary society.[92]

---

87 Park, *Race and Ethnicity*, 64.
88 Brown and Roberts, *Matthew*, 184.
89 These themes are heightened by the evangelist in comparison with Mark's Gospel. Matt. 18:1–5 is emphasised and expanded from Mark (by its placement and additions) and 23:8–11 is unique to Matthew (23:12 has parallels in Luke 14:11; 18:14).
90 For the status emphases and implications of 19:1–15, see Brown, *Disciples*, 79–80.
91 Schüssler Fiorenza, *In Memory of Her*, 150–151.
92 Bauckham, 'Egalitarianism and Hierarchy', 124.

Even within its androcentric context, the direction of Matthew's expressed ecclesiology is moving toward 'greater egalitarian relations and allows us to continue in our theologizing along that trajectory'.[93] As such, reading Matthew for theology can invite Christian communities today to consider how to live into an egalitarian ethic that aligns with Matthew's vision—a vision of the ways the kingdom's arrival upends expected status categories and power dynamics of the status quo.[94]

In summary, this exploration of Gentile women in the first Gospel has highlighted their positive contribution to the shaping of Matthean ecclesiology, as they provide examples of persistence, faith, and faithfulness. These contours in their portraits offer a corrective to how these women have routinely been interpreted in the history of interpretation, and especially by male readers. This diverse set of women also suggest an understanding of God's arriving kingdom rich with ethnic distinctiveness. In Matthew's narrative world, the richness of the reign of God includes people of Canaanite, Moabite, Roman, and, of course, Jewish descent. In our own world, the richness is multiplied and holds promise for Christian communities of faith that celebrate and honour ethnoracial differences even while centring their community around their Jewish Messiah.

Jeannine K. Brown
Bethel Seminary, Saint Paul, MN
j-brown@bethel.edu

---

93 Brown and Roberts, *Matthew*, 423.
94 Gnadt, 'Gospel of Matthew', 616, suggests that '[Jesus'] leading enables and requires life together as brothers and sisters instead of hierarchy (23:6–7)'.

Bibliography

Bauckham, R. — 'Egalitarianism and Hierarchy in the Bible', in *God and the Crisis of Freedom: Biblical and Contemporary Perspectives* (Louisville, KY: Westminster John Knox Press, 2002), 116–127.

Bauckham, R. — *Gospel Women: Studies of the Named Women in the Gospels* (Grand Rapids, MI: Eerdmans, 2002).

Beare, F. W. — *The Gospel according to Matthew: A Commentary* (Peabody, MA: Hendrickson, 1981/1987).

Bond, H. K. — *Pontius Pilate in History and Interpretation* (SNTSMS; Cambridge, U.K.: Cambridge University Press, 1998).

Boxall, I. — *Discovering Matthew: Content, Interpretation, Reception* (Grand Rapids, MI: Eerdmans, 2014).

Brown, J. K. — 'Exodus in Matthew's Gospel', in S. M. Ehorn (ed.), *Exodus in the New Testament* (New York, NY: T & T Clark, 2022), 31–47.

Brown, J. K. — 'Living Out "Justice, Mercy, and Loyalty": Discipleship in Matthew's Gospel', in J. K. Goodrich and M. L. Strauss (eds.), *Following Jesus Christ: The New Testament Message of Discipleship for Today* (Grand Rapids, MI: Kregel Academic, 2019), 9–26.

Brown, J. K. — 'Reconstructing the Historical Pharisees: Does Matthew's Gospel Have Anything to Contribute?', in D. L. Bock and J. E. Komoszewski (eds.), *Jesus, Skepticism, and the Problem of History: Criteria and Context in the Study of Christian Origins* (Grand Rapids, MI: Zondervan, 2019), 164–182.

Brown, J. K. — *Matthew* (Teach the Text New Testament Commentary; Grand Rapids, MI: Baker, 2015).

Brown, J. K. — 'Genesis in Matthew's Gospel', in M. J. J. Menken and S. Moyise (eds.), *Genesis in the New Testament* (New York, NY: T & T Clark, 2012), 42–59.

Brown, J. K. — *The Disciples in Narrative Perspective: The Portrayal and Function of the Matthean Disciples* (SBLAB 9; Atlanta, GA: Scholars Press, 2002).

Brown, J. K. and K. Roberts — *Matthew* (Two Horizons New Testament Commentary; Grand Rapids, MI: Eerdmans, 2018).

Brown, R. E. — *The Birth of the Messiah: A Commentary on the Infancy Narratives in the Gospels of Matthew and Luke* (Anchor Bible; Yale, CN: 1999).

Carter, W. — *Pontius Pilate: Portraits of a Roman Governor* (Collegeville, MN: Liturgical Press, 2003).

Carter, W. — *Matthew and the Margins* (Maryknoll, NY: Orbis, 2000).

Case-Winters, A. — Matthew (Belief: A Theological Commentary on the Bible; Louisville, KY: Westminster John Knox Press, 2015).

Davies, W. D. and D. C. Allison	*A Critical and Exegetical Commentary on the Gospel according to Saint Matthew* (3 vols.; London: T & T Clark International, 1988–1997).
France, R. T.	*Matthew* (NICNT; Grand Rapids, MI: Eerdmans, 2007).
Gibson, M. D. (ed.)	*The Commentaries of Isho'dad of Merv, Bishop of Hadatha (c. 850 A.D.) in Syriac and English. Volume 1: Translation* (Horae Semiticae, no. V; Cambridge: Cambridge University Press, 1911).
Gillman, F. M.	'The Wife of Pilate (Matthew 27:19)', *Louvain Studies* 17 (1992), 152–65.
Gnadt, M. S.	'Gospel of Matthew: Jewish Christian Churches in Opposition to the Pax Romana', in L. Schottroff and M. Wacker (eds.), *Feminist Biblical Interpretation* (Grand Rapids, MI: Eerdmans, 2012), 607–625.
Hagner, D. A.	*Matthew* (WBC; Dallas, TX: Word Books, 1993–1995).
Jerome, and T. P. Scheck	*Commentary on Matthew (The Fathers of the Church, Volume 117).* (Washington, D.C: Catholic University of America Press, 2008).
Keener, C. S.	*A Commentary on the Gospel of Matthew* (Grand Rapids, MI: Eerdmans, 1999).
Kany, R.	'Die Frau des Pilatus und ihr Name: Ein Kapitel aus der Geschichte neutestamentlicher Wissenschaft', *Zeitschrift für die neutestamentliche Wissenschaft* 86 (1995), 104–110.
Lawrence, L. J.	'"Crumb Trails and Puppy-Dog Tales": Reading Afterlives of a Canaanite Woman', in C. E. Joynes and C. C. Rowland (eds.), *From the Margins, Vol. 2: Women of the New Testament and Their Afterlives* (Sheffield: Sheffield Phoenix, 2009), 262–78.
Levine, A.-J.	'Matthew and Anti-Judaism', *Currents in Theology and Mission* 34 (2007), 409–416.
Levine, A.-J.	'Matthew's Advice to a Divided Readership', in W. G. Thompson and D. E. Aune, *The Gospel of Matthew in Current Study: Studies in Memory of William G. Thompson, S.J.* (Grand Rapids, MI: Eerdmans, 2001), 22–41.
Levine, A.-J.	'Discharging Responsibility: Matthean Jesus, Biblical Law, Hemorrhaging Woman', in D. Bauer and M. A. Powell (eds.), *Treasures New and Old: Recent Contributions to Matthean Studies* (Atlanta, GA: Scholars, 1996), 379–397.
Levine, A.-J.	'Gospel of Matthew', in C. A. Newsom and S. H. Ringe (eds.), *The Women's Bible Commentary* (Louisville, KY: Westminster John Knox, 1992), 465–477.
Levine, A.-J.	*The Social and Ethnic Dimensions of Matthean Salvation History* (Lampeter, PA: Edwin Mellen, 1988).
Luther, M.	'*Reminiscere* Sunday Sermon (1534)', in J. F. Thornton and S. B. Varenne (eds.), *Faith and Freedom: An Invitation to the Writings of Martin Luther* (New York, NY: Vintage Books, 2002).

Luz, U. and H. Koester.	*Matthew 21–28: A Commentary* (Hermeneia; Minneapolis, MN: Fortress, 2005).
Luz, U. and H. Koester	*Matthew 8–20: A Commentary* (Hermeneia; Minneapolis, MN: Fortress, 2001).
McGing, B. C.	'Pontius Pilate and the Sources', *CBQ* 53 (1991), 416–438.
Nolland, J.	*The Gospel of Matthew* (NIGTC; Grand Rapids, MI: Eerdmans, 2005).
Origen and R. E. Heine.	*The Commentary of Origen on the Gospel of St Matthew* (Oxford, U.K.: Oxford University Press, 2018).
Park, W.	*The Politics of Race and Ethnicity in Matthew's Passion* (Cham, Switzerland: Palgrave Macmillan, 2019).
Runesson, A.	'Giving Birth to Jesus in the Late First Century: Matthew as Midwife in the Context of Colonisation', in C. Clivaz, et al. (eds.), *Infancy Gospels: Stories and Identities* (WUNT; Tübingen: Mohr Siebeck, 2011), 301–327.
Schüssler Fiorenza, E.	*In Memory of Her: A Feminist Theological Reconstruction of Christian Origins* (New York, NY: Crossroad, 1984).
Sechrest, L. L.	'Enemies, Romans, Pigs, and Dogs: Loving the Other in the Gospel of Matthew', *Ex Auditu* 31 (2015), 71–105.
Simonetti, M.	*Matthew 1–13* (Ancient Christian Commentary on Scripture; Downers Grove, IL: InterVarsity Press, 2001).
Simonetti, M	*Matthew 14–28* (Ancient Christian Commentary on Scripture; Downers Grove, IL: InterVarsity Press, 2001).
Turner, D. L.	*Matthew* (BECNT; Grand Rapids, MI: Baker Academic, 2008).
Van der Bergh, R. H.	'The Reception of Matthew 27:19b (Pilate's Wife's Dream) in the Early Church', *Journal of Early Christian History* 2 (2012), 70–85.
Wainwright, E. M.	*Shall We Look for Another? A Feminist Rereading of the Matthean Jesus.* (Maryknoll, NY: Orbis Books, 1998).
Weaver, D. J.	*The Irony of Power: The Politics of God within Matthew's Narrative* (Eugene, OR: Pickwick, 2017).
Wilkins, M. J.	*Matthew* (NIV Application Commentary; Grand Rapids, MI: Zondervan, 2004).
Woods, S.	'Lanyer, Aemilia', in M. A. Taylor and A. Choi (eds.), *Handbook of Women Biblical Interpreters: A Historical and Biographical Guide* (Grand Rapids, MI: Baker Academic, 2012), 315–321.

Orality and Gospel Research
Revisiting Mark's Gospel

ALAN H. CADWALLADER

Abstract

The oral dimension of the gospel became a key explanation for the Synoptic problem in nineteenth-century Gospel interpretation (Westcott). The burgeoning, critical hunt for the *ipsissima verba* of Jesus drove two subsequent modulations: the retroversion of the written Greek sources to a postulated Aramaic original (for at least some of Jesus' sayings) (Dalman); the form-critical excisions of authorial embellishments on gospel traditions, which were content with reliance on the Greek language of the written Gospels (including Thomas and other apocryphal texts) for their reconstructions (Bultmann; Robinson). The assumption of substantial continuity and unity between the oral and written Gospels was challenged in the second half of the twentieth century (Kelber). A reaction against the resultant polarisation of oral and written has swung attention to the oral/aural dimensions of the written Gospels (Dewey; Horsley). A bifurcation of research has developed, one accenting the performantial elements in the delivery of the Gospels, a second returning to the poiesis of the text, particularly emphasising what is called 'sound-mapping' (Lee-Scott; Nässelqvist). This paper seeks to provide an overview of the changes in the understanding and development of orality in relation to Gospel research and then to apply some insights from socio-anthropological linguistics to Mark's Gospel to explore three elements crucial to its oral/aural dimensions. Firstly, what poetic and rhetorical structures are found in the text that invite an audiential response so as to produce a speech event—here reference is made to the mega-euphonic opening of Mark 1:1, the onomatopoeic extension of Mark 5:38, the assonantial associations of Mark 8:11 and the iambic abuse of Mark 7:27; secondly, what might these constructed speech events imply about the personnel involved in the delivery of Mark's Gospel demanded in Mark 13:14; and thirdly, what settings or spatial contexts can be inferred from such elements, building on the expansive territory of Mark 4. It will be argued that there is yet considerable mileage to be gained from studies in the oral dimensions of the Gospels.

Oral beginnings

In 1850, a twenty-four-year-old bright spark from Trinity College, Cambridge, was awarded the prestigious Norrisian Prize. The essay initially pursued a title 'The plenary Inspiration of the

Four Gospels is not invalidated by the alleged discrepancies which are objected against them'.[1] Fortunately, the polemical ring to the title did not survive the publisher's cutting-room and it was published in 1851 more in line with its positive contribution, 'The Elements of the Gospel Harmony'. Brooke Foss Westcott went on to thoroughly revise the work, add chapters and yet maintain that his basic ideas had not changed.[2] The *Introduction to the Study of the Gospels* passed through eight editions and became a standard for undergraduate study in England, the United States, and India.[3] The question of revelation continued to ferment in Westcott's thinking,[4] and, in an appreciation written thirty years later, W. H. Simcox accented this aspect of his thought: 'the Gospels are not—even when all four are combined—adequate materials for what is called a Harmony, for a biography in chronological order, they yet are not only adequate for their actual purpose as a Revelation, but are trustworthy, though incomplete, as historical documents'.[5] The historical incompleteness was compounded by the differences between the Gospels, from entire blocks such as Luke's 'great omission'[6] to substantial differences in detail and language. In today's parlance this is 'the Synoptic problem'. But for Westcott, the accent on the written is anachronistic because the beginnings of Christianity were marked by the oral, both in terms of the training in the Judaism of the day (which he considered was adverse to the written undertaking)[7] and in the shape of the 'original oral Gospel' which he considered to be in both Aramaic and Greek.[8] He considered resemblances between the written Gospels, to be explicable not by mutual dependence but by separate derivation from a common source which was oral.[9] The differences between the Gospels represent 'the successive remoulding of the oral Gospel according to the peculiar requirements of different classes of hearers'. This 'furnishes a natural explanation of the general similarity in form and substance between the several Gospels, combined with peculiarities and differences in arrangement and contents'.[10] Westcott regarded the teaching of Jesus as having the greatest oral fixity and the narrative being more free. In his view, the Gospel of Mark represented 'most closely the original from which they [each] started'.[11] Accordingly, any harmony of the Gospels needs to eschew a mechanical rationalization of the four written canonical Gospels but rather, given the prompt by the vast witness of their resemblances, look rather to the original oral form from which the four sprang.[12] Once only, Westcott signals that he understands the oral

---

1. Westcott, *Elements*, vii. Curiously, his filial biographer, Arthur Westcott, *Life and Letters*, 1.114, gives the title as 'On the Alleged Historical Contradictions of the Gospels'. This lacks his father's subtlety of understanding history. As he later wrote, 'The science of history is altogether of modern date'; Westcott, *On the Canon*, 8.
2. Westcott, *Introduction*, ix. The assertion by Stephen Neill (and Tom Wright), *Interpretation*, 115—'Unfortunately he [Westcott] allowed the book to be reprinted time and time again without ever subjecting it to a thorough revision'—is completely misleading. Others have been similarly dismissive. For a more appreciative evaluation see Porter, 'Legacy'.
3. Boyce, *Higher Criticism*, 373.
4. See Westcott, *Gospel of Life*.
5. Simcox, 'Canon Westcott', 26.
6. The excision of Mark 6:45 to 8:27—this includes the following pericopae: the water walking, healing at Gennesaret, disputation about clean and unclean, the Syrophoenician and her daughter, the healing of the deaf-mute, the feeding of the 4000, the leaven of the Pharisees and Herod, travel in Caesarea Philippi. The occasional sighting of material from within this Markan block (such as the demand for a sign) implies Luke's knowledge of this block and a decision to omit it, with very few exceptions.
7. Westcott, *Introduction*, 166-7.
8. Westcott, *Introduction*, 192.
9. Westcott, *Introduction*, 208-9.
10. Westcott, *Introduction*, 210.
11. Westcott, *Introduction*, 211.
12. Westcott was not the first to make such a suggestion, though his fulsome exposition renewed attention. See Thiselton, 'New Testament Interpretation', 16-17.

gospel to furnish an aural reception, the function of which, in part, was to retain, during a period of eye-witnesses, a hold on the oral tradition.[13] But this received no elaboration.

Westcott accepted the early Christian testimony (Papias) to a Hebrew/Aramaic version of Matthew, but he was not prepared to sacrifice a Greek version ('for the Hellenists') nor posit a temporal sequencing of a Greek version as derived from the Aramaic.[14] He affirmed that these languages were part of the linguistic frame for Jesus and the early disciples / authors.[15] But this coincidence of languages for the written Gospels, did not sufficiently answer the question of Jesus' own preference in his teaching, given that Westcott had affirmed that the teaching showed the greatest similarity between the Synoptic Gospels. (He admitted that John's Gospel was distinct here.) For those who followed after Westcott, the words of Jesus became the focus.

At the cusp of the twentieth century, Gustaf Dalman was struck by the semitisms that survived in transliterated form in the Synoptics. For him, Aramaic was the language of speech amongst the Jews of Palestine. This Aramaic, furthermore, was not devoid of written witness, including, most importantly, the translations and commentary on the Hebrew Scriptures, and was even used in connection with the temple cult. Hebrew itself had adopted Aramaic letter-forms. Moreover, he fostered the sense that the Greek spoken by Jewish Hellenists was influenced in its structures—and he would add 'thought'—by the Aramaic language.[16] These structures began especially with what has long been classified as *parallelismus membrorum*, that is, the repetition of a short saying by a roughly-synonymous rendition. A good example is Luke 6:28, 'Bless those who curse you; pray for those who abuse you'. Ben Meyer claims that *parallelismus membrorum* occurs in eighty percent of Jesus' sayings.[17] Dalman was quite prepared to acknowledge that the Greek of the Gospels may have had an oral form before being written down—there were clearly what he calls 'Graecisms' that resisted retroversion into Aramaic or Hebrew.[18] However, he was in no doubt that the original oral gospel was Aramaic.[19] The parallelisms can be analysed more closely, looking to rhythm, rhyme, assonance, consonance, alliteration, and onomatopoeia,[20] and Dalman was reassured of his manifold suggestions by equally manifold corroborations in Jewish Aramaic literature. He allowed that absolute certainty in minutiae was impossible; indeed sometimes he offered more than one Aramaic retroversion for the Greek text of a Gospel saying.[21] But he was clear on two fronts; firstly, that Aramaic was the language of Palestine, albeit not exclusively, and that the primary appropriation of Jesus' message by Jewish hearers requires an understanding of the meaning (and one might add, the sound qualities) of that language; secondly, for Dalman, the necessary retroversions from the extant Greek Gospels were an instrument fulfilling an historical imperative. He wrote,

> The more one is convinced that the Gospels contain historically trustworthy communications

---

13   Westcott, *Introduction*, 211.
14   In recent times, note the salutary, balanced contributions of Moule, *Birth*, 215–9, and Kloppenborg, *Formation*, 51–64.
15   Westcott, *Introduction*, 204–5. Westcott noted the 'habitual use of "hearing" in connexion with the contents of the Gospel', citing Eph. 4:21; 1 John 2:7,18,24 etc. (*Introduction*, 172 n.1) but did not explore either the nature of aural reception nor the intricacies of oral delivery that might facilitate that reception.
16   Dalman, *Words of Jesus*, 1–17. The German edition, *Die Worte Iesu* was published in 1898. See also Burney, *The Poetry of our Lord*.
17   Meyer, 'How Jesus charged Language with Meaning', 84–5, citing Reisner, 'Der Ursprung', 507.
18   Dalman, *Words of Jesus*, 18, 71. One example is Matt. 11:7–8 which, in the transposition of letters from κάλαμος to μαλακός, creates a pun that only works in Greek.
19   Dalman, *Words of Jesus*, 17–19.
20   Meyer, 'Language with Meaning', 85.
21   Dalman, *Words of Jesus*, 119; cf. Dalman, *Jesus-Jeshua*, 228.

in regard to the teaching of Jesus, the more important must it appear to get even one step nearer to the original by a fresh apprehension of His message in the light of the primary language and the contemporary modes of thought.[22]

There remains an acknowledgement of Aramaic as key to the teaching of Jesus in a standard introduction to New Testament studies,[23] little disturbed by either a *redivivus* of commonly spoken Hebrew,[24] nor gradations (hierarchical?) even dialectical forms of Aramaic itself.[25] The seventeen Aramaisms preserved in the Gospels continue to be trumpeted,[26] though the awkwardness in some of the authorial translations in text (such as Mark 5:41), combined with the thirty or so Latinisms found in Mark alone, have urged caution. There is an uneasiness in working at a foundational level on retroverted constructions. Semitic or semitic-influenced Greek has been heavily criticised in recent times, especially given that elements of koine Greek found in papyri and inscriptions have provided multiple examples of the Greek of the New Testament that were previously claimed to have been either semitically-influenced or translated from Aramaic or Hebrew. As John Muddiman succinctly puts it, 'the number of "Jewish peculiarities" admitted in biblical Greek has continued to reduce'.[27] Scholarship returned to the Greek text, albeit still in search of the *ipsissima verba* of Jesus.

The form-critical approach to the analysis of the Gospels in search of both the words of Jesus and the experience of the church in shaping and supplementing them is frequently connected with the brilliance of Rudolph Bultmann. However, the claim for an Aramaic original became problematised particularly when the isolation of the now-non-extant document, Q, seemed to point in the direction of, at the very least, an early entrance of Greek into the writing of the gospel traditions. This movement into writing also fundamentally brought a shaping, an editing, usually into clusters. James Robinson pointed out that the Q-saying about considering the lilies of the field (Q12:27) probably involved an illustrative triplet from the textile craft, that is, 'Consider the lilies of the field, how they neither card, nor toil nor spin'.[28] The saying in this form takes into account the (reconstructed) reading found in an early papyrus witness for the Gospel of Thomas, Saying 36, that is, *P.Oxy.* 655, dated to the early third century. It reads, 'you are better than the lilies which neither card nor spin'. The key point hinges on the expression 'do not card', that is, οὐ ξαίνουσιν. The Gospel text, in Matthew and Luke, reads, 'how they grow', πῶς αὐξάνουσιν (Matt. 6:28, singular in Luke 12:27, as in *P. Oxy.* 655).[29] The foundation for Robinson's argument was laid by the papyrologist T. C. Skeat who noted that the original hand of Codex Sinaiticus, the massive four-columned Greek bible (fifth century), at Matthew 6:28, read similarly to *P. Oxy.* 655, that is, not 'grow' but 'card',[30] an expression much more in keeping with the overall textile metaphor.

---

22 Dalman, *Words of Jesus*, 72.
23 See, for example, Perrin, *The New Testament*, 41; Burkett, *An Introduction*, 144, 382; Ehrman, *The New Testament*, 80, 191–2. Chancey, *Greco-Roman Culture*, 122–165, argues strongly for a limited use of Greek by ordinary Galileans. On the multilingualism of Palestine see Ong, *The Multilingual Jesus*.
24 See Birkeland, *The Language of Jesus*.
25 See Taylor, 'Bilingualism and Diglossia'; Wise, *Language and Literacy*.
26 Jeremias, *New Testament Theology*, 3–8.
27 Muddiman, 'The Greek Language', 2.28.
28 The argument appears a number of times in varying degrees of detail. See Robinson and Heil, 'Zeugnisse'; Robinson, 'Pre-Q Text'; Robinson, 'A Written Greek Sayings Cluster'; Robinson, Hoffmann, and Kloppenborg, *A Critical Edition of Q*, lxv, xciii, xcix–ci.
29 This difference in the singular and plural between Matthew and Luke, with Luke having the same reading as *P. Oxy.* 655 has been noted by Baasland, *Parables and Rhetoric*, 382–3.
30 Skeat, 'The Lilies of the Field'.

Indeed, like Craig Evans, I am inclined to drop the 'toil' altogether from the original saying,[31] seeing the triplet as a developing embellishment of the textual (originating in oral?) tradition. The implication, as Stanley Porter admits, is that the hypothetical document Q, at least in this section of sayings, was in written form for long enough for a copyist's error to slip into the text before the Gospels of Matthew and Luke were written.[32] It is a Greek textual variant, only possible on the basis of a written Greek text of at least this section of Jesus' sayings. We need to recall that the accent of Dalman's work was that the sayings of Jesus were those most to be found in the posited Aramaic.[33] Here it is the written Greek which belongs to the period before Matthew and Luke (that is, prior to 80 CE or so). The suggestion therefore is that Greek from an early period—before the written, canonical Gospels—entered the gospel traditions. Moreover, those written sayings and deeds were determinative in shaping the resultant Gospels. The question of whether Jesus delivered this sermon or part thereof in Greek was, needless to say, not treated,[34] even though both Westcott and Dalman had allowed that Greek was or might have been part of the early oral period.

The fundamental heuristic distinction between the oral and written Gospel had to this point remained largely congenial. The written was seen as an avenue to the oral, whether Aramaic or Greek. Form-critical work might peel back layers towards an original form of discrete sayings, might then point to the aggregation of these sayings into lists and then mini-collections, and might allow the layers that were peeled away to point to the *tendenz* or interests of an author or community, but it was generally assumed that such a process was an unproblematic continuity.

However, Werner Kelber's *The Oral and Written Gospel* threw a grenade into scholarly complacency by suggesting that the writing down of the oral was an effort to fetter, re-direct and re-shape the traditions, both to construct a different expression of the gospel and also to reconfigure the power relations involved in the holding of the tradition and the delivery of the gospel.[35] He wrote:

> we cannot flatter ourselves with the path-breaking significance of the written gospel [here a nod to Bultmann] and simultaneously insist on its unbroken connectedness with tradition; if with Mark a creative stage had come when memories were woven into a new form, we must learn to discern and accept the price that was paid for this achievement. Truly creative stages in tradition involve alienation, and genuine innovation is destructive to tradition. That is the reality of the medium transit from the oral to the written gospel, and a religious truth as well [....] With Mark a world was written into being by distanciation from oral dialogue and remembering. To keep Jesus' own preferred medium at arm's length [ie parables] was indispensable for resurrecting him into the written medium. After he had fully passed into written language, a new world of linguistic reification had come into existence.

Fundamental questions were raised:

1. Did textualisation bring an end to the creativity of oral story-telling?
2. Did the elitism of literacy carry a demarcation or stratification of authority within society?
3. What were the tensions and changes involved in the move from an oral delivery of gospel to a written delivery?

---

31 Evans, *Matthew*, 159.
32 Porter, 'P. Oxy. 655 and James Robinson's Proposals'. By contrast, Gundry, *Old is Better*, 149–70, has tried to argue that *P. Oxy.* 655 is nothing other than a redaction of Q 12:22b–31 (little different from Skeat, Porter or Robinson) or even the canonical texts (a common difficulty in accepting that written texts can pre-date the canonical Gospels).
33 This saying is not treated in Dalman, *Words of Jesus*.
34 Compare, Silva, 'Bilingualism'.
35 Kelber, *Oral and Written Gospel*, 215.

Werner also fundamentally challenged the basis for not only form-critical work but for textual work generally, by pointing to how much such an enterprise was executed by scholars nurtured in the fixity of print culture.[36]

Joanna Dewey later developed this issue of power and control in a feminist direction, suggesting that writing, whilst not absent from women in the ancient world, was nonetheless marshalled, publicly marshalled, by men.[37] There are occasional references to women writing in the ancient world, fragments of women's poetry, and even some evidence of women scribes in Egypt, but the general picture of women's creativity in language is confined to the oral—and in male texts reporting on women's orality, rarely in flattering terms. The fluidity of the oral realm, fluid as to the gender of its exponents as much as to the content being delivered, was now being straitened, strait-jacketed by the transmogrification into a written text. Textualisation therefore meant the withdrawal of the Gospel from most women, at least in terms of its shaping. The Gospel of Matthew might exalt the scribe of the kingdom bringing out of his—and it is definitely a 'his' (ὅστις ... αὐτοῦ)—treasure things old and new (Matt. 13:52). But the cost of elevating this male clerk trained for the kingdom (to the equivalent of οἰκοδεσπότης) is that others were pushed down and even forgotten, most especially women. The oral and written Gospel was transformed into a clash between what was dubbed the 'little tradition' and the 'great tradition', between popular and elite culture, sometimes with a peasant modulation,[38] sometimes with a feminist one.

Kelber's challenge ultimately was directed to the assumptions of modern biblical scholarship, less to the movement into writing of the ancient evangelical traditions. But because modern approaches assumed that they were operating in continuity with ancient approaches to writing, a clash between oral and written became even louder than a noisy gong. 'It makes sense in typographic culture', he wrote, 'to visualize texts as palimpsests, with layer superimposed upon layer, and stratum superseding stratum, building up to layered edifices'.[39] But the fundamental question is 'whether Jesus and the early tradition that delivered him unto writing have played by our rules [...] Were they committed, as we are, to the ethos of pure formality, compartmentalization of language, stratigraphic causality'.[40] Of course, it is admitted at least tacitly that this brings a reconfiguration of the elements that are brought in to construct the story but here the attention is given to the time of mission and community nurture and less to the historical Jesus.[41]

The recall of focus to the realm of the oral in the ancient world has highlighted that written texts are not only recipients of the oral delivery (whether play, oratory, poetry and/in song or preaching), they are also or can be contributors and supports to continued oral performance. This has lead recently to the development of two disciplines, sometimes discrete, sometimes complementary, sometimes competing. The first is performantial studies which oscillates between, on the one hand, how the text, usually in the language of the practitioner today, might be delivered with aesthetic punch in a performance and usually built on memorising the text and conceiving strategies of embodied delivery, and, on the other hand, how performance occurred in the ancient world—whether in theatre, law-court or market-place. Some cross-over of course occurs, though the second—attention to performance in the ancient world—is probably less developed in Gospel studies.

---

36 See, especially, Kelber, 'History'.
37 See Dewey, 'From Storytelling to Written Text'.
38 Horsley, 'Introduction'.
39 Kelber, 'Jesus and Tradition', 140.
40 Kelber, 'Jesus and Tradition', 145.
41 This is notwithstanding Larry Hurtado's strident protest at the 'over-simplification' of the emphasis on the oral (as in James Dunn's later work, amongst many). See Hurtado, 'Oral Fixation'.

The second discipline returns to the text of the canonical Gospels, not as sacrosanct print media for distribution, but as holding their own rich oral prompts and even as suggestive of a continued fluidity wrought not by scribal intrusions but by the demands of delivery, reception and context—what socio-linguists call a 'speech event'. This orality is not found by mining for some hidden vein trapped beneath the text, but instead lies on the surface, in the intricacies of the language of the text itself. It has usefully been classified as 'sound-mapping'. The ancients called it *poiesis*. It is to this that I want to devote the remaining part of the essay.

I want to amplify especially the poetic elements for two reasons, without suggesting that Mark is a poet at heart, rivalling Sappho. Firstly, the poetic is rarely dealt with in New Testament studies, even with the return of orality and performance studies.[42] Secondly, the poetic sensibility lay at the heart of Greek linguistic participation even at its most basic educational level with its emphasis on syllabification and phonemic quality.[43] (Homer has a lot to answer for!)[44] The linguistic shift to the accent on stress was still in process.[45] Even if a limping Greek writer, like the anonymous petitioner in *P. Col. Zen.* II 66 (=*P. Col.* IV 66), could not reproduce the niceties of Greek form, metre and its related category of rhythm, she or he could recognise this sophistication of language, perhaps occasionally try to emulate it, as in his own expansive metaphor of 'both summer and winter' (καὶ θέρος καὶ χειμῶνα).[46] Indeed some untrained speakers were begrudgingly recognised as having an innate capacity for successfully deploying rhetorical and poetic devices.[47] The poetic quality is what arrests the ear. It not only draws attention to the content of a section of speech, shaping it into an agreeable or confronting style that attends to the aesthetics of language. But it also has an immense capacity to generate other associations that a concentration on the 'textual manifestation of the enunciation process' cannot plumb.[48] Jeffrey Walker calls it the psychagogy of speech, that 'word-magic' that grabs the ear before the conative grasps the mind.[49] It essentially demands an embodiment of communication, a somatic performance that is irrational in its effect—which is why it was inherently untrustworthy according to the philosophers of language such as Aristotle and Quintilian,[50] much as they deployed the very aspect that was suspect.[51]

Oral and Aural in Mark's Gospel

Four examples from Mark will illustrate this poetic creation.

a) The sonorous opening (mega-euphonic evocation)

Mark 1:1 Ἀρχὴ τοῦ εὐαγγελίου Ἰησοῦ Χριστοῦ υἱοῦ θεοῦ

This 'phonosyllabic' opening to the Gospel gains increasing intensity from the succession of

---

42 For significant exceptions, see Gordley, *The Colossian Hymn*; Standhartinger, 'Der Kolosserhymnus'.
43 See Wachter, **'BA-BE-BH-BI-BO-BY-BΩ'**. This coheres with the report in the *Corpus Glossiorum Latinorum* 3.646; See Cribore, *Writing, Teachers and Students*, 191, and Appendix II, nrs. 78–97; *Gymnastics of the Mind*, 169.
44 On the fundamental resource of Homer for primary Greek education, see MacDonald, *Christianizing Homer*, 17–22; *The Homeric Epics*, 4–5, 171; *The Gospels and Homer*.
45 Horrocks, *Greek*, 162–70.
46 I. 17; for refined usage see Cleomedes, *Cael.* 2.1; Posidonus, Fr. 290a; cf. Thucydides, *Hist.* 2.1.1; Demosthenes *Or.* 9.50.
47 Aristotle, *Rhet.* 1.1 (1354a), Quintilian, *Inst.* 2. §§11–13.
48 Calame, *Craft*, 32.
49 Walker, *Rhetoric and Poetics*, 128; see also Russo, 'The Poetics', 124.
50 Aristotle, *Rhet.* 3.4 (1407a); Quintilian, *Inst.* 10.7.12.
51 Slippage into magic, particularly if the speaker was a woman, was especially fearful; see Schiappa, *Beginnings*, 127.

diphthongs ending every word, requiring in five of the six instances to be drawn out to confer full weight upon each of those magical elements called vowels. But this is more than mere euphony[52] and only partially diminished by the textual critic who might rob the verse of two words![53] The ancient style critic, Demetrius, approves a 'concurrence of the same long vowels' because it suggests a song.[54] Clearly, the opening was to be voluble.

Indeed, by comparison with a ritual context from the sanctuary of Zeus Panamaros just outside of Stratonikeia in Caria (south-western Turkey), volubility is the order of the day when the proclamation of the divine advent is made. One inscription recounts the epiphany of the god that saved the sanctuary, its people and the neighbouring city of Stratonikeia.[55] The reconstructed line 13 of the inscription reads:

[καὶ αὐτίκα πλῆθος ἦν? τῶν αὐτομολ]ούντων τῶν <συ>νγ<ν>ώ<μ>ην φωνούντω[ν,] ἔτι δὲ ἀναβοών[των] μεγάλῃ τῇ φωνῇ Μέγαν εἶναι Δία Πανάμαρον

[At once there was a multitude] of deserters bellowing out for a pardon and others bawling with a loud cry, 'Great is Zeus Panamaros'.[56]

No doubt the narrative of epiphany was recounted in the course of later cultic celebrations and processions, with the implicit cultivation of a megaphonic, audiential acclamation: 'Great is Zeus Panamaros'. Loud cries are of course familiar in Mark's Gospel, from demoniacs and from Jesus (Mark 1:26; 5:7; 15:34,37) but 'loud cries' are not confined to the categories of Spirit or a demon, as some New Testament myopia would have it. 'Loud cries' are everywhere in the ancient world from auctioneering,[57] to epitaph reading,[58] to cultic performance.[59] They are especially associated with the function of heralds, the messengers bringing critical information into a public sphere.[60] Whilst frequently distilled by the narrative description of μεγάλῃ φωνῇ (as in the inscription and Mark), the inscription brings a phonic increase in anticipation with its succession of long-vowel syllables—ων—at the end of words that finally erupts into the acclamation. In fact, extreme care has been given to the lexical manipulation by a duplication of the sound within the verbal forms, that is φωνούντων and ἀναβοώντων. Here has been generated what the linguist, Alessandro Duranti calls 'phonosymbolism', that is 'the use of intonation, lengthening, and volume to emphasise particular emotional states or stances'[61] precisely because such elements are associated with certain situations. A loud voice is coming, and the antici ... pation is not disappointed: 'the

---

52   Curiously, Nässelqvist, *Public Reading*, 153–4, omits the importance of diphthongs to the construction of euphony. They can only with heavy qualification be included under 'long vowels' in a phonic environment.
53   *Pace* Head, 'A Text-Critical Study of Mark 1.1'; Ehrman, *Orthodox Corruption*, 72–5. The more we attend to the oral-aural dimensions of the text, the more text-critical analysis of Mark 1:1 needs to be revisited. The variants do not demand to be passed through a theological grid as Ehrman suggests. Rather the longer opening may reflect the legacy of performance embellishment that sonorously incorporates other elements of the developing (creedal?) tradition; in tensive contrast, the shorter text may reflect a growing hold of a textual focus. This competition awaits further exploration. For other arguments supportive of the longer reading, see Voelz, *Mark 1:1–8:26*, 96–7.
54   Demetrius *Elec.* 2.73–74.
55   *I.Stratonikeia* 10. See N. Belayche, '"In Dieu est né ..."' (French translation at 209–10); Cadwallader, 'Epiphanies and Religious Conflict', 115–116 and 120–121 (English translation).
56   *Translation* adapted from my own rendition (previous note), in order to draw out some salient Markan parallels.
57   *SEG* 12.100; cf *I.Lindos.* II 419.
58   *SEG* 35.1604, 39.937.
59   *Lucian, Alex* 39; cf Hippolytos, *Ref* 5.8. Angelos Chaniotis, 'Staging and Feeling', stresses the importance of the controlled use of a 'loud voice'.
60   Plutarch, *Cor.* 25.3. See Brown, 'The Common Voice'.
61   Duranti, *Linguistic anthropology*, 205.

voice of one bellowing in the wilderness' (Mark 1:3a).[62] Participants in the event at Panamara are positioned in a public sphere; whether cultic, theatrical or agoral, is not absolutely clear, but they are in the open. Volume is required.[63] Mark's text is replete with words that likewise depend on volume.[64] And likewise, open space and invitation to participation are implied. At Panamara, as in Mark's Gospel, the inscription as also the written text, were not centripetally, silently frozen, but were the means by which a voice was energised. One epitaph from Philadelphia now in the museum at Manisa in Turkey, which utilises three different meters in the course of its short testimony, leaps from the cold, inscribed stone into vibrant voice with the assertion μάνθαν' ἐμῇ φωνῇ τοισίδε τοῖς ἔπεσιν 'learn from my voice through these verses'. In fact the stone too is made participant in the speaking with its own alliterative device: στήλλη λαλεῖ 'the stone speaks'.[65] The accent is on the oral and aural, not the textual.

b) The ululation of grief (onomatopoeic extension)

Towards the end of the intercalating miracle story of Jairus and his daughter, there is a scene of abject grief: καὶ κλαίοντας καὶ ἀλαλάζοντας πολλά (Mk 5:38). If the poetic intensity is noted at all, attention has been drawn to the onomatopoeia and derivation of ἀλαλάζοντας (cf ὀλολύζω Jas 5.1).[66] Onomatopoeia was a recognised linguistic category in the ancient world. It is fundamentally about the linguistic appropriation of sound. As L. P. E. Parker explains it, 'the meaning suggests the sound, as well as the sound the meaning'.[67] The Roman teacher of oratory, Quintilian, though he regarded the practice more developed in Greek, nevertheless recognised elements in Latin. He calls onomatopoeia the creation of language that suits sound to sensation.[68] Dan Nässelqvist considers that onomatopoeia is always connected with individual words,[69] though one of Quintilian's examples (from Ovid) accents the repetition of sound in two words.[70] In Mark, one example might be the name Βοανηργές given to James and John (Mark 3:17) though even here Mark takes up the probably Hebraic sound in his rough translation υἱοὶ βροντῆς.[71] But this redirects emphasis from sound to term, and fails to recognise that ancient writers, including the very ones Nässelqvist quotes,[72] frequently used an onomatopoeic word to initiate an extension

---

62 φωνὴ βοῶντος ἐν τῇ ἐρήμος.
63 Compare Demosthenes, Or. 19.338, Aristophanes, Eccles. 30 on the requisite for a loud voice.
64 ἀνακράζω (1:23; 6:49); βοάω (1:3; 15:34), θορυβέω (5:39), θόρυβος (5:38; 14:2) κράζω (3:11; 5:5, 7; 9:24, 26; 10:47, 48; 11:9; 15:13, 14, [39]; sometimes φωνή / φωνέω carries the sense of loudness (eg 14:68, 72; 15:35); the 'seizure' of 9:18 (ῥήγνυμι) seems to imply considerable volubility. Significantly, Strabo's examples of onomatopoeia configure around explosions of sound (Geography 14.2.28).
65 TAM 5.3.1903 = I.Mus. Manisa 318 (corr.) (2nd century ce). Here the stone speaks the name of the deceased father (lacuna).
66 See for example, Gould, St Mark, 100; Zwiep, Jairus's Daughter, 51, 67.
67 Parker, 'Dionysius' Ear', 305.
68 Quintilian, Inst. 8.6.31–2.
69 Nässelqvist, Public Reading, 159, 160. He takes issue with Lee and Scott, Sound Mapping, 178–179, for accenting onomatopoeia as a series of sounds (in their case, the imitation of birdsong in Matt. 6:26). There is some point to the criticism in that there is no instigating onomatopoeic word that prompts the phonic succession; nonetheless the suggestion has merit, not to mention the literary flexibility demanded by ancient stylists. Herodotos, Hist. 3.14 seems in the alliterative repetition of lambdas—ἀνακλαύσας μέγα καὶ καλέσας ὀνομαστὶ τὸν ἑταῖρον ἐπλήξατο τὴν κεφαλήν ('he collapsed into loud wailing howling his friend by name and clubbing his head')—to evoke the lululation of grief.
70 Quintilian, Inst. 8.6.33.
71 Onomatopoeic resonance may in fact provide an explanation for Mark's otherwise infelicitous 'translation' noted by Guelich, Mark 1–8:26, 162; cf. Collins, Mark, 219–20.
72 Aristophanes, Eq. 285–287.

of the word's sound to emphasise and underscore that sound (not provide an illustration of the word).[73] It may even foster the use of certain rhythms or the effort to transliterate sounds that have yet to fix a formal lexeme, as in Aristophanes' *Birds*.[74] I have called this an onomatopoeic extension. The alliterative repetition of the lambdas across an entire phrase in Mark 5:38 is designed to convey more than a single word's onomatopoeia. Sound is exploited into extended resonance. The actual sound of ululation is worked into the passage, not to connote grief but to emote it. The animator of the text begins to ululate through the alliterative sequence and so attracts the commotion from an inner imagining (at least amongst a consensual audience) into an actual performance of lament. That is, the phonic expression of the text dissolves into the extreme rendition of emotion that frequently accompanies death.

Ululation, the shrill trill of sound through the warbling of the tongue, was sometimes transliterated as ἐλελεῦ or ἀλαλά and frequently attracted gender distinctives, with male ululation called ἀλάλαγμα and women's called ὀλολυγμός.[75] Hence, if the evangelist was sensitive to this distinction, he has imbued a gender-specific term with a setting usually given to women, namely lament at death,[76] which some have seen as a derivative from the ululation that women unleashed when a victim was ritually sacrificed.[77] Male ululation was usually associated with a military war-cry,[78] though both male and female ululation might erupt in a cultic setting, especially during Bacchalian or Cybelan rites.[79] Accordingly, Mark may have attempted to augment the intensity of grief at the death of Jairus' daughter by drawing male ululation into the lament. This is not unparalleled in ancient writings. The anguish at imminent disaster in Achilles Tatius' story *Leucippe and Clitophon* is brought to abject panic: ὀλολυγμὸς γυναικῶν, ἀλαλαγμὸς ἀνδρῶν, κελευσμὸς ναυτῶν, πάντα θρήνων καὶ κωκυτῶν ἀνάμεστα ('shrieking of women, shouting of men, the calling of the sailors' orders; all was full of wailing and lamentation').[80]

Like Mark, the tragic dramatist, Aeschylus, uses the technical onomatopoeic term and then proceeds to demonstrate its affect within the language he deploys. So when, in *Agamemnon*, the Watchman, having caught sight of a beacon signal, wakes Clytemnestra so she can 'praise the signal fire with the hallowed cry [ὀλολυγμός]' the cause for celebration (in this case) unfolds that 'the city of Ilium has fallen, as the fire-light vividly declares'. The Greek alliteration captures the ululation noise noted by ὀλολυγμός: Ἰλίου πόλις ἑάλωκεν, ὡς ὁ φρυκτὸς ἀγγέλλων πρέπει.[81]

---

73 Nässelqvist, *Public Reading*, 160, is forced to speak of 'repetitions which accentuate the onomatopoeic word'.
74 Aristophanes, *Av.* 227–8, 237, 242, 260–62.
75 See Stanford, *Greek Tragedy*, 56, and especially, Suter, 'Male Lament in Greek Tragedy'.
76 *Greek Anthology* (Meleager) 7.182; Aeschylus, *Cho.* 387.
77 Gender division meant that the male performed the actual sacrifice. Aeschylus, *Sept.* 267–269. See Kearns, 'Religious Practice and Belief', 320.
78 Xenophon, *Anab.* 5.2.14.
79 Plutarch, *Suav. Viv.* 1098C; *Greek Anthology* 6.173 (Rhianus).
80 Achilles Tatius, *Leuc. Clit.* 3.8–9. Compare Dio Cassius, *Hist. Rom.* XLI.9.5, *Epit.* LXII.16.5 where everyone (children, women, men, the aged, outsiders) engage in ὀλολυγή.
81 Aeschylus, *Ag.* 28–30. Here I have used (with slight changes) the translation of Meineck, 'Cognitive Theory', 165. For another example from the same play see ll. 594–596. It should be noted that the use of the onomatopoeic word is not demanded in order to evoke the sound; see, for example, Aristophanes, *Birds* 211–214 οὓς διὰ θείου στόματος θρηνεῖς τὸν ἐμὸν καὶ σὸν πολύδακρυν Ἴτυν, ἐλελιζομένη διεροῖς μέλεσιν γένυος ξουθῆς ('that from your divine lips bewail deeply mourned Itys, your child and mine, trilling forth fluid melodies from your vibrant throat') where the lambdas in πολύδακρυν ... ἐλελιζομένη ... μέλεσιν create an alliteration that evokes an ululation scene.

c) The serpentine hissing (assonantial associations)

When Jesus and the disciples disembark in the district of Dalmanutha (8:10), a group of Pharisees approaches. Mark's assonance is extensive in length and expansive in the sibilant letters (ξ, σ, and ψ) dominating the period, capturing the ζ into the 'distinctive aural feature':[82] καὶ ἐξῆλθον οἱ Φαρισαῖοι καὶ ἤρξατο συζητεῖν αὐτῷ, ζητοῦντες παρ'αὐτοῦ σημεῖον ἀπὸ τοῦ οὐρανοῦ, πειράζοντες αὐτόν (Mark 8:11).

There is no doubt that rhetoricians, style critics and grammarians strongly advised against an aggregation of sibilant sounds.[83] The particular description was evocative of the hissing of a snake (συρίζω).[84] But it was also the noise of disapproval and castigation, an audiential response that brought a performance to an untimely or disreputable end. The character of Momus in Lucian's *Parliament of the Gods* whines that Πολλὰ ἔτι ἔχων εἰπεῖν καταπαύσω τὸν λόγον· ὁρῶ γοῦν πολλοὺς ἀχθομένους μοι λέγοντι καὶ συρίττοντας, ἐκείνους μάλιστα ὧν καθήψατο ἡ παρρησία τῶν λόγων[85] ('I still have plenty to say, but I will bring my speech to an end, for I notice that many are annoyed with me for my remarks, and are hissing, particularly those who have been touched to the quick by my frankness'). Here the hissing (συρίττοντας)[86] is followed by a sequence of sibilants making the point that Momus' *parrêsia* has struck home too well. Similarly, Cicero recognises that applause meant immortality, hissing meant death.[87] It was only a short step for the association to be turned to an 'othering', a stigmatising of a person or group. Thus Jerome commented that hissing noises were a mark of barbaric nations.[88] And Petronius' character Plocamus, throws a jibe at Greek speech by labelling it 'whistling'.[89]

Quintilian observed, in the course of emphasising the importance of control in the voice, that breathing was an essential component to master. He commented on those who hiss by sucking in breath through their teeth or who pant and wheeze like pack-animals under load. Significantly, he suggests that some orators do this deliberately.[90] The same can be said of texts which, in the face of the general rejection of sibilant succession, yet deploy it. The sense is that the hissing caught in the words is being directed against another. Nässelqvist admitted as much, noting that 'the rough nature of Jesus' address to Simon [Jn 1:42] and Nathaniel [Jn 1:50] may well have caused listeners to interpret these examples of discourse as doubtful, dismissive, or even antagonistic'.[91]

Examples from Mark can be multiplied.[92] But in every instance, sound is being used to express a negative attitude towards the ones being described or addressed. The injunction to avoid the leaven of the Pharisees (Mark 8:15) makes the point bluntly through the character of Jesus, but the attitude has already been conveyed powerfully by the author once the text is animated into its hissing modulation. The sound fits the draconian intent of the Pharisees in the plot; they, after

---

82 So, Nässelqvisat, *Public Reading*, 170.
83 Quintilian, *Inst.* 9.4.37; Dionysius of Halicarnassus, *Comp.* 20, 22.
84 Dio Chrysostom, *Or.* 5.14; Nemesianus 30–32.
85 Lucian, *Deor. conc.* 12–14. Compare Demetrius, *Eloc.* 250.
86 Lucian uses the Attic form of συρίζω.
87 Cicero, *Sest.* 115–16.
88 Jerome, *Ep.* 130.5,
89 Petronius, *Sat.* 64.
90 Quintilian, *Inst.* 11.3.55–57.
91 Nässelqvist, *Public Reading*, 230.
92 See Mark 15:30 σῶσον σεαυτὸν καταβὰς ἀπὸ τοῦ σταυροῦ, noted by Lee and Scott, *Sound Mapping*, 178, who call it onomatopoeia, though here I would be looking for the word συρίζω / συρίττω as the onomatopoeic launch. A further example is found in the first half of the Syrophoenician woman's reply—τῆς τραπέζης ἐσθίουσιν (Mark 7:28). See my *Beyond the Word*, 163.

all, provide the first of three temptations (Mark 8:11; 10:2; 12:13–15) that illustrate the operations of the archetypal enemy (Mark 1:13). The danger that is unfolding is explosively marked with the succession of sound.[93] And given the indications from Cicero, Lucian, and Demetrius that hissing is a crowd activity, the turning of a performance into a speech event is likely to have envisaged the eruption of hissing that added a volume to the sibilant sequence in the words. The sounding of the text acted as an invitation to make the sounds that are found in the text and heard in its animation. If the crowd were caught into the performance, then the hissing would have been seen as an appropriate response every time the Pharisees appeared thereafter, generating an event where they—the crowd—are not only participants in the performance but energisers of the animator of the story.

d) The rustic repulsion (iambic abuse)

I have analysed the exchange between Jesus and the Syrophoenician woman at length elsewhere.[94] Here I want simply to draw attention to the words of Jesus directed to the woman: λαβεῖν τὸν ἄρτον τῶν τέκνων καὶ τοῖς κυναρίοις βαλεῖν (Mark 7:27). The metathesis of λαβεῖν and βαλεῖν generates a related phonemic clash (σύμπληξις) within the paronomatic repetition that according to Demetrius captures attention more effectively than a prosaic rendition.[95] However, the value ought not be overstated. It is a common ornament of writing reaching back to Homer and forward to Archbishop Eustathius of Thessalonike.[96] It received a caution from Quintilian against overdoing the device.[97] This media manipulator knew only too well that overuse leaches power.

This metathesis clearly marks out the unit, two cola of equal parts (isocolon). Apart from the aggregation of harsh sounds held within the unit—the growling of the dog-letter, *rho*, for example—the invitation is to look further. Seneca noted that 'single maxims sink in more easily when they are marked and bounded off like a line of verse'.[98] Here the maxim is formed through the addition of οὐ γὰρ ἐστιν καλόν, but it introduces a proverb.[99] We know also from the Suda that proverbs were frequently aided in memory by being arranged metrically. When this is checked against the text, it falls neatly into iambics, the first line an iambic dimeter, the second half an iambic trimeter.

‿ — ‿ — ‿ — ‿ —

λαβεῖν τὸν ἄρτον τῶν τέκνων
(καὶ)

— ‿ ‿ ‿ — ‿ —

τοῖς κυναρίοις βαλεῖν

Iambics generated an immediately recognisable ambience. Dan Ben-Amos comments, 'the existence or absence of a metric substructure in a message is the quality first recognized in any

---

93 It might be argued that the hissing has already begun with earlier appearances of the Pharisees (Mark 2:16,18,24; 3:6; 7:1) but here the sequencing is more restrained. After all, the noun Φαρισαῖος readily lends itself to sibilant multiplication.
94 See *Beyond the Word* previously cited.
95 Demetrius, *Eloc.* 2.105–106; Cicero, *De or.* 4.29.
96 Homer, *Od.* 21.359; Aristotle, *Hist. an* 611b; Plutarch, *Mor.* 442d; Ps-Galen, *Rem.* 3.461.12–13; Gregory of Nazianzus, *Poe.* 1270.5; Eustathius, *Comm. Il* 3.166.3.
97 Quintilian, *Inst.* 8.5.13–14, 20.
98 Seneca, *Ep.* 33.6.
99 On the proverb being relied upon see *Beyond the Word*, 106–111.

communicative event'.¹⁰⁰ Here the iambics combine with the phonic quality of the letters and syllables and the idea being communicated, but they also undergird what is being communicated. David Gerber argues that iambic was not just a metre; it was a style and that style communicated base language, scornful abuse, bitter tone, even sexual license.¹⁰¹ Key elements to its literary province were metaphor and diminutive—just as here.¹⁰² The metrical rhythm and sound of this delivery leave no room for exonerating Jesus. Rejection and abuse are layered into his reply. The associations conveyed by metre, iambics especially, were simply part of the sonic world of the time, so pervasive that Cicero could speak of it as natural, and therefore readily recognised, even if replicated only with training.¹⁰³

However, not all approved of its use and certainly its use in a prose work. Iambic was the key meter of mime and comedy, genres dismissed by the dour Plutarch as 'bad art and bad taste'.¹⁰⁴ Similarly, Aristotle regarded the iamb and trochee as not conducive to dignity.¹⁰⁵ And prose writing, whilst viewed as refined and exemplary when given a rhythm that drew upon poetic meters, was regarded as ill-formed if particular meters began to dominate the language. Quintilian quipped that the problem was that the audience would start to tap their feet along with the delivery, an unwanted participation in the speech event.¹⁰⁶ A 'general metrical effect' was sufficient to produce the desired effect.¹⁰⁷ Further Quintilian denounced a succession of short syllables mid-colon—precisely what appears with κυναρίοις—which appears to have displaced the simple iambic foot of κύσιν.¹⁰⁸ For him, it 'would cause a sound similar to that of children's rattles (*paene puerilium crepitaculorum*)'.¹⁰⁹

Accordingly, by reliance on a proverb given a puerile mnemonic, Jesus is revealed, in this instance, as a boorish rustic, limping along to a most basic meter, deploying a proverb without any finesse or refinement. This was the educational attainment expected of rural farmers and labourers.¹¹⁰ Such reliance on proverbs learned in the simple formulae that children were trained in gained none of the accolades lavished on those who provided flamboyant improvisations on the basic theme.¹¹¹ In the text it is immediately exposed by the brilliance of the woman's reply (Mark 7:28), a diva-like performance that is underscored by the combination of main verbs (ἀπεκρίθη καὶ λέγει—unique in the Gospel)¹¹² and is recognised by Jesus as the efficacious λόγος in the encounter—not his (Mark 7:29). Space requires me to refer the reader elsewhere for the substantiation of this judgement.¹¹³

---

100 Ben-Amos, 'Analytical Categories', 228. This replicates ancient insights; see Dio Chrysostom, *Or.* 12.71.
101 Gerber, *Greek Iambic Poetry*, 'Introduction', 1–7.
102 Aristotle, *Poet.* 22.19 (1459a).
103 Cicero, *De or.* 3.191, 195–197; Quintilian, *Inst.* 1.10.32–33.
104 Plutarch, *Mor*, 706d.
105 Aristotle, *Rhet.* 3.8 (1408b–1409a). Compare also Longinus, *De subl.* 41. Quintilian noted Aristotle's comments, but argued that the iambic was unavoidable at times—what was important was to surround the common with the superior! See *Inst.* 9.4.87–91.
106 Quintilian, *Inst.* 9.4.104, 107; cf. Cicero, *De or.* 3.183.
107 Demetrius, *Eloc.* 3.181.
108 For details, see Cadwallader, *Beyond the Word*, 88–91.
109 Quintilian, *Inst.* 9.4.66, himself adopting the rhythm that he criticises to make the point!
110 Theocritus, *Id.* 5. Here Theocritus portrays two shepherds trading proverbs with little attempt at sophistication or multiple applications.
111 Demetrius, *Eloc.* 2.108–110.
112 Elsewhere, Mark preferences a syntax of main verb plus participle.
113 Cadwallader, *Beyond the Word*, 157–196.

Let There Be a Speaker …

These few examples, exploring euphonics, onomatopoeia, assonance and rhythm have amply demonstrated that phonic rendition is crucial to an appreciation of a text and opens up dimensions that no distribution of written texts can deliver. As such it demands a speaker, or better, what Erving Goffman calls the 'animator',[114] whose primary task is to bring the full dimensions of the story to bear upon an audience, to become the characters, to make present the scene. Clarity of speech, control of volume, adoption of tone, instinct for rhythms have all been flagged as crucial not for the text but for its performance. Some traces of the audience's participation have been indicated in their reception of some of the phonic renditions. Their anticipation of a loud voice is engendered in Mark 1:1. The emotional impact of ululation would be recognised if not experienced in Mark 5:38. The invitation to hiss at the appearance of Pharisees in Mark 8:11 might be too much to resist. The wry nodding of accompaniment to the simple iambics of a rustic's proverb in Mark 7:27 may well have been a gestural response to whatever embodiment of delivery was performed. But in every instance (even the Syrophoenician's storming of a closeted Jesus, Mark 7:24–5), the atmosphere is open and expansive. The resonance of the text is not built within the walls of a building such as a house, a synagogue, or church, but in the exchange, the event of an animator, and active participants in the open.

Of course, the famous aside of Mark 13:14 appears to direct, parenthetically, the presentation of the warning about the desolating sacrilege.[115] Codex Bezae narrowed the attention to the written text by adding τι ἀναγινώσκει to the wording ὁ ἀναγινώσκων νοείτω, that is, 'let the reader understand what he is reading', which shifts the text away from performance into the study or ecclesial teaching circle. In so doing the semantics of the word are restricted to a later ecclesial development that privileged textual literacy and manuscript. However, the meaning of the word is broader, and can accent persuasion, publication, delivery of a text—just as one historian was honoured by an inscription and statue at a pan-hellenic sanctuary at Epidauros.[116] Angelos Chaniotis paraphrases the inscription thus, 'I Philippos, son of Aristeides from Pergamon, the master of divine history, have been dedicated by Epidauros; but all the Greeks took delight in me when with loud voice (ἔκλαγον) I recited the written account of wars, treating the world of mortals'.[117] Here a distinction is made between the text and the recitation; moreover the audience responded warmly not to the text but to the quality of its oral delivery.

In Mark 13:14, the aside does not stand apart from the performance. Rather it functions as a stage-whisper, designed to pull the audience (further) into a participation with the animator in the performance event. It functions similarly to the retardation of information that Mark indulges in, so that the audience is surprised, challenged and shifted in their perceptions—as occurs in the withholding of critical data about the Syrophoenician woman (not till 7:26) or the women followers from Galilee (not till 15:40–41!). As such, the auditors and viewers are 'overhearers or eavesdroppers' being drawn more closely into the drama. Duranti sees this as part of the process of shifting an audience or members thereof from an unratified position in relation to the speech

---

114   Goffman, *Forms of Talk*, 121.
115   Similarly, Hearon, 'Mapping Written and Spoken Word', 380–1, 386. Others take the advice as directing attention to Dan. 12:5–13 thereby providing the text with a didactic frame and purpose rather than a performance text. See Evans, *Mark 8:27–16:20*, 320. Others take it as advice to the one who is already reading the Daniel text: Dewey, *Oral Ethos*, 82–83, 118 n.28.
116   *IG* IV 2 1 687.
117   Chaniotis, 'Travelling Memories', 260.

event to that of a ratified place;[118] in Christian terms, from an outsider to the faith to the position of an insider, a believer. Accordingly, rather than Mark 13:14 demanding a textual focus it functions as part of the performance of the text designed to draw the audience closer, building the experience of the speech as an event. This has already been signaled earlier in Mark, in what John Crossan has called 'participatory pedagogy'.[119] In the parables chapter, one parable introduction stands out in its singularity: 'How shall we liken the kingdom of God? Or in what parable shall we set it forth?' (Mark 4:30, RV). The 'we' is set into the chapter as referring to the multitudinous crowd (ὄχλος πλεῖστος) 'drawn together' (συνάγεται) with him on the land (Mark 4:1). However, the constant lack of definition given to the repeated words of 'land' and 'sea' enables a sense of flexibility of location that can incorporate the crowd gathered into the speech event. In this sense, if there is a necessary flexibility to be allowed to an audiential reception and response, so also there must be a flexibility in the delivery as animators continually evaluate the responsiveness of their audience[120]—AND a flexibility in regards to spatial setting. Consequently, there cannot be a fixed text at least at the point of the performance participation. Goffman therefore prefers to adopt the metaphor of the stage for whatever social interaction is occurring at a linguistic level; that is, we give 'shows'.[121] After all, Quintilian recommended that would-be orators take lessons from the theatre.[122]

A Spatial Turn for the Oral and Aural

Here we need to return to the setting already named … the open. Although setting has occasionally been listed as an element in linguistic analysis it has tended to be fairly static and under-developed. In New Testament commentary this has been consigned to the expansive and ill-defined context that an interpreter adjudicates as necessary to exploit the meaning of the text. But this pushing at the walls of the written text tends also to be textual, an intertextual symbiosis mutually reinforcing of the basic assumption of writing. However, once the frame of encounter with a text is shifted from writing to performance, to the speech event, another factor becomes crucial, which I now wish briefly to explore.

Alessandro Duranti lays the foundation for the 'spatial turn' in linguistics at the feet of Karl Marx. In his *Theses on Feuerbach*, Marx posited the necessity of recognising (indeed fostering) the connection between consciousness and humanity's material lives, their actions in the world:

> The chief defect of all hitherto existing materialism … is that the thing, reality, sensuousness, is conceived only in the form of the object of contemplation, but not as human sensuous activity, practice, not subjectively. Hence it happened that the active side, in contradistinction to materialism, was developed by idealism—but only abstractly, since, of course, idealism does not know real, sensuous activity as such.[123]

Duranti builds on this, accenting that words cannot be detached from the physical objects of human labour. Words are embedded in human cultural practices and are part thereof. Even when

---

118   Duranti, *Linguistic Anthropology*, 298.
119   Crossan, *Power of Parable*, 134. This is a step beyond H. Hearon's accent on 'hearing' in Mark 4: 'Mapping Written and Spoken', 387.
120   Duranti, *Linguistic Anthropology*, 299.
121   Goffman, *Frame Analysis*, 508.
122   Quintilian, *Inst.* 1.11.1.
123   Marx, *Theses on Feuerbach*, 143.

a performance is turned into an act of ratification, as in the historian's recitation of history that reinforced Epidauros' identity already mentioned, or the delivery of the Gospel of Mark as a means of building faith, no attention is paid to 'the material world in which and through which social interaction, communication included, takes place'.[124]

Duranti's focus is on the human built environment. And of course, that environment is neither static, nor confined to one type of building and material context. Chaniotis has noted that even when armed with a stock-pile of basic material, an itinerant speaker (poet or not) deliberately adjusted their material not only to the assessed audience but also to the environment, the surroundings within which the speech event was to take place. That event thus becomes a socio-spatial linguistic performance. Environments shape the body and the embodied performance. 'Our body does not operate in an empty space. We move in a space that has been shaped by others before us, a space that has history, meaning, that is, a range of possibilities'.[125]

Duranti accents the built environment, the product of human activity. Without in any way wanting to diminish this spatio-temporal accent, I would suggest that there is no necessary marginalisation of the natural environment that carries less of the built materiality of human culture. The desert, the country, the sea all are signalled as spatial players in the speech events of Mark, in addition to the more obvious places of human settlement.

I would like to test this spatial component in two brief locations for the parables chapter, based on the familiar alternative for the provenance of the Gospel, that is, Rome and Syria.[126] Firstly, we need to recognise some of the accents of Chapter 4. Unlike parallels in Matthew and Luke, Mark hammers the setting for the unfolding of the parables in terms of sea and land. Three times in the opening there is the reference to a gerneralised 'sea' (θάλασσα), compared to once in Matthew (13:1) and not at all in Luke (8:4). The importance of the sea will return in the climactic question about the sea's subjection to him (Mark 4:41). No specific toponym is given to this body of water.[127]

Similarly, running through the parables of the chapter, there is a constant repetition of 'land' (γῆ), lost in the variety of synonyms deployed in English translations. The land had been announced in 2:10 as that over which this Jesus had authority, but the great preponderance of occurrences lies in Chapter 4. These observations, especially as regards the land are nothing new.[128] However, the combination of the sea, in which Jesus sits for his teaching (ἐν τῇ θαλάσσῃ v.1) and which is subject to him (v.41) and the land, over which his authority is spread (ἐξουσία ... ἐπὶ τῆς γῆς Mk 2:14), calls for comment.

In city after city within the Roman empire, *sebasteia* or other buildings honouring the emperor(s) were erected, marking by their display, inscription, statuary, and relief, the authority of Rome. That at Aphrodisias is the best preserved and has received the greatest appropriation.[129] Suffice to note the proclamation at the head of a three-tiered display of the emperor as ruler of land and sea. The conceit is not new. It runs back at least to the Persians who demanded that newly conquered peoples bring a bowl of land and a bowl of water to the King as a sign of their subjection and of the conferral of the resources of their territory.[130] But Rome built a material and

---

124 Duranti, *Linguistic Anthropology*, 321.
125 Duranti, *Linguistic Anthropology*, 322.
126 See Incigneri, *The Gospel to the Romans*—Rome; Collins, *Mark*, 7–10 and Mack, 'The Spyglass and the Kaleidoscope'—both opting for Syria; Roskam, *The Purpose of the Gospel of Mark*, 94–114 (specifically Galilee).
127 Throughout Mark's Gospel, the sea is ill-defined; only twice in eighteen instances is it located in Galilee (Mark 1:16a, 7:31). See Cadwallader, 'The Young Man and the Sea'.
128 See especially, Tolbert, *Sowing the Gospel*.
129 See Maier, 'Reading Colossians in the Ruins'.
130 See Munn, 'Earth and Water'.

literary environment saturated with the propaganda not only of the subjection of land and sea but also the prosperity that flowed from that imposition of *pax*—all projected as ordained by the gods.

Mark's Gospel by contrast not only portrays Jesus (and in part the crowd of Chapter 4)[131] as co-constructers of an alternative *basileia*. The headquarters of that *basileia* is located in the desert[132]—the antithesis of the Roman built environment, and the general region constantly portrayed as harbouring the enemies of Roman control.

These are broad-brush sketches of two material environments, one laden with the markings of human cultural artefacts, one bearing the weight of inherited literary traditions. I do not want to decide between them as providing the spatial setting for the performance of Mark's Gospel, loosely configured, as they are, around the two main claimants upon the provenance of the Gospel, Rome and Syria. Rather I want to suggest that the participation of the spatial environment in the animating production of the Gospel will have a vastly different impact on the speech event of the gospel, depending on where one might posit a delivery.[133] This 'deictic function' of the speech event highlights that 'the spatio-temporal anchoring of linguistic expressions can only be interpreted vis-à-vis such anchoring'.[134] If in Rome, or any urban environment under the governance of Rome, Mark's Gospel will become visual and auditory graffiti on the built environment of, say, the agora or the streetscape. If in Syria, within sight of desert environments, Mark's Gospel will turn to a confirmatory and expanding ideation of a natural asylum from Rome's rule. Significantly, one *hapax legomenon* in the Gospel sits astride these two options, the *komopoleis* of Mark 1:38—those places of human settlement that (usually) do not have walls but are large enough and with sufficient contacts to foster regular market days, even when located as stations in wilderness areas.[135]

And the markets, as Martial and Seneca moan (albeit about Rome), are places filled with the bombast of sellers, hawkers, prostitutes, policing, animals, and the like. So, if you want to be heard, make a noise! But then, as time unfolded, there was always someone in the church who said 'ssshhh'.

Afterthoughts

Where does this sweep leave us?

1. The oral is now firmly established as a necessary part of the text both for its analysis and its delivery.
2. The aural is also established not merely as something to configure but as something that involves, pulls into participation.
3. The oral always requires an embodied voice. Consequently, what happens to the reception of the oral, that is, the aural appropriation, when that embodiment is different—as between a male or female animator, or someone from Hicksville, such as Galilee (see Mark 14:70), whose accent grates on certain ears in an audience?

---

131 See my 'The Peasant, the Farmer and the Gardener'.
132 See Marcus, *Mark 1–8*, 204.
133 This has been explored at the level of the impact of a material setting on textual semantics rather than phonic appropriation for the letter to the Romans by Oakes, *Reading Romans in Pompeii*. However, it does provide a valuable example of the level of examination of the material culture preparatory to the examination of the spatial component of a speech event.
134 Duranti, *Linguistic Anthropology*, 209.
135 See Cadwallader, 'Sometimes one word makes a world of difference'.

4. The oral and aural as always spatially contextualised demand that the text be adjusted to place. Further, given that space is never identical it allows that the text does not have a fixed determinacy.

Consequently ...

5. How must the text change when the prime training and language exchange is no longer Greek? This is the issue of translation and contextualisation understood in broad terms.
6. How has the mode of reception been constrained by the invention of printing and a privileging of a university, solitary, silent study as the prime mode of engagement with the text? Dare I say, as in this publishing outlet?
7. How have we been disembodied through an accent on the text alone as the conveyor of gospel? In connection with this question, how have we lost the oral, poetic, performantial elements both of the delivery of the text and the adjuncts to the text, in factors such as gesture, movement, musicality and tonality, stance *et cetera*?
8. And how has the gospel been distorted through dogmatic requirements of unchangeableness which constrain the performance of the text?
9. More particularly, are these forces of constraint and delimitation already visible in the writings of the New Testament, given that, clearly, Matthew and Luke were not satisfied with Mark's open event?

One can see (and, of course, hear) that there is still considerable distance to run in the analysis (and inculcation) of the orality and aurality of the gospel. Time and sound will tell ...!

Alan H. Cadwallader
Australian Centre for Christianity and Culture
Charles Sturt University

Bibliography

Baasland, E. — *Parables and Rhetoric in the Sermon on the Mount: New Approaches to a Classical Text* (Tübingen: Mohr Siebeck, 2015).

Belayche, N. — '"In Dieu est né ..." À Stratonicée de Carie (I Stratonikeia 10)', in C. Bartsch and M. Vârtejanu-Joubert (eds.), *Manières de penser dans l'Antiquité méditerranéenne et orientale: Mélanges offerts à Francis Schmidt par ses élèves, ses collègues et ses amis* (Leiden: Brill, 2009), 193–212.

Ben-Amos, D. — 'Analytical Categories and Ethnic Genres', in D. Ben-Amos (ed.) *Folklore Genres* (Austin: University of Texas Press, 1976), 215–241.

Birkeland, H. — *The Language of Jesus* (Oslo: Jacob Dybwad, 1954).

Boyce, W. B. — *The Higher Criticism and the Bible: A Manual for Students* (London: Wesleyan Conference Office, 1881).

Brown, A. S. — 'The Common Voice of the People: Heralds and the Importance of Proclamation in Archaic and Classical Greece with Special Respect to Athens', PhD Thesis, Wadham College, 2011.

Burkett, D. — *An Introduction to the New Testament and the Origins of Christianity* (Cambridge: Cambridge University Press, 2002).

Burney, C. F. — *The Poetry of our Lord: An Examination of the Formal Elements of Hebrew Poetry in the Discourses of Jesus Christ* (Oxford: Clarendon Press, 1925).

Cadwallader, A. H. — *Beyond the Word of a Woman: Recovering the Bodies of the Syrophoenician Women* (Adelaide: ATF Press, 2009).

Cadwallader, A. H. — 'The Peasant, the Farmer and the Gardener: Approaches to the Environment of the Mustard Seed', in A. H. Cadwallader with P. L. Trudinger (eds.), *Where the Wild Ox Roams: Biblical Essays in Honour of Norman C. Habel* (Sheffield: Sheffield Phoenix, 2013), 129–44.

Cadwallader, A. H. — 'Epiphanies and Religious Conflict: The contests over the Hagiasma of Chonai', in W. Mayer and C. L. de Wet (eds.), *Reconceiving Religious Conflict: New Views from the Formative Centuries of Christianity* (London: Routledge, 2018), 110–135.

Cadwallader, A. H. — 'Sometimes one word makes a world of difference: rethinking the origins of Mark's Gospel', in P.G. Bolt and J. R. Harrison (eds.), *The Impact of Jesus of Nazareth: Historical, Theological and Pastoral Perspectives. Vol.1: Historical and Theological Studies* (CGAR 1; Macquarie Park, NSW: SCD Press, 2020), 233–64.

Cadwallader, A. H. — 'The Young Man and the Sea: Reconceiving Ancient Water Resources', in R. Myles et al. (eds.), *Habitats of the Basileia* (Sheffield: Sheffield Phoenix, 2023), forthcoming.

Calame, C. — *The Craft of Poetic Speech in Ancient Greece* (translated by J. Orion; Ithaca, NY: Cornell University Press, 1995).

Chancey, M.	*Greco-Roman Culture and the Galilee of Jesus* (Cambridge: Cambridge University Press, 2005).
Chaniotis, A.	'Staging and Feeling the Presence of God', in L. Bricault and C. Bonnet (eds.), *Panthée: Religious Transformations in the Roman Empire* (Leiden: Brill, 2013), 169–89.
Chaniotis, A.	'Travelling Memories in the Hellenistic world', in R. Hunter, R. L. Hunter and I. Rutherford (eds.), *Wandering Poets in Ancient Greek Culture: Travel, Locality and Pan-Hellenism* (Cambridge: Cambridge University Press, 2009), 249–69.
Collins, A. Y.	*Mark* (Hermeneia; Minneapolis, MN: Fortress, 2007).
Cribore, R.	*Writing, Teachers and Students in Graeco-Roman Egypt* (Atlanta: Scholars Press, 1996).
Cribore, R.	*Gymnastics of the Mind: Greek Education in Hellenistic and Roman Egypt* (Princeton, NJ: Princeton University Press, 2001).
Crossan, J. D.	*The Power of Parable: How Fiction by Jesus became Fiction about Jesus* (New York: HarperOne, 2012).
Dalman, G.	*Die Worte Iesu* (repr. Whitefish, MT: Kessinger, 2010 [1898]).
Dalman, G.	*The Words of Jesus: considered in the light of post-biblical Jewish writings and the Aramaic language* (translated by D. M. Kay; Edinburgh: T & T Clark, 1902).
Dalman, G.	*Jesus-Jeshua* (London: SPCK, 1929).
Dewey, J.	'From Storytelling to Written Text: The Loss of Early Christian Women's Voices', *BTB* 26 (1996), 71–78.
Dewey, J.	*The Oral Ethos of the Early Church* (BPC 8; Eugene, OR: Cascade, 2013).
Duranti, A.	*Linguistic Anthropology* (Cambridge: Cambridge University Press, 1997).
Ehrman, B. D.	*The Orthodox Corruption of Scripture* (Oxford: Oxford University Press, 1993).
Ehrman, B. D.	*The New Testament: A Historical Introduction to the Early Christian Writings* (5th edn., New York: Oxford University Press, 2012).
Evans, C. A.	*Mark 8:27–16:20* (WBC 34B; Nashville, TN: Thomas Nelson, 2000).
Evans, C. A.	*Matthew* (NCBC; Cambridge: Cambridge University Press, 2012).
Gerber, D. E.	*Greek Iambic Poetry* (LCL; Cambridge, MA: Harvard, 1999).
Goffman, E.	*Forms of Talk* (Philadelphia: University of Pennsylvania Press, 1981).
Gordley, M. E.	*The Colossian Hymn in Context: An Exegesis in Light of Jewish and Greco-Roman Hymnic and Epistolary Conventions* (WUNT 2.228; Tübingen: Mohr Siebeck, 2011).
Gould, E. P.	*A Critical and Exegetical Commentary on the Gospel According to St Mark* (ICC; Edinburgh: T & T Clark, 1912).

Guelich, R.	*Mark 1–8:26* (WBC: Waco, TX: Word, 1989).
Gundry, R. H.	*The Old is Better: New Testament Essays in Support of Traditional Interpretations* (Eugene, OR: Wipf & Stock, 2010 [2005]).
Head, P.	'A Text-Critical Study of Mark 1.1: "The Beginning of the Gospel of Jesus Christ"', *NTS* 37 (1991), 621–29.
Hearon, H.	'Mapping Written and Spoken Word in the Gospel of Mark', in A. Weissenrieder and R. B. Coote (eds.), *The Interface of Orality and Writing* (Tübingen: Mohr Siebeck, 2010), 379–92.
Horrocks, G.	*Greek: A History of the Language and Its Speakers* (2nd edn., Oxford: Wiley-Blackwell, 2010).
Horsley, R. A.	'Introduction', in R. A. Horsley (ed.), *Oral Performance, Popular Tradition, and Hidden Transcript in Q* (Leiden: Brill, 2006), 1–22.
Hurtado, L. W.	'Oral Fixation and New Testament Studies? "Orality," "Performance" and Reading Texts in Early Christianity', *NTS* 60 (2014), 321–40.
Incigneri, B.	*The Gospel to the Romans: The Setting and Rhetoric of Mark's Gospel* (Leiden: Brill, 2003).
Jeremias, J.	*New Testament Theology: The Proclamation of Jesus* (New York: Scribners, 1971).
Kearns, E.	'Religious Practice and Belief', in K. H. Kinzl (ed.), *A Companion to the Classical Greek World* (Oxford: Wiley-Blackwell, 2006), 311–26.
Kelber, W.	*The Oral and Written Gospel: The Hermeneutics of Speaking and Writing in the Synoptic Tradition, Mark, Paul and Q* (Philadelphia: Fortress, 1983).
Kelber, W.	'Jesus and Tradition: Words in Time, Words in Space', *Semeia* 65 (1994), 139–167.
Kelber, W.	'The History of the Closure of Biblical Texts', in A. Weissenrieder and R. B. Coote (eds.), *The Interface of Orality and Writing* (Tübingen: Mohr Siebeck, 2010), 71–99.
Kloppenborg, J. S.	*The Formation of Q* (Philadelphia: Fortress, 1987).
Lee, M. and B. Scott	*Sound Mapping the New Testament* (Salem: Polebridge, 2009).
MacDonald, D. R.	*Christianizing Homer, "The Odyssey," Plato and "The Acts of Andrew"* (New York: Oxford University Press, 1994).
MacDonald, D. R.	*The Homeric Epics and the Gospel of Mark* (New Haven / London: Yale University Press, 2000).
MacDonald, D. R.	*The Gospels and Homer: Imitations of Greek Epic in Mark and Luke-Acts* (Lanham: Rowman & Littlefield, 2015).
Mack, B.	'The Spyglass and the Kaleidoscope: From a Levantine Coign of Vantage', in B. S. Crawford and M. P. Miller (eds.), *Redescribing the Gospel of Mark* (Atlanta, GA: SBL, 2017), 181–205.

Maier, H. O.	'Reading Colossians in the Ruins: Roman Imperial Iconography, Moral Transformation, and the Construction of Christian Identity in the Lycus Valley', in A. H. Cadwallader and M. Trainor (eds.), *Colossae in Space and Time: Linking to an Ancient City* (Göttingen: Vandenhoeck & Ruprecht, 2011), 212–31.
Marcus, J.	*Mark 1–8* (AB27; New York: Doubleday, 2000).
Marx, K.	*Theses on Feuerbach* in R. C. Tucker (ed.), *The Marx-Engels Reader* (2nd edn., New York: Norton, 1978 [1845]).
Meineck, P.	'Cognitive Theory and Aeschylus: Translating beyond the Lexicon', in S. Constantinidis (ed.), *The Reception of Aeschylus' Plays through Shifting Models and Frontiers* (Leiden: Brill, 2016), 147–175.
Meyer, B. F.	'How Jesus charged Language with Meaning: A Study in Rhetoric', in B. D. Chilton and C. A. Evans (eds.), *Authenticating the Words of Jesus* (Leiden: Brill, 1999), 81–96.
Moule, C. F. D.	*The Birth of the New Testament* (2nd edn., London: A& C Black, 1966).
Muddiman, J.	'The Greek Language', in J. Barton (ed.), *The Biblical World* (2 vols; London: Routledge, 2002), 2.25–32.
Munn, M.	'Earth and Water: The Foundation of Sovereignty in Ancient Thought', in C. Kosso and A. Scott (eds.), *The Nature and Function of Water, Baths, Bathing* (Leiden: Brill, 2009), 191–210.
Nässelqvist, D.	*Public Reading in Early Christianity: Lectors, Manuscripts, and Sound in the Oral Delivery of John 1–4* (NovTSupp 163; Leiden: Brill, 2016).
Neill, S and T. Wright.	*The Interpretation of the New Testament 1861–1986* (2nd edn., Oxford: Oxford University Press, 1988).
Oakes, P.	*Reading Romans in Pompeii: Paul's Letter at Ground Level* (Minneapolis: Fortress, 2009).
Ong, H. T.	*The Multilingual Jesus and the Sociolinguistic World of the New Testament* (Leiden: Brill, 2016).
Parker, L. P. E.	'Dionysius' Ear', in P. J. Finglass, C. Collard and N. J. Richardson (eds.), *Hesperos: Studies in Ancient Greek Poetry. Essays Presented to M. L. West on his Seventieth Birthday* (Oxford: Oxford University Press, 2007), 297–305.
Perrin, N.	*The New Testament: An Introduction* (New York: Harcourt Brace Jovanovich, 1974).
Porter, S. E.	'*P. Oxy.* 655 and James Robinson's Proposals for Q: Brief Points of Clarification', *JTS* 52.1 (2001), 84–92.
Porter, S. E.	'The Legacy of B. F. Westcott and Oral Gospel Tradition', in A. Avery-Peck, C. A. Evans and J. Neusner (eds.), *Earliest Christianity within the Boundaries of Judaism: Essays in Honor of Bruce Chilton* (Leiden: Brill, 2016), 326–44.

Reisner, R.   'Der Ursprung der Jesus-Überliefering', *TZ* 38 (1982), 493–513.

Robinson, J. M.   'The Pre-Q Text of the (Ravens and) Lilies: Q 12:22–31 and P. Oxy. 655 (Gos. Thom. 36)', in S. Maser and E. Schlarb (eds.), *Text und Geschichte: Facetten historisch-theologischen Arbeitens aus dem Freunds- und Schülerkreis, Deiter Lührmann zum 60. Geburtstag* (MThSt 50; Marburg: Elwert, 1999), 143–80.

Robinson, J. M.   'A Written Greek Sayings Cluster Older than Q: A Vestige', *HTR* 92 (1999), 61–77.

Robinson, J. M. and C. Heil   'Zeugnisse eines schriftlichen, griechischen vorkanonischen Textes: Mt 6.28b, ℵ*, P. Oxy. 655 l, 1–17 (EvTh 36) und Q 12,27', *ZNW* 89 (1998), 30–44.

Robinson, J. M., P. Hoffmann and J. S. Kloppenborg   *A Critical Edition of Q* (Hermeneia; Minneapolis: Fortress, 2000).

Roskam, H. N.   *The Purpose of the Gospel of Mark in its Historical and Social Context* (Leiden: Brill, 2004).

Russo, J.   'The Poetics of the Ancient Greek Proverb', *JFR* 20 (1983), 121–130.

Schiappa, E.   *The Beginnings of Rhetorical Theory in Classical Greece* (New Haven, CT: Yale University Press, 1999).

Silva, M.   'Bilingualism and the Character of Palestinian Greek', *Biblica* 61 (1980), 198–219.

Simcox, W. H.   'Canon Westcott', *The Expositor*, 3rd Series 25 (1887), 22–38.

Skeat, T. C.   'The Lilies of the Field', *ZNW* 37 (1938), 211–14.

Standhartinger, A   'Der Kolosserhymnus im Lichte epigraphischer Zeugnisse', in J. Verheyden, M. Öhler and T. Corsten (eds.), *Epigraphical Evidence Illustrating Paul's Letter to the Colossians* (WUNT 411; Tübingen: Mohr Siebeck, 2018), 69–91.

Stanford, W. B.   *Greek Tragedy and the Emotions: An Introductory Study* (Routledge Revival; London: Routledge, 1983).

Suter, A.   'Male Lament in Greek Tragedy', in A. Suter (ed.), *Lament: Studies in the Ancient Mediterranean and Beyond* (Oxford: Oxford University Press, 2008), 156–80.

Taylor, D. G. K.   'Bilingualism and Diglossia in Late Antique Syria and Mesopotamia', in J. N. Adams, M. Janse and S. Swain (eds.), *Bilingualism in Ancient Society: Language Contact and the Written Word* (Oxford: Oxford University Press, 2002), 298–331.

Thiselton, A. C.   'New Testament Interpretation in Historical Perspective', in J. B. Green (ed.), *Hearing the New Testament: Strategies for Interpretation* (Grand Rapids, MN: Eerdmans, 1995), 10–36.

Tolbert, M. A.	*Sowing the Gospel: Mark's World in Literary-Historical Perspective* (Minneapolis: Fortress, 1989).
Voelz, J. W.	*Mark 1:1–8:26* (Saint Louis: Concordia, 2013).
Wachter, R.	'BA-BE-BH-BI-BO-BY-BΩ ... Zur Geschichte des elementaren Schreibunterrichts bei den Griechen, Etruskern und Venetern', *ZPE* 146 (2004), 61–74.
Walker, J.	*Rhetoric and Poetics in Antiquity* (Oxford: Oxford University Press, 2000).
Westcott, A.	*Life and Letters of Brooke Foss Westcott* (2 vols., London: Macmillan, 1903).
Westcott, B. F.	*The Elements of the Gospel Harmony: with a Catena on Inspiration, from the Writings of the Ante-Nicene Fathers* (Cambridge: Macmillan, 1851).
Westcott, B. F.	*On the Canon of the New Testament* (4th edn., London: Macmillan, 1875).
Westcott, B. F.	*An Introduction to the Study of the Gospels* (7th edn., London: Macmillan, 1888).
Westcott, B. F.	*The Gospel of Life* (London: Macmillan, 1892).
Wise, M. O.	*Language and Literacy in Roman Judaea: A Study of the Bar Kokhba Documents* (New Haven: Yale University Press, 2015).
Zwiep, A.	*Jairus's Daughter and the Haemorrhaging Woman* (Tübingen: Mohr Siebeck, 2019).

Making a Mark: Biography, Gospel, Apocalypse?

KEITH DYER

Abstract

The word becomes 'flesh' on papyrus too, and then is handed over to copying, editing, analysis, classification, translation, and interpretation. These are all necessary and worthy pursuits, but when do our standard texts, translations, and genre stereotyping begin to inscribe the word as if on tablets of stone, rather than in our hearts and ears? In particular, what is the significance of genre classification for interpretation? Does a Gospel by any other name read as well? Do the genres ascribed to Mark trickle down from high culture to the masses, or do they bubble up from below?

This paper explores the benefits and problems of genre classification, how it can ossify the Gospel of Mark in various ways, and how we might allow the text to challenge us again in new ways.

Questions about genre labels

The Gospel of Mark has been described variously as a Graeco-Roman biography (*bios*), as a parody of a *bios*, as a Jewish biography in OT and Rabbinic style, as the prototype of a new 'Gospel' genre, as 'apocalyptic', and as a rhetorically shaped narrative or novel. Further sub-categories and hybrid genres within and between these classifications are favoured by other commentators.[1] Given this

---

1 For Mark as Graeco-Roman *bios*, see Burridge, *What Are the Gospels*, and for the implications of this for interpretation, see Bond, *The First Biography of Jesus*. For the suggestion that Mark parodies such *bioi*, see Aune, 'Genre Theory'. For Mark as Gospel (*sui* generis), see Bultmann, *Synoptic Tradition*, 373–4: 'while we need analogies for understanding the individual components of the Synoptic Tradition we do not need them for the Gospel as a whole', since for Bultmann such literary analogies 'serve only to throw the uniqueness of the Gospel into still stronger relief'. For a recent argument that Mark narratises Paul's *euangelion*/Gospel, see Mitchell, 'Mark, the Long-Form Pauline εὐαγγέλιον'. For 'apocalyptic' readings of Mark, see Shively, *Apocalyptic Imagination*; Nel, 'The Gospel of Mark in Light of its Apocalyptic Worldview'; and Macaskill, 'Apocalypse and the Gospel of Mark'. For Mark as rhetorically shaped narrative see Dinkler, 'What is a Genre?'; and Van Oyen's emphasis on oral performance in 'Action according to Quintilian'. For distinctions within, and overlaps between these genres, and an emphasis on Jewish biography, see Baum, 'Biographies of Jesus'. For extended analyses of these Markan genre debates, see Collins, *Mark*, 15–43, updating her earlier monograph, *Is Mark's Gospel a Life of Jesus?*; Calhoun, Moessner, and Nicklas, eds., *Modern and Ancient Literary Criticism*; Aune, 'Genre Theory'; Burridge, *What Are the Gospels?* (3rd edn); and Bond, *First Biography*, 15–37. I note my appreciation of the interaction from the Centre for Gospels and Acts Research with an earlier version of this article.

proliferation of possibilities, and despite the current near-consensus that Mark is the first *bios* of Jesus, do these genre labels make any difference for our interpretation of Mark and the 'Gospels' that followed afterwards?

Such questions about the genre of New Testament writings go to the heart of the relationship between faith and culture, the church and artistic and critical literature, and to the nature of historical and hermeneutical method. Graham Stanton argued that:

> The first step in the interpretation of any writing, whether ancient or modern, is to establish its literary genre. [...] A decision about the genre of a work and the discovery of its meaning are inextricably inter-related; different types of texts require different types of interpretation.[2]

Yet even if this were to be conceded, how is the literary genre of any given text to be established? Do we receive it as an established truth from previous scholars (as if they all agreed)? Surely even at a popular level it would be better to begin by first reading each text on its own terms, in its own language (if possible), and so far as we can determine, set in its own context? Is it not good historical method to allow our primary sources to speak for themselves before we classify them and impose our interpretive categories—however helpful they may later turn out to be? As Edwin Judge has pointed out in relation to other terminological assumptions that are made as we translate and interpret these same texts, '(i)t is a productive historical exercise to use only the terminology of the times'.[3] So I will argue here that 'establishing a literary genre' should be suspended until due consideration is given to the language used within the text itself (emic terminology), rather than imposing at the outset etic concepts, sometimes from much later periods in the history of interpretation.[4] Etic categories retrospectively applied are a significant part of the process of attending to the history of interpretation of particular texts, but they need to be measured against the language of the text itself in order to confirm their ongoing relevance. Hebrews was once thought by some to be a letter of Paul, but closer analysis of the text reveals it is neither a letter nor Pauline.

So are *bios, euangelion,* and *apokalypsis* emic or etic terms in the Gospels, and when were they first used in relation to literary genre? The use of *bios* (life) in titles may have been a feature of the Graeco-Roman literary world well before the four Gospels were written, but the word *bios/bioi* is not used by any of the Gospels in relation to genre, nor as a self-description.[5] 'Gospel' (*euangelion*) is at least used prominently by Matthew (4:23; 9:35; 11:5; 24:14; 26:13) and especially Mark (1:1,14;

---

2   Stanton, 'Matthew: βίβλιος, εὐαγγέλιον, βίος?', 1187. Quoted also by Bond, *First Biography*, 1.
3   Judge, 'No King But Caesar', 399–400.
4   For the use of emic and etic in relation to discussions of genre, see Collins, 'Genre Apocalypse', 23–24.
5   The word *bios* occurs once in Mark (12:44) of the widow's 'whole living', and five times in Luke (8:14,43; 12:12,30; 21:4, with similar meanings). It is not used in Matthew or John. Just when the word *bios* was understood to constitute a genre (a distinct category of writing) is less clear. Breytenbach suggests this does not happen until Plutarch (c. 45–125 C.E.), in 'The Gospel According to Mark', 179–200. Baum, 'Biographies of Jesus', 39, describes Plutarch and Suetonius (c. 70–125 C.E.) as two of the best-known Hellenistic biographers, and adds Klaus Berger's list of biographers going back to the fourth century B.C.E. (including Isocrates and Xenophon). See Berger, 'Hellenistische Gattungen'. Yet I can only find *bios* used in a title (which perhaps suggests an emic 'genre' but which may well be a later *superscriptio*), in Aristoxenus (fourth century B.C.E.), Mus. *Fragmenta* (*bios* of Socrates, *bios* of Plato), and Nicolaus (2nd cent. B.C.E.), Hist. *Fragmenta* (*bios* of Caesar), before its use in Philo (first century B.C.E–first century C.E.), *De Josepho* (*bios* of a political operator, about Joseph) and *De vita Mosis* (concerning the *bios* of Moses), and an even longer title involving *bios* in *De Abrahamo*. When does a passing reference (as in Aristotle, fourth century B.C.E. in Phil. *Fragmenta varia*) to '*bios* of Pythagoras' become a genre? Is it when it becomes an emic title or an etic *superscriptio*? This same issue emerges in relation to the use of Gospel (*euangelion*), as Aune has argued ('Genre Theory', 33–42)—see further below.

8:35; 10:29; 13:10; 14:9; [16:15]) as some kind of self-description, if not as a new genre. But it is not used by Luke or John, though Luke has a fondness for the verb form (1:19; 2:10; 3:18; 4:18,43; 7:22; 8:1; 9:6; 16:16; 20:1). How then is it that we call all four Gospels, Gospels?[6] 'Apocalypse' (used once only among the Evangelists, by Luke in 2:32, 'a revelation to the *ethnē* ') was not used to designate a literary genre until the mid-nineteenth century,[7] and although it appears as the first word in the Book of Revelation, it is not used again in that book. John the Seer is clear that he is writing prophecy (Rev. 1:3; 10:11; 22:7,9–10,18–19). It may sound pedantic, but we should let the text speak on its own terms first, before we begin using other labels in a way that determines what we expect to read before we even begin.

So in dialogue with the proponents of Mark as biography, apocalypse, and gospel in particular, I want to question the prioritising of decisions about genre in the hermeneutical process. Comparisons with other contemporary literature are helpful and necessary, but not before a thorough evaluation of the text itself, on its own terms. Blanket statements that all four Gospels are biographies distort the interpretive process, as do claims that all four Gospels are Gospels (as a new genre), or that Mark is an apocalypse (or even 'apocalyptic'—though that depends on what we mean by that slippery adjective). The first rule for the interpretation of any text is read the text, the whole text, and nothing but the text—initially. Read it alone, read it in a group, and wrestle with it—before exploring plausible accounts of its earliest contexts, and then the interpretations and genre classifications of others. Reading in Greek is ideal, but unrealistic in most contexts, so in the tradition of my *Doktorvater,* Athol Gill, I use my own translation of Mark with all the so-called 'historic present tenses' retained, the repetitive 'and' (*kai*) at the start of nearly every paragraph, and all forty-one of that urgent word *euthus* (immediately, straightaway)—seeking to hear Mark as it would have been heard amongst those earliest communities of Jesus followers.

I am aware that this can seem like a naïve return to primitivism—a desire to make the earliest form of the text normative for our interpretation and guidance today—but my concern initially is simply that we respect our primary sources. Whatever form or interpretation of the text we think is to be understood as authoritative (if any) I leave to the various faith communities and/or scholarly guilds to decide, as befits their different contexts. My aim is to argue that these texts (particularly in this case, the one now known as the Gospel of Mark) should be heard on their own terms (so far as is possible), in relation to the material culture of their day (so far as it can be known), and the literary environment in which they arose (which may involve discussions about genre). This is good historical practice and an essential part of the interpretive process, and not just at the academic level, but also for those who teach and preach these texts for formation and transformation. Historical context, both literary and socio-political, do not determine meaning, but they help to set reasonable limits within which our hermeneutical imaginations can operate more realistically.

The extent of the hermeneutical problem concerning these matters is evident in the way we read Mark at the popular level, but perhaps also increasingly at the scholarly level. For unless we pay close attention to the Greek text, we read a post-digested Mark, blended linguistically into a Gospel smoothie with its successors, stripped of the annoying idiosyncrasies of Mark's rough

---

6   Aune points out that 'both Matthew and Luke chose not to use Mark's εὐαγγέλιον as a description of their narratives (Matthew substituted the term βίβλος in Matt. 1:1, while Luke described his work as a διήγησις in Luke 1:1)'. 'Genre Theory', 38. Note that the Fourth Gospel uses βιβλίον of itself in John 20:30. None of these terms are genres from a contemporary literary critical point of view, but they still must be taken seriously as self-descriptions within each text.
7   The first use of the word 'apocalypse' (from Rev. 1:1) to describe a distinct genre of literature has been attributed to German scholar K. I. Nitzsch in 1822 (Aune, *Revelation 1–5*, lxxvii). See also Collins, 'Genre Apocalypse', 23: 'It is important to note that the classification "apocalyptic" or "apocalypse" is a modern one'.

Greek so that it sounds much like the other Gospels.[8] The most obvious argument for the priority of Mark disappears immediately due to this homogenising tendency of our translations. So too, if we are not careful, does the sense of narrative and theological development between and within the early Gospel traditions, and an awareness of their extraordinarily creative diversity—and this happens not just at the level of popular translations. Scholarly classifications of genre can cause the same problems by emphasising similarities rather than distinctive features, particularly when all four canonical Gospels are lumped together in the same category.[9] Stanton goes on to state that:

> The gospels are now widely considered to be a sub-set of the broad ancient literary genre of βίοι, biographies. Even if the evangelists were largely ignorant of the tradition of Greek and Roman βίοι, that is how the gospels were received and listened to in the first decades after their composition.[10]

Does this mean that genre can be determined by the eye of the beholder, or the ear of the hearer—regardless of the language of the text and its authors? Was that actually how all the narrative Jesus traditions were heard and understood in the second half of the first century and beyond, regardless of different locations and sub-cultures? If the genre *bioi* can stretch so widely to cover all these texts in the ears of their hearers, does it have anything to offer of particular value for interpreting each Gospel text—and in this case, Mark, the first one circulated?

Mark as *bios*

It could be said on one level that the earliest written account of the story of Jesus' life and death was an extraordinary literary failure. Today only four papyrus fragments of the Gospel of Mark remain from the first 600 years of its existence (compared with twenty-three for Matthew, eleven for Luke, and thirty for John), and the first full commentary on its text dates to the end of that period (seventh century). The grammar of this first surviving document to incarnate the Word in ink, on papyrus, was so uncouth, that the Church Fathers were embarrassed, and even later scholars have tried to suggest that it was written in a specially inspired 'Holy Ghost Greek' in order to explain its lack of classical style.[11] But mostly, Mark was simply ignored for centuries.

---

8   See further detailed evidence of this below.
9   A notable exception to the tendency to tar all Gospels with the same brush is provided by Vines, *Problem*, who argues that Matthew and Luke conform more closely than Mark to Graeco-Roman *bioi* because they include birth and resurrection accounts. I would add that the naming of the Roman authorities and the Socratic death of Jesus in Luke make that Gospel's implied audience very clear, even as Luke also mimics Septuagintal style to maintain links with Jewish salvation history.
10 Stanton, *Jesus and Gospel*, Summary statement, ch. 9, 'What are the gospels?', 192–206.
11 See Edgar McKnight's critique of Nigel Turner's attempt to return to a pre-Deissmann view of biblical Greek as a special dialect of *Koine* Greek, perhaps even re-opening the question of 'a Holy Ghost language'. McKnight, 'Is the New Testament Written', 87–93, commenting on Turner, *Syntax*, 1–9.

Table 1: Earliest New Testament Papyri (Matthew–Romans)

Book	Early (to 400)	Total (to 600)	100-200 CE 𝔓 no.	200-300 CE 𝔓 no.	300-400 CE 𝔓 no.	400-500 CE 𝔓 no.	500-600 CE 𝔓 no.
Matthew	16	23	104	1, 45, 53, 64, 70, 101	25, 62, 71, 86, 110		83, 96
				77, 103		19, 21	44
				37, 102		35, 105	
Mark	3	4		𝔓45	𝔓88		𝔓84
				𝔓137			
Luke	7	11		4, 45, 69, 75, 111, 138, 141			
						7, 82	3, 97
John	20	30	52, 90	5, 22, 28, 39, 45, 66, 75, 80, 95, 106, 107, 108, 109, 119, 121	6, 120	93	2, 36, 63, 76, 84
					122		44, 55, 128
				134			
Acts	7	15		29, 45, 48, 53, 91	8, 38	112, 127, 140	33, 56, 136
						50, 57	
Romans	7	9		27, 40, 46, 113, 118, 131	10	99	
							94

Online Sources: Peter M. Head, 'Early Greek Bible Manuscript Project: NT Mss. on Papyrus'. Wieland Willker, 'Complete List of Greek NT Papyri'.

On the other hand, it can be pointed out that the literary endeavours behind Mark were so successful that ninety percent of this Gospel was effectively plagiarised by the later Gospels of Matthew and/or Luke, as they adapted the Markan narrative in ways that made it more fitting for their own networks of gatherings. In so doing, they polished Mark's grammar—converting many of his present tense verbs into proper historical tenses; removing much of his *kai* parataxis; greatly reducing the forty-one occurrences of that annoying word *euthus*/immediately; and disambiguating the repeated use of 'he' for various people in the same paragraph by specifically naming Jesus more than twice as many times as does Mark. Then they made such 'minor additions' as the birth narratives, the resurrection appearances, the large teaching discourses known as the Sermon on the Mount or Plain, and the many additional parables.

How well do these processes accord with the view that the most significant literary genre shaping the writing of all four Gospels is ancient biography, the *bioi* of notable men? And how conscious, if at all, are the Gospel authors that they write within the constraints of this genre?

That all four Gospels are in fact *bioi* is not a new idea—it was thought possible, to some extent, by various scholars throughout the centuries (though not in the earliest centuries, when the title 'Gospel', not *bios*, was attached to all four manuscripts)—but it has become a working assumption since Richard Burridge baptised all four Gospels as biographies in his book *What Are the Gospels? A Comparison with Graeco-Roman Biography* (1992, but now in its third expanded edition). Just what this actually meant for the interpretation of each Gospel has been less clear, apart from drawing parallels between certain characteristics: 'how they display character, their (frequently) episodal structure, and their (commonly) ethical interest',[12] and particular literary artifices such as the *chreiai* (brief anecdotes, 'useful' for illuminating the main character), *synkrisis* (comparative juxtapositions of people and events) and other narrative and rhetorical devices.

Helen Bond's recent book—*The First Biography of Jesus: Genre and Meaning in Mark's Gospel*—seeks to give the first detailed reading of Mark as biography in order to demonstrate the efficacy for exegesis and interpretation of such a genre classification. After affirming Stanton's views on the necessity of genre classification, Bond recalls her own essay as a schoolgirl on why the Gospels were *not* biographies, since the evangelists 'were compilers and editors rather than authors, that the transmission of the Jesus tradition within the early Christian communities had more in common with folklore than any kind of literary process, and that the gospels were, in consequence, a unique phenomenon in the history of literature'.[13] But she soon put away her childish ways and became convinced, along with most of the scholarly world these days, that 'what we have in the first four books of the New Testament are *bioi,* or lives of Jesus. In a complete reversal of the former position, the "correct" answer to my schoolgirl question was now, "The gospels are biographies"'.[14] So Bond is now explicit in her intentions to let the genre shape her interpretation of the text itself: 'I aim to read Mark's work according to the literary conventions of ancient biographical literature'.[15]

This results in a very engaging and persuasive analysis of the biographical genre, its relationship to Gospel interpretation, and an insightful comparison with Mark that demonstrates an extraordinary grasp of biblical and classical literature. But I am always suspicious of such precipitous swings of the pendulum in scholarly fashions and the binary opposites that they reinforce. We do well to consider what gets lost in such 'complete reversals'. I am not arguing here for a return to the other extreme, that Mark was a mere collector of oral traditions already well formed, like pearls, nor simply an arranger of extended pre-Markan texts such as the passion narrative, the eschatological discourse, the parables chapter, and perhaps the cycle of conflict stories. But nor am I convinced by Bond's description of an individual author with full creative licence, yet knowingly operating within a formal literary genre. In her words:

> My approach in this study is both literary and historical. I imagine the gospel to have been written by a reasonably educated, creative author, who consciously selected and adapted his material. His adoption of a simple, 'popular' style should not blind us to his theological insight, sensitivity, and literary sophistication.[16]

This suggests that we read the author of Mark as 'dumbing down' his *bios* of Jesus for popular consumption, or could we argue together with the proponents of Mark as oral performance that the vivid and rough language of this Gospel sits closer to the vernacular of 'low culture' networks

---

12   Bond, *First Biography,* 6.
13   Bond, *First Biography,* 1.
14   Bond, *First Biography,* 2.
15   Bond, *First Biography,* 6.
16   Bond, *First Biography,* 6.

of early Jesus followers, resulting in an account that later writers polished and shaped in accord with the more cultured expectations of their audiences?

Bond reads Mark as if a reasonably educated individual provides a bridge by shaping disparate Jesus traditions into a *bios*, so that the benefits of this literature can 'trickle down'[17] to the masses, due to their partial exposure to such elite literature at various public performances at festivals, games, and speeches on grand occasions. As Bond suggests:

> Thus the rhetorical and literary conventions of the educated elite would have effortlessly percolated down to the lower levels of society. Even with only a basic level of education, an intelligent and thoughtful writer would be perfectly able to mimic the genres with which he had come into contact, and even to ape some of their standard conventions and practices. And, we can assume, many in his audience would have understood what he was doing.[18]

So for Bond the writing of Mark's Gospel is an educated literary process making sense of chaotic and diverse oral traditions and re-formulating them for public consumption in the identifiable form of the *bios*. It is 'an attempt actively to reappropriate and reconfigure selected material from the mass of unstructured, ahistorical sayings and anecdotes in circulation at the time into a formal, literary creation'.[19]

In words that to me are more fitting for the Lukan narrative, Bond suggests that:

> By imposing a biographical structure onto traditional material, Mark simultaneously gave it a historical framework. His work was thus the conscious shaping of a normative Christian past, intimately connected to the life of the founding figure, in such a way that it spoke to his own present as he and his audience sought to articulate their own sense of identity within the Roman world.[20]

Again, this describes the Lukan agenda very well, I suggest, as he gives Mark's narrative a wider political and historical framework, tidies up his Greek grammar, and grants Jesus a more appropriate Graeco-Roman death, as he calmly surrenders his spirit surrounded by 'all his acquaintances, including the women who had followed him from Galilee' (Luke 23:46,49). The rough Greek, the village and wilderness orientation,[21] and the horrific God-and-friend-forsaken death of Jesus in Mark, however, suggests that it acts as a bridge operating in the other direction—a means by which the transformative power of the Jesus story as experienced by the lowest strata of society begins to influence also the layers of society above them, particularly as the later Gospels adapt Mark's crude language and narrative into forms (including *bioi*) more persuasive to the cultured ear.[22] But the narrative and style of Mark originates amongst the tax-

---

17 For Bond's explanation of 'the trickle down effect', see *The First Biography of Jesus*, 71–73, 86 n.37.
18 Bond, *First Biography*, 72.
19 Bond, *First Biography*, 5.
20 Bond, *First Biography*, 5.
21 The Markan narrative resolutely avoids the urban centres that feature more prominently in the more urban (and urbane) text of Luke. See Dyer, *'Polis* and *Topos'*.
22 Bond's account of the death of Jesus in Mark succeeds in showing how his death is appropriate to his life and teaching on one level, but fails to convince that the public humiliation of crucifixion could ever be a fitting conclusion to a Graeco-Roman *bios*—unless indeed it was some kind of parody or grisly satire—or perhaps if Jesus could just suffer it all calmly (which is how Luke and John portray it). See Bond, *First Biography*, 224–246; and 'Fitting End?'. Bond describes it powerfully: 'Like a slave, Jesus endures it all, disempowered, humiliated, shamed, violated—nothing less manly and honourable could be imagined' (*First Biography*, 228), but fails to show how this could in any way be a 'good death' befitting a *bios*, especially given Jesus's cry of dereliction in Mark, when she has previously described a 'good and noble death' for a Graeco-Roman *bios* as 'a calm, courageous, dignified acceptance of one's fate' (*First Biography*, 62).

collectors, slaves, and notorious sinners—the 'crucifiable ones' for whom the 'crucified one' brings most hope.

One clear measure of the stylistic differences between the *bioi* that Bond compares with Mark, and the language of Mark itself, is the ratio of the common conjunction καί ('and') to the more refined use of δέ (also 'and' or 'but', but often left untranslated). Beginning sentences with καί in Greek reflects a low cultural origin, particularly if it is frequent, and probably also reflects the influence of Semitic languages (Hebrew and Aramaic). It is *Koinē* Greek, common Greek, or GSL (Greek as a second language, or third), and together with the 'historic present' may well be just a matter of 'personal preference',[23] though as the figures below show, it also correlates in some way with an awareness of culture (Jewish connections perhaps) and literature (the model texts of Hellenistic culture). Of course, genre is not determined by a fixed set of rules or features, or the measurement of style in this way—but rather is a family likeness dependent on various strands of DNA—yet such a marked difference in language for Mark (and especially Revelation) demands explanation.

Table 2: καί/δέ ratios in Ancient Literature
Greek Lives of Philosophers ('closest analogies to Mark')

	Occurrences of καί	Occurrences of δέ	καί/δέ ratio
Xenophon's *Memorabilia*	1915	861	2.224
Philo's *Life of Moses*	1883	505	3.729
Life of Aesop ('lower culture')	1909	1383	1.381
Lucian's *Demonax*	203	102	1.990
Philostratus's *Life of Apollonius of Tyana*	4424	3213	1.377
Diogenes Laertius' *Lives of Eminent Philosophers*	6548	3147	2.081

The Gospels and the Book of Revelation

Gospel of Matthew	1194	494	2.417
Gospel of Mark	1100	163	6.748
Gospel of Luke	1483	542	2.736
Gospel of John	868	213	4.075
Revelation	1128	7	161.143

---

23 As Bond, citing E.P. Sanders points out: *First Biography*, 83.

Are these differences best satisfied by Bond's suggestion that Mark is adapting the *bios* genre to appeal to the lower classes and so deliberately changes his style to that end, or does it suggest a closeness to the oral traditions of the Jesus followers (as Bond herself points out elsewhere),[24] as if these rumours of the crowd in common Greek bubble up from the slaves and other non-Roman dispensables and eventually demand a written account in a form digestible by the more literary minded. Is Mark that later account, or is Mark the one prior to Matthew and Luke, who attempt that task? In either case, the movement here is the reverse of what Bond and Burridge imply—the impetus for social and cultural change comes from below ('the humble will inherit the Earth') until it is given voice and written form by those who no longer wish to suppress it. The evidence for this lies not just with the text of the Gospels and *bioi*, but with their material remains—the papyri and manuscripts. As Bond points out, the formal high literature *bioi* of the philosophers and other notables often survive in only a few later manuscripts[25]—sometimes hundreds of years later, whereas the Gospel accounts are attested by fifty papyrus fragments from the first 350 years alone (notwithstanding Mark's meagre contribution to the total). Many of these are palimpsests (written on scrubbed and re-used papyrus) and double-sided using very ordinary handwriting, but their existence supports the contention that the earliest copies of the Gospels circulated widely amongst the lower classes—and not as simplified high literature trickling down from the elite, but as expressions (via Mark) of their lived experience as those given hope by the idea of a God who affirms the crucified one.

The attempt by Bond to read Mark in the context of Graeco-Roman *bioi* yields many profound insights, sometimes despite her insistence that Mark too is a *bios*. Often, as conceded also by Hägg, and Aune,[26] this is because Mark doesn't quite fit the expectations generated by the other *bioi*—Jesus in Mark is not given a pedigree or a prologue, nor a panegyric at the end,[27] his death hardly fulfills the ideal of a good or noble death (nor do the events that follow),[28] and the use of *chreiai* and *synkrisis* often falls short of the 'proper' *bioi*, not to mention his crude Greek. So why insist that Mark too is a *bios*, when so much of what Bond and others say about that genre fits better with Luke's Gospel, and perhaps Matthew too, if we allow a sub-category of Hellenistic Jewish biography? There is still value in comparing Mark with other genres in order to highlight and evaluate similarities and differences, but it is not necessary to pre-emptively assert the genre of Mark to undertake this analysis. Nor does the failure to identify a genre at the outset limit the effectiveness of other types of analysis, as the many informative narrative analyses of Mark have demonstrated.[29] So is the first step in the interpretation of any writing to establish and name its literary genre, as Stanton asserted and Bond has affirmed? Reader beware. If that genre is not emic to the text being examined, it may well be a misstep, as can be seen even more clearly in the strange ways the genre of 'apocalypse' (or worse still, 'apocalyptic') has been applied to biblical literature.

---

24 Bond, *First Biography*, 73, referring to Grammatiki Karla's description of such grammatical features as indicating the spoken word.
25 Bond, *First Biography*, 71.
26 For references by Bond to their comments on Mark, see *First Biography*, 35, 157 (Hägg), 89–90 (Aune).
27 Bond, *First Biography*, 251, is refreshingly honest: 'I cannot claim that reading Mark as biography solves the problem of Mark's ending'.
28 While discussing Mark's choices for portraying Jesus' death, Bond suggests that 'the final product needed to produce a pleasing effect and to speak to the present needs of the anticipated audience' (Bond, *First Biography*, 226).
29 Here I think of the work of Rhoads and Michie, Tolbert, Geddert, Bolt, Broadhead, Shively, and many others for whom genre was not the primary concern.

Apocalypse and Mark

The *Sitz im Leben* of the genre 'apocalypse' in the nineteenth-century German theological schools has already been alluded to above.[30] Prior to that, the noun 'apocalypse' was used very sparingly in Greek, Jewish, and early Christian literature simply to mean uncovering, revelation, or disclosure. It is not used by Philo or Josephus at all, occurs only four times in the Septuagint, and seven times in the Pseudepigrapha—three of those instances paralleling, and perhaps imitating, the single use as the first word in the Book of Revelation.[31] 'Apocalypse' is not used in Enoch or Daniel at all. Only the verb (*anakalyptō* = reveal) appears twice in Enoch, with no verb form in Daniel. They have been described as apocalypses retrospectively, as have most of the books that now carry the title apocalypse.

Even if we accept that this etic use of 'apocalypse' as a literary genre is valid and has retrospectivity,[32] apocalypses today are not what they used to be, and this is the first reason why the word, together with 'apocalyptic', is better not applied to Mark and should be dropped from our public theology and reflections. In popular usage (as indicated in newspaper headlines) 'apocalypse' is understood to mean disaster, a world-ending catastrophe, even when (perhaps especially when) it is associated with the last book of the Bible. So we read in any number of online dictionaries that 'apocalypse' is a noun meaning 'the complete final destruction of the world, as described in the biblical book of Revelation', and its synonyms are listed as 'annihilation, cataclysm, catastrophe, devastation, holocaust, Armageddon, decimation, and end of the world'. In graphic endorsement of these meanings, the number of movies in the genre of apocalyptic and postapocalyptic films has grown from four in the years before 1950 to over 100 in the last decade alone, many containing images and symbols derived from the visions of John the Seer. How then, is the person in the street to understand the relationship between the 'beginning of the Good News (the *euangelion*) of Jesus Christ' (the first five words of the Gospel of Mark) and the '*apokalypsis*, the Catastrophe of Jesus Christ' (the first three words of Revelation 1:1)? How can Good News seemingly threaten such catastrophic consequences for creation?

Even though James Barr convinced us long ago that widespread usage is more important in shaping the meaning of words than etymology, we are inclined to retreat to our classrooms to set the record straight. At least there we can teach students what 'apocalypse', 'apocalyptic eschatology', and 'apocalypticism' *really* mean, rather than the way they are misused by the newspapers, films, Tweeters, and social media of our age. And such education is important if we are going to equip our students to understand past interpretive traditions, but if we wish to persist in using words with special meanings inside the academy, we ought to make provision for the way that we will be heard outside.

I suggest that this common understanding of 'apocalypse' as disaster/cataclysm has deeply affected popular Christian theology, even though the 'rapture and left behind' heresy is not as prominent in Australia as it has been in the USA. There is still a sense that in the face of the imminent crises facing us, many think that Revelation, and Mark 13 and parallels too, call the church to wait quietly and passively witnessing and worshipping until an interventionist God is moved to sort it all out for us. The repeated calls in Revelation for the *ekklēsiai* to repent, to change

---

30 See footnote 7 above.
31 It appears in 2/4 Ezra/Esdras 1:0 'word and apocalypse of the holy prophet Esdras' and in 3 Baruch 0:1 'An apocalypse of Baruch', and is repeated in the next verse, 0:2.
32 The word 'apocalypse' is emic to Revelation, and especially to the Pauline corpus as we shall see, but is used in the sense of 'uncovering' or 'revelation', and not as a literary genre.

our ways, to live up to our priestly, prophetic and *basileic* commission and work as God's 'slaves'[33] to challenge the consequences of human abuse of power, continue to fall on our deaf ears. The common understanding of apocalypse as disaster is not Good News, and leads to a fatalistic quietism at best, and ethical paralysis and despair at worst.

A second reason for caution in using the term 'apocalypse' is that even within scholarly circles its meaning has become confused and unclear. Those weightier dictionaries that do give the first meaning as 'a revelation' and/or a 'literary genre', often go on to list a taxonomy of descriptive features of some kind, derived from the scholarly literature. For example:

> Apocalypse. 1a: one of the Jewish and Christian writings of 200 B.C. to A.D. 150 marked by pseudonymity, symbolic imagery, and the expectation of an imminent cosmic cataclysm in which God destroys the ruling powers of evil and raises the righteous to life in a messianic kingdom.[34]

We might wish here to clarify the difference between the literary genre, 'Apocalypse', and the three phases of 'apocalyptic eschatology' (present crisis–coming judgement–final vindication), but such neat distinctions are difficult to maintain even in scholarly circles. The taxonomy of possible features of the genre apocalypse is a long and variable one, and often overlaps with the characteristics of apocalyptic eschatology. The J. J. and A. Y. Collins team produced the most helpful comparative list delineating twenty-eight features potentially present in fifteen Jewish Apocalypses, twenty-four Christian Apocalypses, and twelve related works.[35] The only features they see as common to all of these 'apocalypses' are the presence of 'otherworldly beings' and 'otherworldly mediators', with all Jewish apocalypses also characterised by 'pseudonymity' and the 'judgment/destruction of the wicked', and all Christian ones referencing the 'afterlife'. This process is helpful for mapping the characteristics of the literature of the second Temple period, but it results in a rather shaky foundation for establishing a new literary genre—even given the contemporary preference for genres with fuzzy boundaries. Unsurprisingly, John Collins has since reviewed the resulting lengthy definitions of 'apocalypse' and re-affirmed a focus on the 'prototypical core'—the heart of the genre—such as his earlier formulation 'the transcendence of death'.[36]

Genre taxonomies like these may be helpful in a general descriptive way, but not if they lead us to impose later distinctions on texts anachronistically. For a start, these categories assume a premature judgement of what is Jewish and what is Christian (especially at the time of the Book of Revelation), and modernist views about what is 'this worldly' and what is 'other worldly' (constructing a cosmic duality)—polarities not evident in the texts themselves. The three-tiered cosmos is just that—all that can be seen from the standpoint of Earth—and does not in itself constitute two opposing worlds. Further problems emerge when binary polarities are multiplied in the lists of apocalyptic characteristics given by other scholars: a moral duality (good and evil); temporal duality (this age and the age to come); social duality (the elect and the damned/sons of light and sons of darkness); and an epistemological duality (revelation and hiddenness). These categories may be appropriate in themselves, but pairing them as polarities suggests they are equal and opposite and dualistic in nature. It is possible to detect elements of this thinking and

---

33 Again the text (and John) identifies with the dispensable classes, but our translators invariably give us 'servants' for *doulos* (used fourteen times in Revelation from 1:1 onwards) to give a more comfortable reading.
34 Merriam-Webster Dictionary online.
35 Collins, 'Jewish apocalypses', and Collins, 'Early Christian apocalypses'.
36 Collins, 'Apocalyptic Eschatology', and later, 'Genre Apocalypse', 40.

terminology in some Second Temple texts, but to suggest that they are characteristic of all so-called apocalypses, Revelation included, is not a helpful way to begin reading such documents. If such lists are to constitute a definition or description of 'apocalyptic literature', then 'apocalyptic' is not just the Mother of Christian theology, as Ernst Käsemann once affirmed it to be, but of all the apocalunatic cults that have arisen since. The genre 'apocalypse' has become so widely defined that everything in the New Testament is said to be 'apocalyptic'— whatever that means, including Mark's Gospel.

This leaves one major user of the noun 'apocalypse' in the New Testament—and indeed in all Greek literature up until the second century, so far as I can see—the Apostle Paul. Thirteen of the eighteen uses of 'apocalypse' in the New Testament (discounting the extra *superscriptio* later given to Revelation) occur in the Pauline corpus, and mainly in the earlier seven letters. But Paul writes letters, not 'apocalypses', and his use of the word does not invoke disaster or cataclysm or indeed any of the many features attributed to apocalypses in the taxonomies I have mentioned. Rather, in the tradition reaching back through J. Louis Martyn to Käsemann, and Karl Barth, Paul's use of 'apocalypse' intensifies the everyday meaning of reveal/uncover. It is 'about God's liberating invasion of the cosmos' (Martyn) through 'Christ's love enacted in the cross' that 'has the power to change the world because it is embodied in the new community of mutual service'.[37] So this is not about the destruction of the world, dualistic thinking, or mysterious sky journeys as such (though apparently Paul had one of those too, 2 Cor. 12.1–5)—but is a way of conceptualising the implications of God's affirmation of the way and faithfulness of Jesus Christ.

As the first substantial user of the noun 'apocalypse' in the Greek language, we should let Paul's meaning inform our thinking and teaching—not the much later descriptions of a supposed literary genre. Even in Paul there are at least two main ways we can interpret the term: as 'eschatological invasion' (following Martyn, as just outlined) and/or as 'unveiled fulfilment', often attributed to the work of Chris Rowland. The former stresses the newness of God's action and the latter the continuity with past revelations through the prophets and Lady Wisdom. In these two carefully defined ways we might even apply the description 'apocalyptic' to Mark's narrative. The former revelatory understanding is evident in the ripping apart of the heavens at the baptism of Jesus (Mark 1:10) and in the ripping apart of the Temple curtain at Jesus's death (Mark 15:38), as pointed out by Grant Macaskill.[38] The latter sense of unveiled fulfilment is apparent in the references to Isaiah that surround the baptism, where wise discernment of the prophetic voices indicates that Isaiah is the hermeneutical key to understanding the identities of John and Jesus. But Mark never uses 'apocalypse' or 'apocalyptic', and we should be careful not to import the misunderstanding of these terms into our reading of Mark. I appreciate the 'apocalyptic' readings of Mark by Shively, Macaskill, and Nel (and others), provided they don't import the modernist polarities so often associated with 'apocalyptic'—dualisms between Jesus and Satan (when Satan is only mentioned five times in Mark, once of Peter, and only in the first half of the Gospel; it is the religio-political powers in Jerusalem that are the ultimate opposition to Jesus); between 'the elect' and the 'the damned' (when the elect in Mark 13 is gathered from the four corners, and those threatened with *Gehenna* are a minority of religious leaders); between 'this world' and 'the next' (when Mark 13 addresses this world and the disasters that befell Jerusalem within a generation of

---

37 Martyn, 'Apocalyptic Gospel', 255.

38 Macaskill, 'Apocalypse', 58. The shift in emphasis in the understanding of apocalypse from eschatology to revelation that is evident in the collected articles in *The Jewish Apocalyptic Tradition and the Shaping of New Testament Thought* (ed. by Stuckenbruck and Reynolds) is to be welcomed. Next step is to jettison the word altogether and leave it as a movie genre only.

Jesus, as he foretold, 13:30). If 'apocalypses' are understood to involve those kinds of binaries, then using such language in reference to Mark will not help our interpretation or our proclamation.

Mark as Gospel

Whatever genre we may assign to the Gospels (and *bios* is wide enough in usage to fit at least Matthew and Luke, I think), they will still be referred to as Gospels, which is not a genre in itself but at least is a clear descriptor. Aune has given us a detailed account of how that word 'Gospel' (*euangelion*) came to be attached to all four canonical Gospels, not yet as a genre label, he argues, but nor did the early church call them *bioi* or *apokalyptika*.[39] Mark is the only Gospel that uses 'gospel' as a self-description, and that sense of 'good news' fits better than simply calling it the *The First Life of Jesus*, for the good news centres on God's affirmation of the death of Jesus as well as his life. This is not just playing semantics, for Jesus in Mark lacks important indicators of 'life' (a birth and a clear family of origin), and is much less the 'subject of the verbs' (one of Burridge's markers of *bioi*) than in the other Gospels. Mark downplays the subject by frequently (and sometimes ambiguously) using 'he' and Jesus himself deflects attention to God and the *basileia* of God. Jesus asks who others think he is, but accepts no labels for himself—the nametags stick to those who would apply them instead. Perhaps that's also how it is with naming the genre of the Gospels—the labels we give say more about us and our interpretive strategies and assumptions.

Keith Dyer
kdyer@whitley.edu.au
Whitley College, University of Divinity

---

39 Aune, 'Genre Theory'.

Select Bibliography

Aune, D. E.	*Revelation 1–5* (Word Biblical Commentary, vol. 52A; Grand Rapids, MI: Zondervan, 1997).
Aune, D. E.	'Genre Theory and the Genre-Function of Mark and Matthew', in D. E. Aune (ed.), *Jesus, Gospel Tradition and Paul in the Context of Jewish and Greco-Roman Antiquity, Collected Essays II* (Tübingen: Mohr Siebeck, 2013), 26–56.
Baum, A. D.	'Biographies of Jesus in Old Testament and Rabbinic Style: The Genre of the New Testament Gospels', in A. W. White, C. A. Evans, and D. Wenham (eds.), *The Earliest Perceptions of Jesus in Context: Essays in Honour of John Nolland on His 70th Birthday* (London: Bloomsbury T&T Clark), 33–58.
Berger, K.	'Hellenistische Gattungen im Neuen Testament', *ANRW* 2.25.2 (1984), 1031–1432.
Bond, H. K.	*The First Biography of Jesus: Genre and Meaning in Mark's Gospel* (Grand Rapids, MI: Eerdmans, 2020).
Bond, H. K.	'A Fitting End? Self-Denial and a Slave's Death in Mark's *Life of Jesus*', NTS 65 (2019), 425–442.
Breytenbach, C.	'The Gospel According to Mark: The Yardstick for Comparing the Gospels with Ancient Texts', in R. M. Calhoun, D. P. Moessner, and T. Nicklas (eds.), *Modern and Ancient Literary Criticism of the Gospels: Continuing the Debate on Gospel Genre(s)* (WUNT 451; Tübingen: Mohr Siebeck, 2020), 179–200.
Bultmann, R.	*The History of the Synoptic Tradition* (trans. J. Marsh; New York, NY: Harper & Row, 1963).
Burridge, R.	*What Are the Gospels? A Comparison with Graeco-Roman Biography* (Cambridge: Cambridge University Press, 1992; expanded 3rd edn; Waco, TX: Baylor University Press, 2018).
Calhoun, R. M., D. P. Moessner, and T. Nicklas, (eds.)	*Modern and Ancient Literary Criticism of the Gospels: Continuing the Debate on Gospel Genre(s)* (WUNT 451; Tübingen: Mohr Siebeck, 2020).
Collins, A. Y.	*Mark: A Commentary* (Minneapolis, MN: Fortress Press, 2007).
Collins, A. Y.	*Is Mark's Gospel a Life of Jesus? The Question of Genre* (Milwaukee, WI: Marquette University Press, 1990).
Collins, A. Y.	'The Early Christian Apocalypses', in J.J. Collins (ed.), *Semeia* 14, *Apocalypse: The Morphology of a Genre* (Missoula, MT: Scholars Press, 1979), 61–121.
Collins, J. J.	'The Jewish Apocalypses', in J.J. Collins (ed.), *Semeia* 14, *Apocalypse: The Morphology of a Genre* (Missoula, MT: Scholars Press, 1979), 21–59.
Collins, J. J.	'Apocalyptic Eschatology as the Transcendence of Death', *CBQ* 36 (1974), 21–43.
Collins, J. J.	'The Genre Apocalypse Reconsidered', *ZAC* 20 (2016), 21–40.

Dinkler, M. B.	'What is a Genre?', in R. M. Calhoun, D. P. Moessner, and T. Nicklas (eds.), *Modern and Ancient Literary Criticism of the Gospels: Continuing the Debate on Gospel Genre(s)* (WUNT 451; Tübingen: Mohr Siebeck, 2020), 77–96.
Dyer, K.	'The Empire of God, the Postcolonial Jesus, and Postapocalyptic Mark', in M. Brett and J. Havea (eds.), *Colonial Contexts and Postcolonial Theologies: Storyweaving in the Asia-Pacific* (New York, NY: Palgrave Macmillan, 2014), 81–97.
Dyer, K.	'*Polis* and *Topos*: Reimagining "Home" in Mark's Narrative', in D. Jackson, D. Cronshaw, and R. Dewerse (eds.), *Reimagining Home: Understanding, reconciling and engaging with God's stories together* (Macquarie Park, NSW: Morling Press, 2019), 249–258.
Judge, E.	'"We Have No King but Caesar". When was Caesar First Seen as a King?' in E. A. Judge, *The First Christians in the Roman World* (ed. J. R. Harrison; Tübingen: Mohr Siebeck, 2008 [first presented in 1986]), 395–403.
Macaskill, G.	'Apocalypse and the Gospel of Mark', in L. T. Stuckenbruck and B. E. Reynolds (eds.), *The Jewish Apocalyptic Tradition and the Shaping of New Testament Thought* (Minneapolis, MN: Fortress/1517 Media, 2017), 53–77.
McKnight, E. V.	'Is the New Testament Written in "Holy Ghost" Greek', *The Bible Translator* 116 (1965), 87–93.
Martyn, J. L.	'The Apocalyptic Gospel in Galatians', *Interpretation* 54 (2000), 246–266.
Mitchell, M. M.	'Mark, the Long-Form Pauline εὐαγγέλιον', in R. M. Calhoun, D. P. Moessner, and T. Nicklas (eds.), *Modern and Ancient Literary Criticism of the Gospels: Continuing the Debate on Gospel Genre(s)* (WUNT 451; Tübingen: Mohr Siebeck, 2020), 201–218.
Nell, M.	'The Gospel of Mark in Light of its Apocalyptic Worldview', *Journal of Early Christian History* 4 (2014), 135–148.
Shively, E. E.	*Apocalyptic Imagination in the Gospel of Mark: The Literary and Theological Role of Mark 3:22–30*, (Vol. 189, BZnW; Berlin: De Gruyter, 2012).
Stanton, G. N.	'Matthew: βίβλιος , εὐαγγέλιον , βίος?', in F. van Segbroeck with C. M. Tuckett, G. Van Belle, and J. Verheyden (eds.), *The Four Gospels, 1992: Festschrift for Frans Neirynck* (Leuven: Leuven University Press, 1992), 2.1187–1201.
Stanton, G. N.	*Jesus and Gospel* (Cambridge: Cambridge University Press, 2004).
Turner, N.	*Syntax,* vol. III of *A Grammar of New Testament Greek* (Edinburgh: T&T Clark, 1963).
Van Oyen, G.	'Action according to Quintilian (*Institutio oratoria* 11.3) and the Performance of the Gospel of Mark', in R. M. Calhoun, D. P. Moessner, and T. Nicklas (eds.), *Modern and Ancient Literary Criticism of the Gospels: Continuing the Debate on Gospel Genre(s)* (WUNT 451; Tübingen: Mohr Siebeck, 2020), 335–356.
Vines, M. E.	*The Problem of Markan Genre: The Gospel of Mark and the Jewish Novel* (Leiden: Brill, 2002).

The Divine Identity of Jesus in John 4

CHRIS SEGLENIEKS

Abstract

The account of the Samaritan woman and her encounter with Jesus places significant attention upon Jesus' identity. Yet like the Samaritan woman it is possible to fail to see beyond the surface presentation of Jesus as an essentially human Messiah and into the deeper significance of Jesus' words and actions that convey his divine identity. Jesus takes on God's role as giver of the Spirit (4:10), by taking on a divine prerogative in determining the location of worship (John 4:21–24) and replacing the temple with himself as God's presence. Jesus is shown as the bringer of divine salvation (4:22). He takes on the role he ascribes to God in seeking true worshippers (4:23), before alluding to his divine identity declaring 'I am' (4:26). This connects Jesus' divine identity with his messianic identity, presenting Jesus as the divine Messiah.

The story of Jesus in Samaria in John 4 is a classic example of Johannine misunderstanding.[1] The Samaritan woman struggles to grasp Jesus' identity, misinterpreting his words about 'living water' (4:10–15), by taking them in a physical rather than symbolic sense. But what if readers interpret the story like the woman interpreted Jesus, understanding the surface meaning but failing to recognise the deeper symbolism of the encounter? John draws attention to Jesus' identity with the question that Jesus raises, 'who is speaking to you' (4:10). The opening scene presents a very human Jesus, arriving at the well tired from his travels (4:6).[2] The following narrative depicts Jesus' identity in terms of prophet (4:19), Messiah (4:25,29), and the 'Saviour of the World' (4:42). For the woman, though, there is the sense of a journey incomplete. While she accepts Jesus is a prophet, she only questions whether he is the Messiah. Her announcement to her village and their confession in 4:42 suggests a positive conclusion to her questioning. Yet Jesus' response in 4:26 also points to her need to continue to go deeper in understanding his identity. On one level, Jesus' words are an admission that he is the Messiah. At the same time, the use of ἐγώ εἰμι (I am) and its divine use in Isaiah form an implicit claim to divinity—a depth to Jesus' identity that the woman does not yet recognise.

The implications of the 'I am' in 4:26 should point the reader towards a deeper understanding. Yet it is possible to overlook the symbolic significance in Jesus' words that, like the 'I am', point

---

1 On Johannine misunderstanding, see esp. Carson, 'Understanding Misunderstandings',.
2 Thompson, *Humanity of Jesus*, 3.

towards his divine identity. A focus on a non-divine messianic presentation of Jesus in John 4 is evident in previous scholarship.[3] It has explored the prophetic and revelatory dimension, including connections to the Samaritan concept of the *Taheb*, a primarily revelatory messianic figure.[4] At other times a royal dimension is seen, as with the imperial resonances of Saviour of the World.[5] A common feature of such approaches is a focus on what the characters within the story could have perceived about Jesus' identity at the time. While this accounts for the interaction between Jesus and his audiences within the narrative, it fails to appreciate the full picture of Jesus' identity as presented to the audience of the Gospel.[6]

When Jesus speaks to the woman, there is a surface meaning and a deeper symbolism, and the situation is similar for the reader. When the significance of Jesus' words is recognised, there are implications for Christology, as we see Jesus taking on divine roles. The connections are conveyed in part through scriptural links, some of which may have been accessible to the woman in the story but are more evident for the reader. Aside from the implications of 'I am' in 4:26, these scriptural links that convey Jesus' divine identity have been given little attention. The close connection between the implicit presentation of Jesus as divine and his identity as Messiah further suggests that beyond a kingly or prophetic messiah, this story functions to present Jesus as a divine messiah. Rather than focusing on the human messianic dimensions, there is a need to see the way scriptural connections are used to construct an implicit presentation of Jesus as divine.

1. A Gospel Communicating to an Audience

In order to appreciate the way in which the Gospel works for the audience, it is vital to recognise the two levels at which the text works. At one level, the Gospel relates the story of the events of Jesus' ministry, while at another level it arranges and frames the elements of the story for the Gospel audience.[7] The work of literary theorist Seymour Chatman has previously been applied to the Gospel, and his categories of the story level and discourse level respectively are useful for understanding the function of the two levels in the text.[8] The story level refers to the characters and events within the narrative. The discourse level, which will be the focus here, is the communication between the author and the audience. It encompasses the way in which the story is told, including the words or actions that are highlighted, the choice of words which may introduce ambiguity, or may link together events. It also encompasses the input of the narrator

---

3   Those considering Jesus in John 4 in human messianic terms include: Loader, *Jesus in John's Gospel*, 76; Kruse, *John*, 148–51; Michaels, *John*, 256–7; Carson, *John*, 224; Beasley-Murray, *John*, 61. Where development in Christology is identified in John 4, it is an expansion of scope from Messiah of Israel to saviour of the world. Thompson, *John*, 95–96. In discussions of Jesus' divine identity, John 4 is overlooked, as seen in Schnelle's chapter where in the section on divine identity, the only reference to John 4:1–42 refers to Jesus completing his work (4:30). Schnelle, 'The Person of Jesus', 322.
4   On Samaritan messianic ideas, see Coloe, *God Dwells with Us*, 101–2; MacDonald, *Theology of the Samaritans*, 359–71.
5   On the imperial connections of 'Saviour of the World', see Koester, 'Saviour of the World', 665–80. Schnackenburg also notes the 'element of majesty and royalty'. Schnackenburg, *John*, 1:458.
6   Botha is one who focuses more on the audience of the Gospel, but the concern is primarily on the effect of the text rather than on Christology. Botha, *Jesus and the Samaritan Woman*.
7   The two levels at which the narrative operates have been recognised by Frey, *Glory of the Crucified One*, 93–7; Carson, 'Understanding Misunderstandings', 81.
8   Chatman, *Story and Discourse*, 19, 43. On the application of Chatman's theory to the Gospel of John, see Seglenieks, 'Faith and Narrative', 23–40. These two levels are not to be confused with the two levels advocated by Martyn, *History and Theology*.

that may explain further the events of the story. The Prologue demonstrates the narrator's role as it sets the readers up as a privileged audience, knowing more of Jesus' identity than the characters within the story. Recognising this way that narratives work facilitates posing two distinct sets of questions, one focusing on the depiction of the events of Jesus' ministry, and the other examining the interaction between the Gospel and its audience. At the story level, John presents Christology with historically plausible details, such as the disciples' lack of christological understanding (2:22; 12:16; 20:9), or the similarly incomplete understanding of the Samaritan woman. Yet the author also explains to the audience his post-resurrection understanding of the true significance of Jesus' words and deeds. To fully come to grips with the Johannine text, we must also ask the question of how the text is shaped to present the identity of Jesus to the Gospel audience.

If we are to consider the interaction between text and audience, we must outline what the audience is assumed to know beyond the text of the Gospel. In what was likely a mixed Jewish and Gentile audience, knowledge of the Jewish Scriptures can be presupposed for the Jewish component, while their prominence in the early church means a Gentile audience would likely also be, or would soon become, familiar with them.[9] Thus, texts such as Deuteronomy and Isaiah can be assumed as part of the repertoire the early audience brings to the text.

More controversially, some of the following arguments will involve reading John alongside Revelation. Rather than arguing for a direct literary connection or common authorship, the two texts represent a shared theological thought world. The texts are connected by a similar place and time of origin. For John, at least the final stages of composition are located by most scholars in Ephesus, often around A.D. 80–90.[10] Revelation is tied to Asia Minor by the text itself, both by placing John on Patmos (1:9) and in the seven churches addressed, including Ephesus (1:11). The predominant dating of Revelation is to the reign of Domitian (A.D. 81–96), following Irenaeus *Adv. haer.* 5.30.3, which coincides with the dating of the Gospel of John.[11] Modern scholars tend to reject common authorship, yet Alan Culpepper and Martin Hengel identify the Gospel and Revelation as either emerging from a common group or showing links at an earlier stage in their composition.[12] This commonality means that Revelation provides evidence of the thought world of the Gospel audience; thus we can use Revelation to add to our understanding of the audience's repertoire. While audience knowledge of the text of Revelation cannot be assumed, the concepts within Revelation can be used to guide the interpretation of what may be implied or assumed in

---

9   On a mixed audience for John, see Klink, *Sheep of the Fold*, 176–7; Koester, 'The Spectrum of Johannine Readers', 5–19; Hengel, *The Johannine Question*, 119. On drawing conclusions about the real audience based upon the implied audience see Culpepper, *Anatomy of the Fourth Gospel*, 211–23; De Boer, 'Narrative Criticism', 35–48.

10 The early sources for locating the Gospel in Ephesus include: Irenaeus, *Haer.* 3.1.1, 2.22.5 and Eusebius, *Hist. eccl.* 3.1.1, 3.23.6, 5.8.4. On the early witnesses to the place and authorship of the Gospel, see esp. Bauckham, *Jesus and the Eyewitnesses*, 412–71. On the date and setting of the Gospel, see Klink, *John*, 59–60; Thompson, *John*, 20–22; Frey, 'The Diaspora-Jewish Background', 190; Hengel, *The Johannine Question*, 119–33; Barrett, *John*, 128–32.

11 On the date and setting of Revelation, see Paul, *Revelation*, 11–22; Beale, *Revelation*, 4–33; Aune, *Revelation*, 1:xlvii–lxx.

12 Culpepper, *The Johannine School*, 1–5; Hengel, *The Johannine Question*, 126–7; Frey, 'Erwägungen zum Verhältnis', 329–49; Beasley-Murray, *Revelation*, 36. Not all scholars reject common authorship. Most recently, the connection between the Gospel and Revelation is advocated by Behr, *John the Theologian*, 72–76. Modern as well as ancient assertions of common authorship (such as Irenaeus, *Adv. haer.* 4.20.11, Clement of Alexandria, *Strom.* 6.16.141.7) add weight to the argument that the two texts are at least theologically aligned. While some early sources reject common authorship (such as Dionysius of Alexandria, in Eusebius, *Hist. eccl.* 7.25.6–7), these come later and often in the context of theological controversies where contested interpretations of Revelation feature.

the Gospel, reflecting how an early audience may have understood the text of the Gospel.[13]

The final methodological consideration is to outline how the Gospel communicates to the reader in John 4. Unlike in the Prologue, in John 4 the narrator does not make explicit chistological statements. The audience is not directly given information beyond what those present could have known. In the absence of such narration, we must consider more implicit features that convey Jesus' identity. The consideration of implicit Christology builds on the work of Jerome Neyrey and Richard Bauckham.[14] Neyrey examines sections of the Gospel, making the argument that the attribution of God's creative and eschatological powers to Jesus in John 5 is the way that the evangelist seeks to portray Jesus as equal to God.[15] Bauckham investigates the ways Jesus shares in the divine identity by taking on roles that are uniquely God's.[16] Bauckham's focus is upon God as creator and as sovereign Lord as the two defining features of God in his relationship to the world. These approaches to implicit Christology can be extended to consider the ways in which Jesus is shown in John 4 as fulfilling a role or acting in a way that is ascribed to God.

2. Divine Identity in John 4

A shift of focus from Jesus' identity as perceived by the Samaritan woman to the way it is presented to the reader, reveals no less than six indicators of Jesus' divine identity.

2.1 Jesus, Giver of the Spirit

The first allusion to Jesus' divine identity comes in the verse which raises his identity as a key issue in the dialogue. Jesus offers to give living water (4:10), a provision that leads to eternal life (4:14).[17] The idea of living water echoes Exodus and the provision of water by God at Meribah, water that sustains God's people in the wilderness (Exod. 17:1–7; cf. Ps. 68:8–9).[18] This is an initial allusion to Jesus as divine, as he takes on the role that God took for his people in Exodus by providing living water.

The image of living water, in the context of the Temple themes of this chapter, also alludes to Ezekiel 47:1–12. There too God provides flowing water, this time coming from the Temple rather than a rock. It is not a natural phenomenon, as the water flowing out gets deeper and wider as

---

13 See for example Keener's use of Revelation to explain 'worship in the Spirit' in 4:21-24; Keener, *John*, 1:616. This approach has a long history, as Origen (*Comm. Jo.* 1.1-3) presents Revelation as providing an interpretative key for the Gospel.

14 Neyrey, *Ideology of Revolt*; Bauckham, *God Crucified*; with further development in his later book *Jesus and the God of Israel*. Cf. McGrath, *John's Apologetic Christology*; Loader, *Jesus in John's Gospel*, 331-7.

15 Neyrey, *Ideology*, 9–36. Cf. Koester, *Word of Life*, 100–1.

16 Bauckham, *God Crucified*, 25–42. While the characteristics explored in this article are not as unequivocally divine as those which Bauckham focuses upon, the framework of Jesus as divine in John (1:1; 20:28) along with the collocation of so many indicators of divine identity, justifies a broader range.

17 While there is no explicit connection, often commentators connect the 'gift of God' with the 'living water' and understand both as referring to the gift of the Spirit, thus: Thompson, *John*, 99–101; Michaels, *John*, 241. Others see the gift as revelatory, linked to Torah, thus: Carson, *John*, 218; Barrett, *John*, 233.

18 Willoughby argues that the water in John 4 is about purification, but the echoes of Meribah and the eschatological temple of Ezekiel both point to a life-giving water, not a cleansing water. The context in John 4 is one of a thirsty Jesus needing water to drink not wash. The mention of Samaritans not having dealings with Jews may suggest an element of clean/unclean in the scene but there is no language of cleansing or purification. Willoughby, 'The Word Became Flesh', 135–6. Curiously, Estelle omits John in his work on Exodus in the rest of Scripture, *Echoes of Exodus*.

it goes. An explanation for the symbolic significance of the water comes in John 7:37–39. Jesus speaks of living water flowing from his belly, adapting the image of Ezekiel in light of the temple replacement theme.[19] The narrator explains to the Gospel audience that the water symbolises the gift of the Spirit. Returning to John 4, by offering the gift of living water, Jesus is offering to give the Holy Spirit.[20] In the Old Testament, it is God who gives his Spirit (Num. 11:25–30; 1 Sam. 16:13–14; Ps. 51:11; Isa. 42:1; 44:3; 61:1; Joel 2:28), while from a Johannine perspective the Spirit is beyond human comprehension (John 3:8) and its gift is not to be understood in worldly terms (14:26–27), thus making the gift of the Spirit an action only God can take. The narrator's explicit commentary in John 7 enables the audience to understand the symbolism of Jesus' words in John 4, and therefore to see how Jesus is presented as sharing the divine identity on account of his ability to give the Spirit.

2.2 Jesus and the Place of Worship

The next indicator of Jesus' divine identity in John 4 is the role he assumes in determining the place of worship.[21] In response to the question about the right place of worship, Jesus states, 'Believe me, woman, an hour is coming when you will worship the Father neither on this mountain nor in Jerusalem' (4:21). This statement functions as a declaration regarding the right place to worship God. The discussion of worship in 4:21–24 is more complex than merely denoting an alternative physical location for worship. Nevertheless, the focus in the opening verses (4:20–21) on physical places of worship means that we must consider earlier biblical paradigms regarding the right place to worship God.

The key passage for framing a biblical perspective on the right place to worship God is Deuteronomy 12.[22] Deuteronomy directs the people of Israel to worship the Lord in the place which he will choose (Deut. 12:5,11,18,21,26). This is an injunction against taking over the sacred places of those in the land before them (Deut. 12:1–4). But it also establishes that the determination of the location of worship is a divine prerogative.

Both Jews and Samaritans accepted this divine injunction. The Samaritans believed that Mt Gerizim was the place that God had chosen for worship. Drawing solely on the Pentateuch, their beliefs rested upon the role of Shechem, located beside Mt Gerizim, as the place where Abraham first sacrificed in the land (Gen. 12:6–7). Further, Mt Gerizim is the place where the terms of the covenant were declared (Deut. 11:29–30; 27:12). The Jews, however, identified Jerusalem as the

---

19 Beale, *Temple and The Church's Mission*, 196. There is debate as to whether the water flows from Jesus or the believer; the role of giving the Spirit is not attributed to believers at any other point, making the latter option unlikely. Favouring Jesus as the source see Brown, *John*, 1:320–21; Lincoln, *John*, 254–5; Bennema, 'The Giving of the Spirit', 199–200; Marcus, 'Rivers of Living Water', 328–30. For the believer as the source see Michaels, *John*, 463–65; Carson, *John*, 322–9.

20 For an extensive argument that in John 4, 'living water' represents the Spirit and not revelation, see Um, *Theme of Temple*, 130–66; cf. Brown, *Spirit in the Writings of John*, 134–5.

21 As a possible further indicator of Jesus' divine identity, Jesus' knowledge about the woman and her situation (4:17–18) may be accounted as an instance of divine omniscience, as suggested by Haenchen, *John*, 1:222. However, the woman does not take it as such, rather interpreting it as merely prophetic knowledge. If the audience of the Gospel accepts the other indicators in this chapter regarding Jesus as divine, then they may read this event as an instance of divine knowledge. However, there are no interpretative clues that lead the audience in this direction within these verses, nor is Jesus' knowledge of people elsewhere presented as divine knowledge (cf. 2:23–25; 5:6; 6:15,61).

22 On the relationship of Deut. 12 to the earlier instructions in Exod. 20, see Foreman, 'Sacrifice and Centralisation', 1–22. While some commentators note the connection between Deuteronomy 12 and John 4:21, they do not draw implications for Jesus' identity, so Beasley-Murray, *John*, 61; Carson, *John*, 222.

place where the LORD was to be worshipped. The word given through Nathan (2 Sam. 7:12–13) constitutes divine authorisation for Solomon to build the Temple in Jerusalem (1 Kgs 5:5). Solomon's actions are endorsed by prophetic word (1 Kgs 6:11–13), and then by the divine presence entering the newly built Temple (1 Kgs 8:10–11, cf. 8:29). Thus, the decision to build the place to worship God in Jerusalem remains a divine prerogative, guided by prophetic words and endorsed by divine action. After the Exile, the prophetic commands to rebuild the Temple indicate a continuing divine endorsement of Jerusalem as the place where God is to be worshipped (Hag. 1:1–2:9; Zech. 6:9–15).

The location of the dialogue in John 4 in the shadow of Mt Gerizim evokes the Deuteronomistic context. Jesus rejects the ongoing significance of Mt Gerizim as the place for worshipping the LORD, which alone is nothing more than a typical Jewish position. However, Jesus also rejects the ongoing significance of Jerusalem as the established place of worship. That is the implication of his declaration that worship will be *neither* here *nor* there.[23] While it does point to the end of geographic limitations, it also speaks to the end of the unique role of the Temple in Jerusalem, which will no longer be the place where the LORD is to be worshipped.[24] Thus, Jesus goes beyond contemporary critiques of the Temple. For while the community of Qumran reject the Temple as corrupted, they still anticipate a messianic cleansing of the Temple, not its permanent rejection.[25]

By rejecting both Jerusalem and Mt Gerizim as the place in which the LORD is to be worshipped, Jesus assumes a divine prerogative. He does not seek to arbitrate between the two positions that claim divine sanction, neither does he seek divine approval for his pronouncement, nor are Jesus' words cast in the form of a prophetic pronouncement.[26] Jesus declares the new situation regarding the proper place where God is to be worshipped, and by taking on this divine prerogative, the Gospel audience is pointed towards the divine identity of Jesus.

Jesus does not replace Jerusalem and Gerizim with yet another physical location. John 4:23 highlights the mode of worship more than the place, saying that God desires worship in spirit and truth. This might be seen to lessen the argument, because Jesus does not establish a physical place for worship. However, the act of setting aside what God has previously established is significant enough. But going further, Jesus establishes a new locus of worship, by making himself the new Temple.

2.3 Jesus the Temple

One area where a higher Christology in John 4 has been considered is in relation to the temple replacement theme.[27] John begins linking Jesus to the temple in the Prologue, describing the

---

23 Ashton notes that 'the holy city of Jerusalem...has lost all relevance', while Loader states that 'both are to be left behind'. Ashton, *Understanding the Fourth Gospel*, 79; Loader, 'Jesus and the Law', 142.
24 This end is pronounced without a note of judgement, not condemning the Jewish system but announcing something new and greater.
25 Regev, 'Community as Temple', 604–31.
26 While in John all of Jesus' words find their origin with the Father (7:16; 8:26; 12:49–50), this is part of the Johannine presentation of Jesus as the Son whose will is entirely aligned with that of the Father. It is distinct from Old Testament patterns where the words of the prophet appear in the form 'Thus says the LORD'. While Haenchen says that Jesus speaks as a prophet, this is on account of assuming that Jesus' words are a prediction of the destruction of the Temple. Yet there is no language of destruction, while it is at odds with the implication that worship at Gerizim will also cease, despite the destruction of that temple being long past. Haenchen, *John*, 222.
27 Works on the temple theme include: Greene, 'Jesus as the Heavenly Temple', 425–46; Hoskins, *Jesus as the Fulfillment*; Salier, 'The Temple in the Gospel', 121–34; Kerr, *The Temple of Jesus' Body*; Coloe, *God Dwells With Us*. Of these, Coloe most emphasises the christological implications of the temple theme in John 4.

presence of the Word made flesh as ἐσκήνωσεν ἐν ἡμῖν (1:14), evoking the Exodus tabernacle (ἡ σκηνή Exod. 25:9).[28] Another allusion that has implications for the temple theme is the image of the ladder to heaven drawn from Genesis 28:12. In John 1:51 this allusion is extended to present Jesus as the place where heaven and earth meet. Furthermore, in 2:19–21, the narrator explains that Jesus spoke of himself as the temple.[29] In John 4 images of the temple continue, as the offer of living water evokes the eschatological temple of Ezekiel 47:1–12.[30] Beale describes the offer as presenting Jesus as 'the beginning form of the true temple from which true life in God's presence proceeds'.[31] The replacement of the temple conveys a new locus for the worship of God, which has, necessarily, christological implications.

At this point, placing John 4 alongside Revelation 21 illumines the christological implications of Jesus as the replacement for the Jerusalem Temple. Revelation points to the future role of the temple within the new creation. More precisely, it speaks of the obsolescence, and thus absence, of the temple from the new Jerusalem because of God's direct, unmediated presence in the city (Rev. 21:22).[32] The cubic city, patterned on the shape of the Holy of Holies of Solomon's Temple (1 Kgs 6:20), will be filled with God's presence.[33] So, when John 4:21 is read in light of Revelation 21 it suggests that to abrogate the physical sanctuary is to say that God is now pervasively present.[34] Jesus in John 4 not only says that we can now worship anywhere, but effectively he declares that the object of worship is immanent.

The implications for Jesus' divine identity are apparent as it is 'the hour' which is the decisive transformation of worship. 'The hour' has as its central focus Jesus on the cross, but the inclusion of 'now is' (4:23) implies that it is the incarnation, not merely the cross, which transforms worship through the presence of the object of worship.[35] Jesus is not explicitly identified as the temple in John 4, but the image of living water evokes the temple of Ezekiel 47. For the reader who has already encountered the connection of Jesus and temple in John 2:19–21, this image confirms that Jesus is the replacement for the Jerusalem temple. The replacement of the temple with a person, in light of Revelation 21, is an indication of the presence of God. The connection is further strengthened as in Revelation 21:3 the same verb is used to describe God's presence in the new Jerusalem as was used for Jesus' incarnation (σκηνόω, cf. John 1:14). There is no further need for an earthly temple for God is now present in the person of Jesus.

2.4 Jesus, Bringer of Salvation

The following verse provides another indicator of the divine identity of Jesus, through the

---

28 Greene, 'Jesus as the Heavenly Temple', 430–1; Brown, *John*, 1:32–33.
29 Beale, *The Temple*, 192–5.
30 Coloe also connects the imagery of Ezekiel 47 to the similarly eschatological image of the harvest in 4:31–38. Coloe, *God Dwells With Us*, 93–6, 111; cf. Beale, *The Temple*, 196.
31 Beale, *The Temple*, 197; cf. Greene, 'Jesus as the Heavenly Temple', 438; Thettayil, *In Spirit and Truth*, 225–7.
32 The connection between the temple and God's presence builds upon the Old Testament presentation of the tabernacle/temple as the dwelling place of God. Beale, *The Temple*, 48.
33 Beale argues that Revelation 21–22 portrays the new creation as the ultimate temple. Beale, *The Temple*, 24–25, 365–72.
34 Um, *Temple Christology*, 190.
35 Contra those who argue a conflation of the time of the narrative and the post-resurrection time of the author (e.g. Haenchen, *John*, 222–3), the Gospel widely presents the effects of Jesus' coming as available in the present, particularly having life now (3:16–18; 4:36; 5:24; 6:50–51). Bultmann also points to the way the Gospel presents the eschatological hour as having come with Jesus (so 3:19, 5:25). Bultmann, *John*, 190. For a discussion of time in relation to this verse and the original context, see Brown, *Spirit*, 99–101, 136–7.

statement that salvation comes from the Jews (4:22). While the full significance of the statement is not evident to the Samaritan woman, the construction of the chapter for the reader brings out the connections. The first indicator that this statement refers to Jesus is the identification of Jesus as a Jew earlier in the discourse (4:9).[36] The subsequent identification of Jesus as 'Saviour of the World' (4:42) by the villagers confirms Jesus as the focus of salvation, for these are the only instances of both σωτήρ and σωτηρία in the Gospel. As with other aspects of Christology in this chapter, the significance of Jesus as 'Saviour of the World' has been explored regarding what it could have meant within the story, with a frequent focus on the use of the term by the Roman emperors, as well as Graeco-Roman gods.[37] Outside of these passages, the verb σῴζω is used occasionally, with a focus on Jesus' role in bringing salvation, which is connected to eternal life and opposed to judgement (3:16; 12:47; cf. 5:34; 10:9).[38] Thus in John 4 the reader is to identify Jesus as the one who brings salvation.

When read in the canonical context, salvation is often an activity of God in the Old Testament, with the Psalms and Isaiah referring to God as 'my salvation' (Ps. 18:2; 25:5; 38:22; Isa. 12:2). There is some sense that God is the only source of true salvation, although this is rarely explicit.[39] The closest indication of this is the statement that salvation belongs to the Lord (Ps. 3:8; Jonah 2:9) which may simply express confidence that God will save. However, it could be an assertion that God is the only one who saves.[40] While the Messiah is connected to salvation and can be seen as the one inaugurating the era of salvation, the language of salvation is rarely connected to the Messiah.[41] Zechariah uses salvation in a way that might be interpreted messianically in 9:9, as the king brings salvation/victory (ישׁע). That said, when the word is repeated soon after, it is explicitly 'the LORD their God' doing the saving (Zech. 9:16). Similarly, 1 Enoch draws some connection between salvation and the Messiah (1 Enoch 48:7), but salvation is still the result of the name of the Lord of the Spirits (i.e. God), and not the Son of Man (also 1 En. 50:3).[42] In the rest of the New Testament, salvation is often depicted as coming through Jesus, but, as with the Old Testament, rarely in exclusive terms (except Acts 4:12).

The Johannine understanding of salvation here in John 4 can be illuminated through attention to the place of salvation in the Book of Revelation. The idea that salvation belongs to God is repeated (Rev. 7:10; 19:1), albeit with several key differences to the Old Testament pattern. First is the eschatological context, which is only occasionally in view in some prophetic material (Isa. 45:17; cf. 51:6,8). Salvation, especially in Rev. 19:1, refers to a final salvation. In the Gospel, Jesus' salvation has both present and future elements (John 3:16–17; 5:28–29) albeit with both elements closely connected (John 11:25–26). The connection to eschatological salvation in John 4 implies

---

36 Coloe, *God Dwells With Us*, 105.
37 Koester, 'The Saviour of the World', 665–7; Thatcher, *Greater Than Caesar*, 136. For inscriptions using 'saviour' with regard to Roman officials or Artemis in Ephesus, see van Tilborg, *Reading John in Ephesus*, 47–51.
38 Barrett, *John*, 216; Michaels, *John*, 270.
39 Beasley-Murray observes that 'saviour' is a divine title, especially in Isaiah, and not applied to the Messiah by Jews. Yet he then speculates with little evidence as to how the Samaritans could have used it as a title meaning 'converter' or 'deliverer' of the world, rather than conveying any implications of divine identity for Jesus. Beasley-Murray, *John*, 65.
40 Thus while Stuart reads the statement in Jonah as implying God as the sole source of salvation, Goldingay, while acknowledging similar views of the statement in Psalm 3, sets it in the context of the question of whether God will save the psalmist. Stuart, *Hosea-Jonah*, 478; Goldingay, *Psalms*, 1:114–5.
41 While Boccaccini sees 1 Enoch reflecting expectation of salvation from the evil of the world by a superhuman saviour, only God is the explicit agent of salvation. Boccaccini, 'From Jewish Prophet', 344. It is indicative of the lack of explicit connection that Novenson, *Grammar of Messianism*, does not discuss salvation language related to the Messiah. Cf. Brown, *John*, 1:175.
42 Gieschen, 'The Divine Name', 393.

a divine role, beyond the scope of this-worldly salvation that could be provided by humans. Additionally, salvation is ascribed to God and the Lamb in the context of worship in both Rev 7:10 and 19:10. Both God and the Lamb are objects of worship, which points to their shared divine identity.[43] Indeed, it is their enacting of salvation which is the basis for worship. Thus when John 4 is read in light of the wider scriptural witness, the depiction of Jesus as Saviour is a depiction of him as sharing in the divine identity of God, as he performs an action that belongs to God, which is also an action that forms the basis for the worship of Jesus as God.[44]

2.5 Jesus and Worship

Alongside Jesus' statement on the nature of worship, God is described as not merely desiring worship but actively seeking (ζητέω) worshippers such as these (4:23). While the Gospel narrative focuses upon the role of Jesus, God the Father plays an active if less visible role in the story, notably as the one sending his Son (3:16–17; 8:42), providing the example for his Son to follow (5:19; 7:16, 8:26; 12:50), and giving his Son authority (5:21–22,26–27).[45] Yet despite the statement that God seeks worshippers, he is not seen to act directly to bring about such worship.

The lack of direct action by God the Father is contrasted with the visibly active role of Jesus. As Jesus speaks with the Samaritan woman and her fellow Samaritans, Jesus himself is actively seeking those who will worship God rightly. His instruction of the Samaritan woman about the nature of true worship forms an invitation. She is invited to perceive Jesus rightly, and, therefore, to come to him and ask for living water (4:10). While worship is not explicitly referred to in the subsequent interaction with the villagers, they too respond to Jesus positively. They ask Jesus to stay with them, an instance of their receiving Jesus (1:11–12). The significance of their response is augmented as the narrator presents both their request and Jesus' action using the theologically significant verb, μένω (remain, 4:40; cf. 15:1–10), which creates an implicit alignment between the Samaritans and the disciples, who begin their relationship with Jesus by staying with him (μένω, 1:38–39).[46] The Samaritans subsequently demonstrate worship in their acclamation of Jesus as the saviour of the world (4:42). The role of Jesus as seeking those who will worship God in spirit and truth is further highlighted by the mission-themed discourse with the disciples that is framed within the interaction with the Samaritans (4:31–38).[47] Thus, John 4 presents Jesus taking on the role of God by seeking true worshippers.[48]

For John, right worship of God is understood in christological terms. While in 4:23 God desires worshippers of himself, there is a broader pattern which centres on the Father's desire that people respond rightly to Jesus (5:22–23; 6:28–29). The Gospel also makes it clear that a right response to Jesus is equally a right response to God. In addition to calling for belief in both the Father and the Son (14:1), Jesus states that to honour the Son is to honour the Father (5:23).[49] The two are unified

---

43 Bauckham, *Jesus and the God of Israel*, 11, 25, points to the role of worship as an indicator of divine identity.
44 Coloe, *God Dwells With Us*, 112, makes a connection that worship is a response to God's salvation, and thus the worship of Jesus is suggested by the presentation of Jesus as God's gift of salvation to the world (3:16–17; 4:42).
45 Cf. Thompson, *The God of the Gospel of John*.
46 The connection is also made through the repetition of 'come and see' (4:29, cf. 1:39,46). Wang, *Sense Perception*, 176–7.
47 While the mission theme of both 4:31–38 and the wider Samaritan context is often noted, the links between the harvest and the divine search for true worshippers is not made. For example, there is no reference to 4:23 and God's seeking in Köstenberger, *Missions of Jesus*.
48 While Coloe observes that the Father is seeking worshippers through Jesus, she does not draw conclusions about Jesus' identity as a result. Coloe, *God Dwells With Us*, 111; similarly Lincoln, *John*, 178.
49 Fletcher-Louis, 'John 5:19–30', 419, argues that to honour Jesus is to worship him in 5:23.

in mission and message, such that a response to one is indistinguishable from a response to the other (5:41–44; 6:29; 8:19, 42; 14:6–7). Thus, Jesus' mission calling for belief in himself is equally a mission to seek true worshippers of God, a role ascribed to God himself.

The connection between Jesus and worship helps tie together the indicators of divine identity argued for in this article, as well as further clarifying this identity through the inclusion of Jesus in the worship that is rightly directed to the Father. Jesus as giver of the Spirit (§2.1) enables right worship of God, as the Spirit is a necessary condition for worship in Spirit and truth (4:23). The call to worship in spirit and truth (4:23) also foreshadows Jesus' self-identification as the truth (14:6), pointing to the inclusion of Jesus in the response of worship directed towards God. In Deuteronomy 12 the one who is worshipped is the one who determines the place of worship. In John 4, Jesus now determines the place of worship (§2.2), therefore he too is to receive that worship. In the identification of Jesus as the Temple (§2.3), the distinction between place and object of worship is blurred, as the place of worship is identified with a person. The implication is that Jesus as the Temple is both the place and object of worship. In bringing salvation (§2.4), Jesus acts in John 4 in a way that is worthy of worship. Finally, the overlap between the response to Jesus and to the Father leads to the conclusion that in seeking worshippers for the Father (§2.5), Jesus is also seeking worshippers of himself. Thus, the way that John presents Jesus as divine does not mean that Jesus participates in the divine identity in some secondary or limited sense (a divine being like the angels) but as one who is to be worshipped as the Father is worshipped.[50]

2.6 Jesus the 'I am'

The final indicator of divine identity is one that has been observed but often rejected. In Jesus' response to the Samaritan woman in 4:26, he uses the expression ἐγώ εἰμι (I am). In the story context, this expression functions as self-identification, and thus is commonly translated 'I am he'.[51] Jesus identifies himself as the expected Messiah—the only time in the Gospel that Jesus explicitly identifies himself as such. The woman responds to Jesus in a way entirely consistent with such a reading, as Jesus' words merely provoke her to ponder whether Jesus is the Messiah (4:29). We might ask if this is another case where the woman ought to have seen deeper into Jesus' words.[52] This may not have been possible in her time, but the Gospel depicts the way that Jesus' words were the basis for later remembrance and deeper christological understanding (2:22; 12:16).[53] Yet it remains understandable why, if the interpretative horizon is limited to the original events, scholars opt for reading this ἐγώ εἰμι as self-identification.

However, it is well recognised that ἐγώ εἰμι can have deeper significance in John.[54] In addition to the predicate 'I am' statements, John also features several absolute uses of this expression. The use in 8:58 has often been taken as an allusion to the divine name revealed in Exodus 3:14 which is used repeatedly by Isaiah and, therefore, the motive for the violent hostility that ensues in John. Similar uses in John 8:24,28 and 18:5 have also been connected with the Isaianic use of the expression to refer to God.[55] While these instances can function within the story as self-identification, their significance appears to extend beyond that. Thus, in John 18:5 Jesus' words

---

50 For the significance of worship for the early formulation of Christology, see Hurtado, *One God, One Lord*.
51 Loader, *Jesus*, 348; Carson, *John*, 227; Barrett, *John*, 239; Thompson, *John*, 106.
52 Stauffer, *Jesus and His Story*, 186–8, suggests that Jesus pointed the woman beyond the established title of Messiah.
53 Kugler, 'New Testament Christology', 373, points to the necessity of words such as this to provide a basis for later recognition of Jesus as divine, and thus as an object of worship.
54 Thompson, *John*, 156–59; Brown, *John*, 1:533–38; Schnackenburg, *John*, 2:79–89.
55 Williams, '"I Am" or "I Am He"', 343–52; Ball, *'I Am' in John's Gospel*.

are followed by the incongruous response of the soldiers who bow down and back away from him, suggesting an awareness (even if subconscious) that the man before them is more than just a criminal they have been sent to arrest.[56] In addition, Williams suggests that John 6:20 may have similar overtones of divine identity, as the use of ἐγώ εἰμι along with the exhortation against fear echoes Isaiah 41:10,13. John draws on Isaiah, both in explicit quotations (John 1:23; 6:45; 12:38–40) and in the titles ascribed to Jesus (1:29,34), and these frequent connections may bring to mind a broader Isaianic context, including the divine use of ἐγώ εἰμι.[57] Thus, while the possible reflection and later understanding of the Samaritan woman remains speculation, for a reader familiar with Isaiah, the use of this language can function as an allusion to divine identity.[58] The implications of divine identity that the reader would have just encountered in 4:21–24 strengthen the case that ἐγώ εἰμι has divine connotations in 4:26. Thus, while Barrett argues that self-identification is the natural sense given the expression is used for self-identification elsewhere in John, the context itself leads towards the symbolic reading.[59] Again, Jesus is presented as divine in John 4.

One further implication of reading the 'I am' in 4:26 as a divine identification is that it connects the divine identity of Jesus to his messianic identity. At times these two aspects can appear as different components of Jesus' identity, with his messiahship treated as his human role as God's anointed representative, while his divine identity entails an ontologically exalted status.[60] Yet Jesus' words in 4:26 constitute both an admission of messiahship and a definition of what sort of messiah he is.[61] The Messiah is often understood in human categories of king, prophet, or priest, and there are prophetic and royal elements present in this passage.[62] There is some suggestion of a divine messiah in Second Temple literature, notably 1 Enoch, although the extent and significance of the exalted position of the Son of Man in 1 Enoch is debated.[63] John goes beyond any previous messianic concepts to present Jesus as the divine Messiah, embodying and acting as God on earth. Thus John 4 defines what sort of messiah Jesus is—the divine Messiah.

3. Conclusion

While John 4 does not explicitly state that Jesus is God, his words and deeds depict him taking on the role of God. Within the story, characters see Jesus as the Messiah and Saviour, but the reader is privileged by the narrator and given further information which presents Jesus as divine. By offering the gift of the Spirit, Jesus assumes the divine role of dispensing the Holy Spirit. Jesus

---

56 On 18:5 see Moloney, *Johannine Studies*, 470.
57 Lincoln, *John*, 178, is confident of the connection between John 4:26 and Isa. 45:19; 52:6 LXX.
58 Coutts, *Divine Name*, 115–6, suggests the impact would be particularly felt upon rereading the Gospel, noting that the double meaning aligns with the irony already evident in the discourse. Coloe, *God Dwells With Us*, 102; Beasley-Murray, *John*, 62; Botha, *Jesus and the Samaritan Woman*, 153.
59 Barrett, *John*, 281; similarly Carson, *John*, 227; Kruse, *John*, 151. Haenchen's suggestion of a Hellenistic revelation formula is less plausible given the extensive use of the OT in John. Haenchen, *John*, 1:224.
60 Thus e.g. Barrett, *John*, 70–72.
61 Similarly, Son of God functions to define Christ in 20:31. Michaels, *John*, 1023; Carson, *John*, 663; Beasley-Murray, *John*, 388.
62 There may be a priestly connection implied through the references to temple and worship.
63 Boccaccini and Gieschen argue that 1 Enoch depicts a divine Messiah, while Kugler and Hurtado reject the proposition. The problem is in part one of definition, whether divine means superhuman, or if it entails some form of equality with the God of Israel. The argument in this essay uses divine identity in the latter sense, and thus John goes beyond what is found in 1 Enoch. Boccaccini, 'From Jewish Prophet', 345; Gieschen, 'The Divine Name', 390–92; Kugler, 'New Testament Christology', 371; Hurtado, *One God, One Lord*, 51–6.

takes the divine role of determining the proper place for the worship of God. As the Temple, Jesus is the presence of God on earth. As the bringer of salvation, Jesus takes on a role that is properly God's, and one that results in Jesus being worshipped alongside God. Jesus takes on the role he ascribes to God in seeking true worshippers. Finally, the form of the self-acknowledgement of Jesus' messianic identity evokes an Isaianic resonance, turning it for the reader into an implicit claim to a divine identity. These features together show that while John reflects an interaction from Jesus' ministry in terms that are consistent with that context, the narrative is at the same time shaped to present to the reader a Jesus who shares in the divine identity of God the Father. By tying this divine identity to messiahship in 4:26, John presents Jesus as the divine Messiah, not only God's anointed representative but God's very presence on earth, and the one to be worshipped.

Chris Seglenieks
Honorary Research Associate
Bible College of South Australia

Bibliography

Ashton, J.	*Understanding the Fourth Gospel* (2nd edn; Oxford: Oxford University Press, 2007).
Aune, D. E.	*Revelation* (WBC, 3 vols.; Dallas, TX: Word, 1997).
Ball, D. M.	*'I Am' in John's Gospel: Literary Function, Background and Theological Implications* (JSNTSup 124; Sheffield: Sheffield Academic, 1996).
Barrett, C. K.	*The Gospel According to St. John* (2nd edn; London: SPCK, 1978).
Bauckham, R.	*Jesus and the Eyewitnesses: The Gospels as Eyewitness Testimony* (2nd edn; Grand Rapids, MI: Eerdmans, 2017).
Bauckham, R.	*Jesus and the God of Israel: God Crucified and Other Studies on the New Testament's Christology of Divine Identity* (Milton Keynes: Paternoster, 2008).
Bauckham, R.	*God Crucified: Monotheism and Christology in the New Testament* (Carlisle: Paternoster, 1998).
Beale, G.K.	*The Book of Revelation* (NIGTC; Grand Rapids, MI: Eerdmans, 1999).
Beale, G. K.	*The Temple and The Church's Mission: A Biblical Theology of the Dwelling Place of God* (NSBT; Downers Grove, IL: IVP, 2004).
Beasley-Murray, G. R.	*John* (WBC; 2nd edn; Waco, TX: Word, 1987).
Beasley-Murray, G. R.	*Revelation* (NCBC; rev. edn; London: Marshall, Morgan & Scott, 1978).
Behr, J.	*John the Theologian and his Paschal Gospel* (Oxford: Oxford University Press, 2019).
Bennema, C.	'The Giving of the Spirit in John's Gospel—A New Proposal?', *EvQ* 74.3 (2002), 195–213.
Boccaccini, G.	'From Jewish Prophet to Jewish God: How John Made the Divine Jesus Uncreated', in B. E. Reynolds and G. Boccaccini (eds.), *Reading the Gospel of John's Christology as Jewish Messianism* (Leiden: Brill, 2018), 335–57.
Botha, J. E.	*Jesus and the Samaritan Woman: A Speech Act Reading of John 4:1–42* (Leiden: Brill, 1991).
Brown, R. E.	*The Gospel According to John* (2 vols.; Garden City, NY: Doubleday, 1966–70).
Bultmann, R.	*The Gospel of John* (Oxford: Blackwell, 1971).
Brown, T. G.	*Spirit in the Writings of John: Johannine Pneumatology in Social-Scientific Perspective* (London: T&T Clark, 2003).
Carson, D. A.	'Understanding Misunderstandings in the Fourth Gospel', *TynB* 33 (1982), 59–91.
Carson, D. A.	*The Gospel According to John* (PNTC; Grand Rapids, MI: Eerdmans, 1991).
Chatman, S. B.	*Story and Discourse: Narrative Structure in Fiction and Film* (Ithaca, NY: Cornell University Press, 1978).

Coloe, M. L.	*God Dwells with Us: Temple Symbolism in the Fourth Gospel* (Collegeville, MN: Liturgical, 2001).
Culpepper, R. A.	*The Johannine School: An Evaluation of the Johannine School Hypothesis Based on an Investigation of the Nature of Ancient Schools* (Missoula, MT: Scholars, 1975).
Culpepper, R. A.	*Anatomy of the Fourth Gospel: A Study in Literary Design* (Philadelphia, PA: Fortress, 1987).
De Boer, M. C.	'Narrative Criticism, Historical Criticism, and the Gospel of John', *JSNT* 47.1 (1992), 35–48.
Estelle, B. D.	*Echoes of Exodus: Tracing a Biblical Motif* (Downers Grove, IL: IVP, 2018).
Fletcher-Louis, C.	'John 5:19–30: The Son of God is the Apocalyptic Son of Man', in B. E. Reynolds and G. Boccaccini (eds.), *Reading the Gospel of John's Christology as Jewish Messianism* (Leiden: Brill, 2018), 411–34.
Foreman, B.	'Sacrifice and Centralisation in the Pentateuch: Is Exodus 20:24–26 Really at Odds with Deuteronomy?', *TynB* 70.1 (2019), 1–22.
Frey, J.	*The Glory of the Crucified One: Christology and Theology in the Gospel of John* (Waco, TX: Baylor, 2018).
Frey, J.	'The Diaspora-Jewish Background of the Fourth Gospel', *SEÅ* 77 (2012), 169–96.
Frey, J.	'Erwägungen zum Verhältnis der Johannesapokalypse zu den übrigen Schriften des Corpus Johanneum', in M. Hengel (ed), *Die johanneische Frage: Ein Lösungsversuch* (Tübingen: Mohr Siebeck, 1993), 329–49.
Gieschen, C. A.	'The Divine Name that the Son Shares with the Father in the Gospel of John', in B. E. Reynolds and G. Boccaccini (eds.), *Reading the Gospel of John's Christology as Jewish Messianism* (Leiden: Brill, 2018), 387–410.
Goldingay, J.	*Psalms* (3 vols.; Grand Rapids, MI: Baker, 2006).
Greene, J. R.	'Jesus as the Heavenly Temple in the Fourth Gospel', *BBR* 28.3 (2018), 425–46.
Haenchen, E.	*Commentary on the Gospel of John* (trans. R. W. Funk. 2 vols.; Philadelphia, PA: Fortress, 1984).
Hengel, M.	*The Johannine Question* (trans. J. Bowden; London: SCM, 1989).
Hoskins, P. M.	*Jesus as the Fulfillment of the Temple in the Gospel of John* (Eugene, OR: Wipf & Stock, 2006).
Hurtado, L. W.	*One God, One Lord: Ancient Christian Devotion and Ancient Jewish Monotheism* (London: SCM, 1988).
Keener, C. S.	*The Gospel of John* (2 vols.; Peabody, MA: Hendrickson, 2003).
Kerr, A. R.	*The Temple of Jesus' Body: The Temple Theme in the Gospel of John* (LNTS; London: Sheffield Academic, 2002).

Klink, E. W.	*John* (ZECNT; Grand Rapids, MI: Zondervan, 2016).
Klink, E. W.	*The Sheep of the Fold: The Audience and Origin of the Gospel of John* (Cambridge: Cambridge University Press, 2007).
Koester, C. R.	*The Word of Life: A Theology of John's Gospel* (Grand Rapids, MI: Eerdmans, 2008).
Koester, C. R.	'The Spectrum of Johannine Readers', in F. F. Segovia (ed), *What is John? Readers and Readings of the Fourth Gospel* (Atlanta, GA: Scholars, 1996), 5–19.
Koester, C. R.	'"The Saviour of the World" (John 4:42)', *JBL* 109 (1990), 665–80.
Köstenberger, A. J.	*The Missions of Jesus and the Disciples according to the Fourth Gospel* (Grand Rapids, MI: Eerdmans, 1998).
Coutts, J. J. F.	*The Divine Name in the Gospel of John: Significance and Impetus* (Tübingen: Mohr Siebeck, 2017).
Kruse, C. G.	*John* (TNTC, rev. ed.; Downers Grove, IL: IVP, 2017).
Kugler, C.	'New Testament Christology: A Critique of Hurtado's Influence', *BBR* 30.3 (2020), 367–78.
Lincoln, A. T.	*The Gospel According to Saint John* (Grand Rapids, MI: Baker Academic, 2013).
Loader, W. R. G.	*Jesus in John's Gospel: Structure and Issues in Johannine Christology* (Grand Rapids, MI: Eerdmans, 2017).
Loader, W. R. G.	'Jesus and the Law', in G. van Belle et al. (eds.), *Theology and Christology in the Fourth Gospel: Essays by the Members of the SNTS Johannine Writings Seminar* (Leuven: Leuven University Press, 2005), 135–54.
MacDonald, J.	*The Theology of the Samaritans* (London: SCM, 1964).
Marcus, J.	'Rivers of Living Water from Jesus' Belly (John 7:38)', *JBL* 117.2 (1998), 328–30.
Martyn, J. L.	*History and Theology in the Fourth Gospel* (New York, NY: Harper & Row, 1968).
McGrath, J. F.	*John's Apologetic Christology: Legitimation and Development in Johannine Christology* (SNTSMS 111; Cambridge: Cambridge University Press, 2001).
Michaels, J. R.	*The Gospel of John* (NICNT; Grand Rapids, MI: Eerdmans, 2010).
Moloney, F. J.	*Johannine Studies 1975–2017* (Tübingen: Mohr Siebeck, 2017).
Neyrey, J. H.	*An Ideology of Revolt: John's Christology in Social-Science Perspective* (Philadelphia, PA: Fortress, 1988).
Novenson, M. V.	*The Grammar of Messianism: An Ancient Jewish Political Idiom and its Users* (New York, NY: Oxford University Press, 2017).

Paul, I.	*Revelation* (TNTC; London: IVP, 2018).
Regev, E.	'Community as Temple: Revisiting Cultic Metaphors in Qumran and the New Testament', *BBR* 28.4 (2018), 604–31.
Salier, W.H.	'The Temple in the Gospel According to John', in T. D. Alexander et al. (eds), *Heaven on Earth: The Temple in Biblical Theology* (Carlisle: Paternoster, 2004), 121–34.
Schnackenburg, R.	*The Gospel According to St. John* (3 vols. New York, NY: Herder & Herder, 1968–1982).
Schnelle, U.	'The Person of Jesus', in J. M Lieu and M. C. de Boer (eds.), *The Oxford Handbook of Johannine Studies* (London: Oxford University Press, 2018), 311–30.
Seglenieks, C.	'Faith and Narrative: A Two-Level Reading of Belief in the Gospel of John', *TynB* 70.1 (2019), 23–40.
Stauffer, E.	*Jesus and His Story* (trans. R. and C. Winston; New York, NY: Knopf, 1974).
Stuart, D.	*Hosea-Jonah* (WBC; Waco, TX: Word, 1987).
Thatcher, T.	*Greater Than Caesar: Christology and Empire in the Fourth Gospel* (Minneapolis, MN: Fortress, 2009).
Thettayil, B.	*In Spirit and Truth: An Exegetical Study of John 4:19–26 and a Theological Investigation of the Replacement Theme in the Fourth Gospel* (Leuven: Peeters, 2007).
Thompson, M. M.	*John* (Louisville, KY: Westminster John Knox, 2015).
Thompson, M. M.	*The God of the Gospel of John* (Grand Rapids, MI: Eerdmans, 2001).
Thompson, M. M.	*The Humanity of Jesus in the Fourth Gospel* (Philadelphia: Fortress, 1988).
van Tilborg, S.	*Reading John in Ephesus* (Leiden: Brill, 1996).
Um, S. T.	*The Theme of Temple Christology in John's Gospel* (LNTS; London: T&T Clark, 2006).
Wang, S. K.-H.	*Sense Perception and Testimony in the Gospel According to John* (Tübingen; Mohr Siebeck, 2017).
Williams, C. H.	'"I Am" or "I Am He"? Self-Declaratory Pronouncements in the Fourth Gospel and Rabbinic Tradition', in R. T. Fortna et al. (eds), *Jesus in Johannine Tradition* (Louisville, KY: Westminster John Knox, 2001), 343–52.
Willoughby, T. N.	'"The Word Became Flesh and Tabernacled Among Us?": A Primer for the Exodus in John', in R. M. Fox (ed), *Reverberations of the Exodus in Scripture* (Eugene, OR: Pickwick, 2014), 121–38.

David in the Gospels and Acts

MARIE MCINNES

Abstract

David is frequently referenced in the Gospels and Acts. He is presented in three principal and very different roles: in the birth narratives and the entry into Jerusalem, as the royal ancestor and forerunner of Jesus; in the accounts of Jesus' ministry as the type of the therapeutic messiah; in Acts, as the prophetic psalmist. The invocation, 'Son of David' by the outcasts of society reflects a melding of several concepts from the Second Temple period: the Shepherd-King, the Isaianic Servant, and perhaps suffering David. Its frequency is due to Matthew's changes to Mark. In Acts, David is presented as an unwitting prophet who, in writing about himself, more importantly writes about Christ. All the narrative blocks are connected by the belief that David, although a worthy forerunner, is eclipsed, in the Passion Narrative and the latter half of Acts, by the risen Christ who is worthy of the name 'Son of God', who brings the salvation which David could not.

Key Words: David, Son of David, therapeutic messiah, *Davidssohnfrage*, Psalm 15 (LXX).

Introduction

Allusions to David in the Gospels and Acts, as in pre-Christian literature, are frequent, complex, and rich. There are thirty-seven direct references to David in the Gospels, many of them clustered in six parallel pericopes, and eleven references in Acts, most often made by Peter and Paul. David is portrayed both as an arguably historical person, and as an ahistorical, idealised and typical figure.[1] This follows the transformation of the David found in the Books of Samuel which develops from the boy shepherd, who is anointed to be a shepherd to his people, to a flawed king who is nevertheless triumphant over his enemies. He is later metamorphosed into the ideal king and cult leader in the writings of the Prophets and the Chronicler, and is further idealised in the Second Temple period, especially in the Psalms of Solomon which have been called 'perhaps the *locus classicus* for belief in a Davidic Messiah'.[2] There are echoes of all these in Gospels and Acts.

---

1   Miuru, *David in Luke-Acts,* divides Luke's use of David into genealogical and typological but this does not always fit, especially in Stephen's speech in Acts.
2   Wright, *Psalms of Solomon,* vii. The most apposite lines from Psalms of Solomon are 17:40–41: 'He shall be strong in his works and mighty in fear of God, shepherding the flock of the Lord faithfully and righteously, and he shall not let any of them become weak in their pasture'.

In the Synoptic Gospels and Acts, David fulfils three main roles: the forerunner of Jesus, biological and royal; the type of the healing Messiah (identified by designation 'Son of David'); the prophetic psalmist (found primarily in Acts).[3] The appellation υἱός Δαυίδ is not found in the New Testament outside the Synoptic Gospels and Acts, occurring in the common Synoptic tradition only twice, in completely different contexts: a healing pericope and the *Davidssohnfrage*.

1. David as Royal Forerunner

Matthew and Luke present very different genealogies in different locations. Matthew attaches great importance to Jesus' pedigree because he is writing primarily for Jews,[4] and he gives it priority in his Gospel. As the last member of a midrashic series of 3 x 14, Jesus is shown to be the goal of history: the long awaited Messiah.[5] Matthew mentions David four times in his opening verses (1:1–6), but Joseph is also addressed as 'Son of David' by the angel (1:20), indicating that Matthew has a racial rather than a messianic focus.[6] In fact, in the birth narrative, David is not mentioned outside of the genealogical context, though the reference to Micah's prophecy about Bethlehem (2:5–6) is strongly suggestive of David with its allusion to 'a ruler who will be the shepherd of my people Israel'. Luke's family tree, on the other hand, is placed at the launch of Jesus' ministry, between his baptism and his temptation, and is more messianic in tone. Luke reverses the genealogy so that it is a list of sons rather than fathers. David is the only king mentioned; the obscure Nathan, not Solomon, is David's heir (3:31). The fact that Jesus is not descended from a long line of kings has the effect of making David, and therefore Jesus, unique.[7] There is a further effect; as Novakovic argues, the insignificance of Jesus' ancestors attunes with his concern for the poor and marginalised.[8]

Luke is often described as the evangelist to the Gentiles with an emphasis on lowliness but the first two chapters of his Gospel indicate that this is only partly true. The lowliness is certainly there, especially in the story of the shepherds, but so also is political power. The Canticles in particular are very Hebraic and have a martial tone, with terms such as David's *throne, horn, salvation from enemies, service in holiness, and righteousness*. A contrast with Roman rule may be intended. The explanation that best fits these inconsistencies is that Luke 1:4—2:52 is a later, very lengthy,

---

3 John's Gospel has a single reference to David and that is by the crowd; it is more important to John that Jesus comes from God. Any reference to David would detract from Jesus' unique kingship; he is not the man of sorrows, as in the Synoptics, but the King of glory (Gibbs, 'Purpose', 447, n.1).
4 The numerous citations of the Tanakh support this assumption.
5 Novakovic, *Messiah*, 42.
6 According to 1:20, he is not Jesus' natural father but is given the role of passing on his Davidic lineage. According to Friedman, 'Davidic Lineage', 249, 266, adoption was a common Jewish custom. Gibbs, 'Purpose', 448, notes that Matthew (13:55) modifies Mark (6.3) to show that Joseph's paternity is not questioned, so 'Jesus the carpenter' becomes 'the carpenter's son'.
7 Adamczewski, *Gospel of Luke*, 49, 79, believes that Luke's emphasis on the house of David is post-Pauline (cf. Rom. 1:3). He sees the genealogy as a heptadic structure with Salathiel representing Judaea and Jerusalem, David both Judaea and Israel, Abraham the whole of Israel and all circumcised peoples, and Adam the whole of mankind. This theory has the merit of explaining the inclusion in the genealogy of Salathiel, father of Zerubbabel, not of Neri, as in Luke's list. Zerubbabel would be out of place in the list of non-entities that fill the family tree from Nathan onwards. (In Zech. 12:12–13, the house of Nathan is mentioned along with the house of David, and Levi and Shimei, representing the priesthood, as mourning apart, perhaps for the good shepherd.)
8 *Messiah*, 39.

prologue.⁹ The opening of Chapter 3 ('In the fifteenth year of the reign of Tiberius Caesar...') reads like the beginning of a conventional history. Both the rhetorical address to Theophilus at the beginning of the Gospel and the detailed positioning of Christ's birth within Roman history indicate that Luke is directing it to 'opinion-formers'.[10] Soteriological concepts, however, counterbalance the martial tone: the shepherds, who are at the bottom of the social pyramid, are directed ἐν πόλει Δαυίδ, because σωτήρ has been born there (Luke 2:11). This statement does not have the preciseness of Matthew's explanation: 'he shall save his people from their sins' (1:21) but the angels' allusion to 'peace on earth' gives a clue.[11] As Harris notes, Bethlehem was not a military site and Jerusalem was in fact David's city. Luke is indicating that Jesus' kingdom will be one of peace, partly in antithesis to the Roman Emperor.[12] John's only reference to David concerns the crowd's agreement about the Messiah's origin (7:40–44). John may assume that his readers have read Matthew's and Luke's nativity stories, and know that Jesus was born in Bethlehem.

In the Triumphal Entry into Jerusalem, Jesus is no longer a biological descendent but a kingly heir. While the announcement of the physical connection to David is made in the birth narratives by angels or spirit-filled individuals, the proclamation of the hereditary kingship is made by οἱ ὄχλοι (Matthew), πολλοί (Mark). According to Mark, many exclaim, 'Blessed is the coming kingdom of our father David' (11:10), an unusual statement where the emphasis is not on the Son, Jesus, but on David as the father of the Jews. According to Moloney, Mark underlines the fact that the crowd displays a false messianic hope that the kingdom of David will be restored, rather than that Jesus has come to Jerusalem to die. This view is shared also by the disciples.[13] Certainly, Matthew and Luke seem to have felt the need to clarify Mark. Matthew has the most Hebraic version: 'Hosanna to the Son of David' (21:9); Luke does not mention David but implies it in the cry, 'Blessed is the king who comes in the name of the Lord' (19:38). As Kinman points out, whereas Mark focuses on the kingdom, Luke draws attention to the person;[14] this is also true of Matthew, perhaps even more so since he has not only a reference to the Son of David but also to the king (21:8) : 'Your king comes to you, gentle and riding on a donkey...' (Zech. 9:9). This is in line with his interest in the fulfilment of prophecy.[15] Again, Matthew adds two further messianic references. When Jesus has entered Jerusalem, the whole city asks, 'Who is this?'; the crowds who have travelled with Jesus do not reply, 'the Son of David' but 'the prophet from Nazareth' (21:11). This has been seen as strange but it is probably just giving basic information to those who are unacquainted with Jesus. After the blind and lame come to be healed in the temple, it is children who invoke the messianic title for the last time: 'Hosanna to the son of David'. Jesus gives his imprimatur to the exclamation of the children in the temple, not to that of the crowd. The expression of indignation on the part of the hierarchy presents Jesus with the opportunity to cite Psalm 8:2: 'from the lips of children you have prepared praise' (21:15–16). By implication, Jesus accepts the acclamation of the crowd as well, although it might be thought that they had a this-worldly salvation in mind.

David, as a historical forerunner rather than an idealised one, appears only once in all three Synoptics, in an altercation between Jesus and the Pharisees regarding the Sabbath. Jesus uses

---

9 Luke 1–2 is seen as both early and late, because of the prominence given to Mary, who is scarcely mentioned in the remainder of the Gospel.
10 Or 'influencers', in today's parlance.
11 The emphasis on Bethlehem rather than Jerusalem may not only be because of the Davidic connection but also because that city had become the centre of opposition to the early Christians; Fox, 'Decentralization', 124.
12 *Shepherd-King*, 53–54.
13 'Ending', 8–9.
14 'Parousia', 288.
15 John also cites Zech. 9:9, but without any reference to David (12:15).

the incident, recorded in 1 Samuel 21:1–6, to justify the disciples' work of reaping on the sabbath (Mark 2:23–28; Matt. 12:1–8; Luke 6:1–5). Jesus is not arguing that, because David broke the law, the disciples could also do so. Rather, as Viljoen argues, it is about authority. If David had authority to reinterpret the law, Jesus has even greater authority, confirmed in his claim to be Lord of the Sabbath.[16] The issue of persecution also arises: David's action is because of his persecution by Saul, Jesus' persecution because of an action by his disciples.[17] The historical David is used ahistorically, to make messianic claims about Jesus. He is proclaiming himself much more entitled than David.

In Acts, Stephen's and Paul's references to the historical David are in a very different context from that of the Gospels. Stephen's speech before the Sanhedrin signals the beginning of Christianity's break from Judaism, which Paul will formalise. In his survey of salvation history, Stephen does not treat David and Solomon sympathetically, because they replaced the tent of testimony, which had been made as God commanded Moses, with a man-made building for which seemingly no permission was granted: 'David asked that he might provide σκήνωμα[18] for the God of Jacob' (7:46). Although David is described as one 'who enjoyed God's favour' (v.46), Solomon is rebuked, in the words of Isaiah 66:1–2, for believing that God would be contained within a building (vv.48–50). As Moore argues, Stephen's consistent focus is on the sanctuary of heaven, with ambivalence toward the land and Jerusalem. The temple is revitalised and humbled with respect to the new cultic reality. Stephen's speech is the turning point.[19] Paul's later focus on the Gentiles means that David and his proposed temple become even more irrelevant. Finally, at the Jerusalem Council (15:26–29), James the Just moves the argument along further. He cites Amos 9:11–12: God will rebuild τὴν σκηνὴν Δαυὶδ τὴν πεπτωκυῖαν ('the booth of David which has fallen down'), an ironic reference to the Davidic dynasty or perhaps to the temple. Whether James intends the verses to refer to the restoration of the kingdom or to the eschatological temple, it will mean the salvation of the Gentiles who are already turning to God.[20]

2. David as Type of Messianic Healer

There are two main problems associated with the use of the term 'Son of David' outside of the birth narratives of Matthew and Luke. First, the association of the title 'Son of David' with Jesus' *healing activity* is somewhat surprising. Secondly, there is a dissonance between the use of 'Son of David' in relation to healing of outcasts and the dynastic pretensions of the title in relation to the royal ancestor. Many scholars view it as a relatively late tradition, because it is not found in the earlier epistles and because the disciples and sympathetic elites do not address Jesus in this way.[21] Those who call Jesus 'Son of David' in this context are the outcasts of society: several blind

---

16 'Sabbath', 2.
17 Matthew adds that in the Temple the priests profane the Sabbath but are blameless (12:5), an even stronger messianic affirmation.
18 This word has the idea of 'embodiment', clear in the only other use in the NT, in 2 Peter 1:13–14. This is in contrast to the word used of the tent of meeting, σκην, which he used in v.44 and James will use in Acts 15:16 (citing Amos 9:11–12).
19 'Heavenly Temple', 44, 51. Stephen's dying vision underlines this point.
20 Meek, 'Gentile Mission', 220–221.
21 The most frequent forms of address are κύριε, ῥαββι and its Aramaic variant ῥαββουνι (Mark 10:51). Διδάσκαλε, διδάσκαλε ἀγαθέ (Luke 18:18) and ἐπιστάτα are found only in Luke, on six occasions, in place of Rabbi (e.g. 5:5), perhaps a concession to Luke's Gentile readership.

beggars and a foreign woman.[22] The explanation, I believe, lies in Matthew's changes to Mark.

2.1 The Healing Shepherd

Most scholarship sees a link between the healing role and the shepherd motif. Chae, for example, argues that the Davidic Shepherd as the 'Therapeutic Son of David' fulfils the role of the eschatological Shepherd of Israel and also that of the Davidic Shepherd-Appointee over the one eschatological flock, as found in the Tanakh and Second Temple Judaism.[23] The shepherd image may be the key to understanding the association of the Son of David and healing. In 9:35, Jesus is described as having compassion on the crowds 'because they were harassed and helpless like sheep without a shepherd'. There are many other references in the Gospels to shepherds and their caring role, based on motifs found mostly in the *nevi' im*. The diatribe in Ezekiel 34 against the shepherds of Israel is particularly apposite to Jesus' therapeutic role: they are condemned because they do not strengthen the diseased, heal the sick or bind up that which was broken (v.4). YHWH promises: 'I will set up over them one shepherd, my servant David, and he will feed them [...] and be their shepherd' (v.23). The message of salvation announced to the shepherds in Luke's birth narrative thus constitutes a strong connection with the Davidic healer.

Another possible source for the healing 'Son of David' is the Isaianic Servant. Matthew (12:15–21) cites Isaiah 42:1–4. Luke (4:18–19), in the programmatic Nazareth Manifesto, cites Isaiah 61:1–2. Matthew's citation mentions justice and hope but not healing, whereas Luke promises good news for the poor, freedom to prisoners and sight to the blind.[24] Messianic healing is also referenced when John the Baptizer sent his disciples to ask, 'Are you the one who is to come?' Jesus answered by pointing out that 'the blind receive their sight, the lame walk, the lepers are cleansed, the deaf hear, the dead are raised and the gospel is preached to the poor' (Matt. 11:4, Luke 7:22). This parallels the Nazareth Manifesto which in turn echoes messianic texts such as Isaiah 35:5, 'Then the lame man shall leap like a deer and the tongue of the mute shall sing', and Isaiah 53:4, 'He took up our diseases and carried our illnesses', which Matthew cites after the healing of many demon-possessed people (8:17). The Servant is not specifically connected to David but the motifs of the therapeutic shepherd and the suffering servant come together in Zechariah's words, 'Strike the shepherd and the sheep will be scattered' (13:7), which Jesus quotes just before Gethsemane (Mark 14:27, Matt. 26:31).[25] The transition from literal shepherding to metaphorical leading is especially noticeable in Ezekiel 34. The notion of healing in Mark and Matthew is implicit in the concept of David the shepherd-king and hence that of Jesus.

Another origin proposed is that of 'suffering David'. Jipp points out that a connection is nowhere made between the Messiah and the Isaianic Servant in Second Temple literature. He argues that the Psalms play an important role in Luke's narrative and it is in the sufferings

---

22 Dvorácek, *Son of David*, 191, notes the contrast with the David of 2 Samuel (5:8) who, when he captures Jerusalem, orders the massacre of 'the lame and the blind whom David's soul hates'. The meaning of the verse is obscure. According to the LXX, the blind and lame resist him and he orders an attack on them and those who hate David's soul. This makes the references to David healer as even more puzzling.
23 *Davidic Shepherd*, 278–9.
24 A figurative freeing of prisoners might include the mentally ill, although they address Jesus as 'Son of the Most High God' in Mark 5:6 and Luke 8:28, and 'Son of God' in Matthew 8:29. Even more appropriate verses are found in Isa. 35:5–6: 'Then the eyes of the blind shall be opened and the ears of the deaf unstopped. Then the lame shall leap like a hart and the tongue of the dumb sing'. As Fox, 'Decentralization', 129, points out, Jesus omits Isaiah's final phrase 'and the day of vengeance of our God'; Jesus' ministry will not include revenge on Israel's enemies.
25 Zechariah's preceding words, 'Awake, O sword against the shepherd, and against the man near unto me' were no doubt well-known and suggestive of 'the pierced one' of Isaiah 53:5.

of *David* that the connection is to be found.[26] Stead argues that it has not been sufficiently appreciated that the sufferings of the servant in Isaiah 40—55 resound with echoes of the psalms of the 'suffering David'. These two streams of tradition have become fused into a single tradition in the post-exilic literature of the Tanakh, particularly Zechariah 9—14, and in intertestamental literature.[27] This is indeed possible.

Two other sources of the therapeutic Messiah are less plausible: Solomon the exorcist and Jesus the priest. The Second Temple belief in the non-messianic Solomon as exorcist, healer and sage[28] seems rather tenuous. The only reference to Solomon in the Gospels (Matt. 12:42, Luke 11:31) is in relation to his wisdom as revealed to the Queen of Sheba. Furthermore, the demon-possessed (Mark 3:11, 5:7 and Matt. 8:29) address Jesus as 'Son of (the most high) God', not 'Son of David'. Spadaro's argument for a priestly subtext in Matthew is debatable. Jesus cleansed physical and mental infirmity,[29] but it was not the priest's role to heal but to confirm God's healing (for example, Matt. 8:4). The term 'priest' is never applied either to David or to Jesus in any of the Gospels.

2.2 Son of David as Healer in the Gospels and Acts

The address 'Son of David' occurs eight times in the Synoptics. Mark and Luke contain only one pericope in which the term is used twice by the same blind man; Matthew includes a doublet of the same incident. Matthew also inserts 'Son of David' in a retelling of Jesus' encounter with the Canaanite woman. He is the only evangelist to record the crowd's reference to the 'Son of David' at the Triumphal Entry. His interest in Jewish genealogy as shown in his first chapter might explain the more frequent use of the term. Matthew is distinctive in another way: apart from one incident, Matthew changes Mark's exorcisms into general healings. He uses the verb θεραπεύειν ('heal') fourteen times. According to Paffenroth, Matthew seeks to show that, while David was king, he was not a healer, but Jesus is both.[30] It is more likely that Matthew favours healing in general over exorcisms because the former is more prominent in messianic texts, especially Isaiah 42 which he cites. In the single pericope (12:23–28), where Matthew describes an exorcism, there is no request for healing from the demon-possessed man but 'all the people were astonished and asked, Could this be the Son of David?' It seems that Matthew has recorded this one exorcism to provide an occasion for Jesus' lengthy attack on the Pharisees that follows (vv.25–31).

In the one pericope common to all the Synoptics (Mark 10:47–48; Matt. 20:30–31; Luke 18:38–39), the petitioners in Mark and Luke repeat the address 'Son of David', thus underlining their urgency. The incident occurs in the context of messianic predictions: just after Jesus tells his disciples that he came not to be served but to serve and to give his life for many, which is a clear reference to the Suffering Servant, a blind beggar whom Mark alone named Bartimaeus, or two blind men in Matthew's case, call/s on Jesus as 'Son of David' as he leaves Jericho. When the crowd tries to silence him/them, he/they to cry out all the more,[31] repeating the address 'Son of David'. Bauckham believes that Bartimaeus calls Jesus 'Son of David' because of Mark's coming focus on the messianic king, for there has been no mention of this theme earlier.[32] Two pericopes peculiar to

---

26 'Suffering Messiah', 256–57.
27 'Suffering David', 62–63.
28 So Duling, 'Solomon'; Shavit, *Trio*.
29 *Reading Matthew*, 19.
30 'Jesus as anointed', 531. All three Synoptics include the incident of the Gadarene swine where the demon-possessed man/men call Jesus 'Son of (the Most High) God' (Mark 5:7; Matt. 8:2; Luke 8:28).
31 Since Mark thinks Bartimaeus important enough to name, perhaps he was a follower of Jesus.
32 'Eyewitnesses', 6.

Matthew consolidate the theme of Jesus' messiahship. In a possible doublet, another pair of blind men call on Jesus as 'Son of David', immediately after the raising of Jairus' daughter (9:27) and earlier than the healing of the pair who are to be equated with Bartimaeus (20:29–34).[33] When 'the people' ask if the healing of a demon-possessed man who was both blind and dumb means that Jesus is the son of David (Matt. 12:23), they are associating Jesus with messianic expectations. Just before this healing miracle, Jesus had healed a man with a withered arm (Matt. 12:9–13). Matthew adds: 'many followed Jesus and he healed them all, but he warned them not to make him known' (vv.15–16). The evangelist links this injunction with Isaiah 42:1–4, of which the most relevant words are: 'He will not quarrel or cry out'. Although the passage does not refer to healing as such, the fact that the Pharisees were plotting how to kill him suggests the Suffering Servant.

The use of the epithet 'Son of David' by a Canaanite woman (Matt. 15:22)[34] has proven difficult to explain. Some commentators think it is highly unlikely that a foreign woman would know of such an appellation. Several explanations are possible. Since the woman had heard of his cures, she might also have heard that he was so addressed. What Connolly calls 'her wit and her understanding of the theology of the abundance of God's grace'[35] might have her use that title, tacitly acknowledging that she is an outsider, and exploiting that fact, as her wonderful riposte shows. Wainwright is surely correct in suggesting that the woman is reminding him that he had healed others who appealed to him under that title and is contrasting his mission to the lost sheep with the dynastic implications of the title given to him.[36] As Dvorácek notes, the emphasis is not on healing but on the persistent request and faith of a Gentile expressed in dialogue.[37] Mark also records Jesus' encounter with 'the Syro-Phoenician woman' but she addresses Jesus only once, as Κύριε (7:28), with no mention of David. Matthew, as usual, shifts Mark's focus on an exorcism to a healing. Luke omits the encounter altogether, perhaps because, according to his schema, Jesus had no dealings with Gentiles—that is Paul's sphere.

To conclude, perhaps we need to ask another question with regard to the 'Son of David' provenance: why did Matthew take the term of address in Mark's pericope and use it again four times? His frequent use of 'Son of David' is no doubt due to his interest in Jewish genealogy, and the connection with healing to the suffering servant of Deutero-Isaiah. Without Matthew's frequent use of the address, it would hardly be a crux. Fitzmyer suggests that the Messiah is the bridge between the Suffering Servant and David's Son along which the ability to perform miracles has passed.[38] One could add a third element: suffering David. The shepherd-king motif, on the face of it, might seem the most relevant but it is the texts concerning the Isaianic Servant that are cited rather than merely suggested. Those who sought healing were petitioning someone with benevolent power which both the Shepherd and the Servant possessed. It is important, however, not to make too much of the use of the designation 'Son of David'. It disappears even in Matthew after its last use by the children in the Temple, to be overtaken by the title 'Son of God', which reaches its

---

33 Gibbs sees the two miracles as representing two different stages in the recognition and acceptance of Jesus' Messianic Davidic sonship: the first pair disobey Jesus' order not to tell anyone but the second pair obey him ('Purpose', 460).
34 The term 'Canaanite' is more symbolic than descriptive, suggesting an outsider or foreigner in the borderland of Tyre and Sidon, or even a sinner (Wainwright, *Habitat,* 141).
35 *Disorderly Women,* 140.
36 *Habitat,* 158–60.
37 *Son of David,* 176.
38 *The One,* 143.

apogee in the centurion's remark: 'Surely this was the Son of God' (Mark 15:39, Matt. 27:54).[39]

3. David as the Prophetic Psalmist

It would be more accurate to say that David is the psalm-writing prophet rather than the prophetic psalmist (Peter calls him a prophet in Acts 2:30).[40] The many citations from the Psalms in Acts are used mostly to show the fulfilment of prophecy in relation to Jesus' Messiahship. In the Gospels, by contrast, David as Psalmist is recruited only once, in a dispute with religious rulers. The paucity of references to the Psalms in the Synoptics can be explained by the quite different context: Jesus who is the main speaker in the Gospels is adhering to the Messianic secret whereas the apostles in Acts use David to bolster Jesus' claims after the resurrection and ascension.

The one incident in the Synoptics in which David is regarded as 'the Psalmist' is the *Davidssohnfrage* (Mark 12:35–37; Matt. 22:41–45; Luke 20:41–44) which illustrates the rabbinical treatment of an apparent contradiction in or between scriptural passages.[41] The argument turns on the twin uses of the title in Psalm 109 (LXX).[42] The difficulty is that, if the psalm is about the Messiah and the author is David, why is the Messiah called κύριος, not υἱός in relation to David? In Mark, it is a dominical saying against the teachers of the law who are not present. There is no indication of any debate, but rather, the great crowd heard him gladly (27b).[43] Luke likewise does not mention a debate and Jesus' riposte is directed against an unspecified 'they'. But, in Matthew, Jesus initiates the exchange with the Pharisees when he bluntly asks, 'Whose son is the Christ?' anticipating that they will reply, 'The son of David'. He is then ready with his retort, 'Why then does he call him Lord?' The passage does not expressly state that David is the king in question or that Jesus is the Messiah. As Gibbs[44] and Strauss[45] argue, 'Son of David' is a valid but *inadequate* description of Jesus. Although descended from David, he is more exalted, to the extent that he can be given the name κύριος which is reserved for YHWH. This is fitting as he moves toward the cross.

The much more frequent attribution in Acts of the Psalms to David can be explained by the contrast between pre- and post-Resurrection settings. Although David does not belong among the *nevi'im*, there is evidence from Qumran that he was so regarded. Fitzmyer believes that this is why there is such use of the Psalms in Acts.[46] For example, Peter, in his sermon to the 120 disciples (Acts 1:16–22), uses a pastiche of verses from the imprecatory psalms that originally referred to the psalmist's personal enemies, in order to explain Judas' end. In the process, he makes very high claims for David: 'the Scripture had to be fulfilled *which the Holy Spirit spoke before* by the mouth of David' (v.16). Smith believes that the Psalms are strongly linked to Luke's Davidic theme and form a lens through which Luke-Acts is read. This connection creates a rich repository of theology about a suffering and rejected one which Luke mines, in the parallel between the lives of

---

39 Other references to Jesus as Son of God have already been made in the Temptation, the Transfiguration, Peter's Confession. In Mark 3:11 and Luke 4:34, unclean spirits call Jesus 'the Son of the Most High'.
40 David is not a prophet anywhere in the Tanakh but he is so named in Qumran texts (Fitzmyer, 'David', 335).
41 Fitzmyer, *Semitic Background*, 123, suggests that what we have may only represent a torso of the full account.
42 The argument is similar to that used with regard to Moses in the burning bush, where the LXX is used, but cannot be sustained with reference to the MT.
43 Luke follows Mark although he does not mention scribes: 'How can *they* say that Christ is David's son?' and substitutes 'in the Book of Psalms' for Mark's 'in the Holy Spirit', perhaps for the benefit of his Gentile readers.
44 'Purpose', 460.
45 *Davidic Messiah*, 70.
46 'A prophet', 333–334.

David and Jesus in the early Acts speeches.[47] After Peter's and John's arrest, however, Psalm 2:1–2 is applied first to David and then Jesus, and is finally transferred to the messianic community, showing fluidity in the way in which Psalms are appropriated: suffering David becomes suffering Jesus; suffering Jesus becomes the suffering Church.

David is a complex of historical figure, ideal king, and prophet in four great discourses: Peter's sermon at Pentecost, Stephen's defence before the Sanhedrin, Paul's sermon at Pisidian Antioch, and James' speech at the Council in Jerusalem. The use of Psalm 15 (LXX) by Peter at Pentecost and by Paul in Antioch indicates that it may already have formed part of a *testimonium*. The meaning of the psalm in Hebrew differs from the Greek, allowing both apostles to make a novel point. Whereas the psalmist, in the MT, declares his confidence that God will protect his pious or faithful one (חֲסִידְךָ) from an untimely death in Sheol,[48] the Septuagint gives an eschatological context: the hope is that the holy one (τὸν ὅσιόν)[49] will not see corruption, in other words, will have eternal life. Cuany argues convincingly that Peter is not using the Davidic psalm as a *proof* or even a *proclamation* of the resurrection but an *explanation* of why Jesus did not die—death has no power over the righteous one. Without 'proving' the resurrection in any way, this type of explanation for Jesus' resurrection, made in the presence of a crowd aware that this man was powerfully attested by God and unjustly crucified, is much more likely to have 'cut the people to the heart and make them take the apostolic claim that Jesus rose from the dead seriously'.[50] Peter argues that the existence of David's tomb, which is 'here to this day',[51] shows that he is not speaking of himself but of another. He then cites a verse from the *Davidssohnfrage*, as proof that Christ has been exalted to the right hand of God. Paul makes a similar point but more briefly. According to Paul, 'After he had served his own generation, David fell asleep, was buried and his body decayed' (13:36), therefore, Psalm 15 does not apply to him but to the one who in fact was raised and did not undergo decay.[52] Paul regards the resurrection of Jesus as the fulfilment of the sure blessings promised to David, a reference to Isaiah 55:3, where the context suggests both prosperity ('wine and milk without money') and peace ('a prince and commander)' (v.5), but, significantly, no longer a king. The idea of David *redivivus* led to a future hope in the restoration without Davidic kings. After the fall of Jerusalem, David has been downgraded and only God is king.

The common thread in all uses of David as psalmist throughout Acts is the idea that he cannot be speaking of himself alone but of someone greater. (This has been true in the Gospels, especially in Matthew who often accommodates the Tanakh to the life of Jesus.) In Acts, there is also a widening in the audience: the Petrine sermon is directed to the Jews, the Pauline address is to both Jews and God-fearers, while James, although addressing Jews, confirms the inclusion of Gentiles. Significantly, after Paul'ss conversion, there is no reference to the Son of David: 'Saul began to preach in the synagogues that Jesus is *the Son of God*' (9:30).

---

47 *Fate*, 20–21.
48 The parallelism in 16:10 indicates that *chesed* refers to David. In Ps. 86:2, David prays, 'Preserve my soul, for I am *chesed*' (MT).
49 This is similar to 4:27: ἐπὶ τὸν ἅγιον παῖδά σου Ἰησοῦν.
50 'Divine Necessity', 403–404.
51 According to Josephus, Solomon buried his father in Jerusalem with great pomp and vast wealth (*Antiq.* 7.3).
52 Sargent, *David*, 90, points out that the Lucan view of history, in a marked departure from traditional Jewish exegesis, enables a text to belong to the past but yet speak of the future.

Conclusion

The references to David in the birth narratives of Matthew and Luke, which are separate from the account of Jesus' ministry, have the effect of placing Jesus in a biological context in the case of Matthew and a political one in the case of Luke. Both are written for a Jewish readership. That fact and the martial tone in Luke suggest an addition to that Gospel which is from another source. The two nativity texts, though very different, are linked by the declaration that the promises to David are fulfilled in the Messiah born in Bethlehem and that salvation from sins, or from enemies, will come through him.

In the account of Jesus' ministry, Matthew with his putative Jewish readership highlights the Davidic connection much more than Mark and Luke. The frequent use of the formula 'Son of David' in healing contexts is due to two changes which Matthew makes to Mark's Gospel. He applies Mark's original formula, 'Son of David' to other healing episodes while also removing the reference to exorcisms. Again, Matthew is the only evangelist to cite David in the Triumphal Entry into Jerusalem, though the other two Synoptics make a veiled allusion. The link between the use of 'Son of David' in both the nativity stories and the ministry pericopes concern two different concepts of power, royal and righteous in the first section, royal and therapeutic in the second, both of which bring salvation.

The example of David in the two unrelated pericopes, the Sabbath-controversy and the *Davidssohnfrage*, is used during disputes with the Pharisees. The first is the only instance where David is presented in any detail as a historical figure and it is in the context of a dispute initiated by the Pharisees. In the second, he is an idealised king and a prophet, in a controversy initiated by Jesus himself. In both instances, Jesus' primacy over David is asserted, as above rabbinical law, and as worthy of the name of God himself.

In Acts, David is presented as an unwitting prophet who, in writing about himself, also and more importantly writes about Christ. Peter and Paul use the same Psalm to prove the Resurrection but at the same time they stress David's mortality. James goes further in anticipating a spiritualised version of the Davidic dynasty and/or the temple.

In all the uses of David's name in the Gospels and Acts, there is a progression from a rather temporal and national salvation to a spiritual and universal one. The superiority of Jesus is everywhere assumed but in the latter half of the Gospels and Acts it is made explicit, when David is no longer named. This is fitting as Jesus goes to the Cross in the Gospels, and later in Acts when the Gospel proclamation is widened to the Gentiles.

Marie McInnes
Independent Researcher

Bibliography

Adamczewski, B.   *The Gospel of Luke: A Hypertextual Commentary* (Frankfurt am Main: Peter Lang, 2016).

Bauckham, R.   'Jesus and the Eyewitnesses, Fourteen Years Later', *JGAR* 3 (2019), 5–14.

Chae, Y. S.   *Jesus as the Eschatological Davidic Shepherd: Studies in the Old Testament, Second Temple Judaism, and in the Gospel of Matthew* (Tübingen: Mohr Siebeck, 2006).

Cuany, M.   'The Divine Necessity of the Resurrection: A Re-Assessment of the Use of Psalm 16 in Acts 2', *NTS* 66.3 (2020), 392–405.

Connolly, M. A.   *Disorderly Women and the Order of God* (London: T&T Clark, 2018).

Duling, D. C.   'The Promises to David and their Entrance into Christianity: Nailing down a Likely Hypothesis', *NTS* 19.1 (1973), 55–77.

Duling, D. C.   'The Therapeutic Son of David: An Element in Matthew's Christological Apologetic', *NTS* 24.3 (1977), 392–410.

Duling, D. C.   'Solomon, Exorcism and the Son of David', *HTR* 68.3–4 (1975), 235–52.

Dvorácek, J.   *The Son of David in Matthew's Gospel in the Light of Solomon as Exorcist Tradition* (Tübingen: Mohr Siebeck, 2016).

Fitzmyer, J. A.   *The One who is to Come* (Grand Rapids, MI: Eerdmans, 2007).

Fitzmyer, J. A.   *Essays on the Semitic Background of the New Testament* (London: Chapman, 1971).

Fitzmyer, J. A.   'David, "Being therefore a Prophet", Acts 2.30', *CBQ* 34.3 (1972), 332–339.

Fox, N. A.   'Decentralization in Luke-Acts', *JGAR* 5 (2021), 123–142.

Friedman, C. T.   'Jesus' Lineage and the Case for Jewish Adoption', *NTS* 66.2 (2020), 249–267.

Gibbs, J.   'The purpose and pattern in Matthew's use of Son of David', *NTS* 10.4 (1964), 446–464.

Harris, S.   The Davidic Shepherd King in the Lucan Narrative (PhD thesis, Otago University, Dunedin, 2011). [online:https://ourarchive.otago.ac.nz/bitstream/handle/10523/2409/HarrisSarahJG2012PhD?sequence=1&isAllowed=y]. Now published as *The Davidic Shepherd King in the Lukan Narrative* (LNTS; London: T&T Clark, 2018).

Jipp, J. W.   'Luke's Scriptural Suffering Messiah: A Search for Precedent, a Search for Identity', *CBQ* 72.2 (2010), 255–274.

Kinman, B.   'Parousia, Jesus' "A-triumphal" Entry, and the Fate of Jerusalem (Luke 19.28-44)', *JBL* 118.2 (1999), 279–294.

Meek, J.	'The Gentile Mission in Old Testament Citations in Acts-Text, Hermeneutic, and Purpose' (2005). PhD, Concordia, St Louis. [online: https://scholar.csl.edu/phd/97]
Moloney, F. J.	'An ending and a new beginning: A study of Mark 11.1–25', *JGAR* 1 (2017), 5–17.
Moore, N. J.	'"He Saw Heaven Opened": Heavenly Temple and Universal Mission in Luke-Acts', *NTS* 68.1 (2022), 38–51.
Miura, Y.	*David in Luke-Acts* (Tübingen: Mohr Siebeck, 2007).
Novakovic, L.	*Messiah, the Healer of the Sick: A Study of Jesus as the Son of David in the Gospel of Matthew* (Tübingen: Mohr Siebeck, 2003).
Paffenroth, K.	'Jesus as Anointed and Healing Son of David in the Gospel of Matthew', *Biblica* 80 (1999), 547–554.
Sargent, B.	*David Being a Prophet: The Contingency of Scripture upon History in the New Testament* (Berlin/Boston: Walter De Gruyter, 2014).
Shavit, J.	*An Imaginary Trio: King Solomon, Jesus and Aristotle* (Berlin/Boston: De Gruyter, 2020).
Smith, S. H.	'The Function of the Son of David Tradition in Matthew's Gospel', *NTS* 42.4 (1996), 523–539.
Smith, S.	*The Fate of the Jerusalem Temple in Luke-Acts: An Intertextual Approach to Christ's Laments over Jerusalem and Stephen's Speech* (London: T&T Clark, 2017).
Spadaro, M.	*Reading Matthew as the Climactic Fulfilment of the Hebrew Story* (Eugene, OR: Wipf & Stock, 2015).
Stanton, G.	*The Gospels and Jesus* (Oxford: Oxford University Press, 2002).
Stead, M. R.	'Suffering Servant, Suffering David and Stricken Shepherd', in M. R. Stead (ed.), *Christ died for our sins: Essays on the Atonement* (The Doctrine Commission General Synod of the Anglican Church of Australia, 2013), 59–79.
Story, J. L.	'The Jerusalem Council: A pivotal and instructive paradigm', *Journal of Biblical Perspectives in Leadership* 3.1 (2010), 33–60.
Strauss, M.	*The Davidic Messiah in Luke-Acts: the promise and its fulfillment in Lukan Theology* (Sheffield: Sheffield University Press, 1995).
Viljoen, F. P.	'Sabbath controversy in Matthew', *Verbum et Ecclesia* 32.1 (Article 418, 1–8, 2011). [Online: doi:10.4102/ ve.v32i1.418]
Wainwright, E. M.	*Habitat, Human and Holy: An Eco-Rhetorical Reading of the Gospel of Matthew* (Sheffield: Sheffield Phoenix Press, 2016).
Wright, R. B. (ed.)	*The Psalms of Solomon: A Critical Edition of the Greek Text* (London: T & T Clark, 2007).

The Rise and Rise of James the Just in Luke–Acts

MARY J. MARSHALL

Abstract

Underlying this study is the hypothesis that the 'historical Jesus' was typically present at meals as a guest, not as the host, and that this is true of his last meal. The fundamental premise is that the host at the Last Supper was Jesus' brother James, and that his surprising rise from obscurity to preeminence can be traced back to his presence at that occasion. Key points of the scenario are that the meal took place on Wednesday evening 1 April 33 C.E. at the start of 15 Nisan according to the Essenic calendar, in a household in southwest Jerusalem, where James was the *mebaqqer*. The essay is based primarily on Luke–Acts but draws on other sources, particularly the Dead Sea Scrolls. While Luke is utilised for comparison with the other Synoptics for discussion concerning Jesus' relationship with his family, and his last meal, Acts is a significant source for demonstrating links between Essenic and early Christian communities, and the context of James' extraordinary elevation in the early church. The Epistle of James is briefly considered in order to affirm Essenic influence upon both James and Jesus, and to explain the division that occurred within nascent Christianity between Jewish and Gentile believers. Despite the speculative nature of the argument, the conclusion assembles several reasons for accepting its plausibility.

1. Introduction

Since the publication of Colin Humphreys' *The Mystery of the Last Supper* in 2011, my research on the chronology of the meal has been based on the concept that it took place on Wednesday evening, 1 April 33 C.E. at the beginning of Nisan 15 according to the lunisolar calendar of the Essenes.[1] Humphreys demonstrates that the use of the Essenic calendar for the paschal celebration would explain the disparity between the synoptic Last Supper narratives, and the account in the Fourth Gospel, in which the feast that year coincided with the Sabbath.[2] While Humphreys and Saulnier

---

[1] The chronology draws also on Saulnier, *Calendrical Variations*.
[2] See Humphreys, *Mystery of the Last Supper*, 163, where according to the official *Jewish* calendar, Nisan 14 in 33 C.E. was from sunset on Thursday 2 April to sunset Friday 3 April. There is scholarly debate as to whether the beginning of the lunar month was calculated by the Qumran Essenes from the *new* moon as asserted by Humphreys and Saulnier, or the *full* moon. See Saulnier, *Calendrical Variations*, 178–203, 226–27. There is controversy also regarding interpretation of the terms X and *dwq* in the scrolls. On the terms' meaning see Saulnier, *Calendrical Variations*, 208–214, 240. I concur with Humphreys and Saulnier that X relates to the day of conjunction, that is, the end of one lunar month and the start of the next. See Humphreys, *Mystery of the Last Supper*, 144, 217 n.24; Saulnier, *Calendrical Variations*, 211, 216, 221.

reach the same conclusion regarding the date of the Last Supper, their methods of calculation differ slightly. Here I follow the method utilised by the latter. X indicated the last time that the crescent moon *was* seen in the morning at the end of the lunation before the conjunction. In 33 C.E, X would have occurred on the morning of Wednesday 18 March. The lunar month began *on the evening* of that day, i.e. Nisan 1 began on the Wednesday evening. Hence the evening of Tuesday 31 March was the beginning of Nisan 14 and it ended on the evening of Wednesday 1 April. The paschal lambs would have been slain on the Wednesday afternoon, and the meal eaten that evening at the start of Nisan 15.[3] This coheres with evidence of the Temple Scroll showing that Passover must always fall on a Tuesday.[4]

In an earlier essay on the topic, based on Luke, I argued that the meal was held in the dining room of an Essene household,[5] and that although it was a commemoration of Passover, there was no lamb on the menu.[6] The hypothesis is that Jesus' extraordinary actions and sayings on the occasion would have convinced his Essene commensals, familiar with the text 1QSa II, 11–22, that he was the anticipated royal Messiah.[7] Following Jesus' death in the mid-afternoon on the Friday, on what was Nisan 14 in the *official* Jewish calendar, those who had been present at the meal might well have identified him as the true passover lamb—reminiscent of Paul's description in 1 Corinthians 5:7.[8]

The present essay builds on that scenario, with the contention that James, the brother of Jesus, was an Essene, and was the host at the Last Supper. My aim is to demonstrate how this could account for the preeminence of James in the early church.

Section 2 explores Luke's references to Jesus' family and compares them with those of the other Synoptic Gospels, before discussing the Last Supper. The following section then discusses how James features in Acts. Section 4 considers the links between the early church and the Essenes, and Section 5 looks at the Epistle of James to provide further evidence of connection with Essenes, and for clues concerning the discord that arose between the first followers of Jesus and the later Gentile believers. The conclusion then sums up the findings and refers to several factors that support the hypothesis.

---

3 Saulnier, *Calendrical Variations*, 118, citing 11Q19 XVII, 6–9, which also agrees with instructions in Jub. 49:1–2 (Saulnier, *Calendrical Variations*, 92, 92 n.4).
4 According to the 364-day year, Nisan 1 would always fall on a Wednesday, and so Passover, on Nisan 14, would always be on a Tuesday. See Maier, *The Temple* Scroll, 71–76, for the structure of the year, esp. p.71 re Passover falling on Tuesday. On Passover, see also Maier, *The Temple* Scroll, 25, 78–79; and Saulnier, *Calendrical Variations*, 118, 120, citing 4Q326. See further on the structure of the 364-day year in Saulnier, *Calendrical Variations*, 206–207.
5 For background on the Essenes, and the surmised links between this movement and early Christianity, see Marshall, 'Essenic Influence on Jesus', esp. pp.52–63; Joseph, *Jesus, the Essenes*, esp. the findings on p.164; and also Capper, 'Distribution of Essene Community of Goods', 10–59, though I find some of his proposals unpersuasive.
6 The essay, 'Rethinking the Last Supper Again—with Insights from Luke', builds on a paper presented in the 'Synoptic Gospels and Allusions in the Gospels' section at the Society of Biblical Literature International Meeting held in August 2017, in Berlin, Germany.
7 For a translation of the passage, see García Martínez, *The Dead Sea Scrolls Translated*, 127–28; VanderKam, *Dead Sea Scrolls and the Bible*, 126; and for commentary, pp.120–27, esp. pp.125–27.
8 The identification also recalls the view of Jesus as 'the Lamb of God', in John 1:29,36. However, my comment does not imply a theological association with the two cited texts.

2. Jesus' Family and His Relationship With Them

2.1 Kinship theories

The existence of actual siblings of Jesus appears to have been accepted in early tradition,[9] and gains support from the statement in Luke 2:7 that he is Mary's 'firstborn' (πρωτότοκον), not her 'only' (μονογενής) son.[10] However, this view changed as the concept of Mary's perpetual virginity became established,[11] with Jesus' 'brothers and sisters' being interpreted in three different ways after the mid-second century.[12]

The first, the Helvidian theory, is that they are the offspring of Mary and Joseph, and hence biological siblings, or if credence is given to the virgin birth, half-brothers and -sisters.[13] The second, the Epiphanian theory, holds that they were children of Joseph from a first marriage, thus allowing belief in Mary's perpetual virginity.[14] Another theory, the Hieronymian, proposes that the offspring are 'cousins' of Jesus, on the supposition that the James known as his 'brother' was actually the son of Alphaeus, that is, one of the Twelve.[15] There are serious defects with the Epiphanian and Hieronymian theories,[16] and I concur with Bernheim's conclusion that: 'James, and also Joses, Jude, Simon and their sisters, were very probably children of Joseph and Mary'.[17] It follows that none of the siblings was among the Twelve.[18] Interestingly, in the narratives about Jesus' rejection at Nazareth, while Matthew and Mark name the four brothers, and mention the sisters, Luke does not.[19] However, Luke does refer to Jesus' mother and brothers in his 'true kindred' account.[20] The next section further explores these disparities.[21]

---

9   See Turner, 'James, the Lord's Brother', 8.
10 Turner, 'James, the Lord's Brother', 14. Note that in Luke's three uses of the term μονογενής in his Gospel (7:12; 8:42; 9:38), it is in reference to an *only* child. See also Bernheim, *James, Brother of Jesus*, 18.
11 Turner, 'James, the Lord's Brother', 8.
12 Bernheim, *James, Brother of Jesus*, 14.
13 Bernheim, *James, Brother of Jesus*, 14.
14 Bernheim, *James, Brother of Jesus*, 15. The theory derives from the mid-second century apocryphal work *Protevangelium of James* (Bernheim, *James, Brother of Jesus*, 15, 19–20). Saldarini, 'Matthew', 1007, notes that while it is stated in Matt. 1:25 that Joseph did not have sexual relations with Mary until the birth, the Greek word ως ('until') 'neither affirms nor denies' that Mary 'remained a virgin for life, as patristic and medieval interpretations affirmed'.
15 Bernheim, *James, Brother of Jesus*, 15–16. According to Catholic tradition, James the son of Alphaeus is known as 'St James the Less' to distinguish him from James the son of Zebedee, who is designated as 'St James the Great'.
16 *James, Brother of Jesus*, 16–29. The main reason for discounting the validity of the virgin birth, is that the word עַלְמָה which features in Isaiah 7:14 and is quoted in Matthew 1:23, refers to a *girl* (of marriageable age), or *young woman* (until the birth of first child); [Holladay, *Hebrew and Aramaic Lexicon*, 274]. Isaiah refers not to a virgin but to a young pregnant woman, yet the evangelist quotes the LXX, which mistranslates עַלְמָה as παρθένος ('virgin'). See Levine and Brettler, *Bible with and without Jesus*, 260; Carrigan, 'Virgin Birth', 1359. Luke's annunciation narrative (1:26–35) has Mary described as a 'virgin' (twice in v.27, implied in v.34), and the historicity of the tradition that a virginal conception occurred is affirmed by many scholars, e.g. Balch, 'Luke', 1106–1107; Bauckham, *Jude and the Relatives*, 369 n.166; Green, *Gospel of Luke*, 90–91; Nolland, *Luke*, 46, 48, 58. However, as Levine and Brettler show, Luke does not explicitly indicate that Mary conceived virginally. 'She is a virgin at the time of Gabriel's annunciation, but the angel does not tell her that she will be so at the time of Jesus' conception' (*Bible with and without Jesus*, 259). Moreover, a significant problem with the notion of a virgin birth is that for Jesus to be truly a son of David, requires that Joseph was his biological father, as I believe to be the case.
17 *James, Brother of Jesus*, 29.
18 For discussion on the 'plainly traditional' ways of distinguishing between the different persons who share the names of Jesus' brothers, see Bauckham, *Jude and the Relatives*, 18.
19 See Mark 6:3; Matt. 13:55–56; cf. Luke 4:22.
20 See Mark 3:31–35; Matt. 12:46–50; Luke 8:19–21.
21 The discussion that follows draws on the Two Source hypothesis, though it is recognised that the concept is not accepted universally. See Tuckett, 'Synoptic Gospels', 1262.

2.2 Relations with Family

Luke's references to Jesus' family differ significantly from those in the other Synoptics. Importantly, only Mark includes the suggestion that Jesus' family sought to restrain him because people were saying he was 'out of his mind' (3:21).[22] However, in the 'true kindred' pericope, Matthew (12:46–50) follows Mark (3:31–35) fairly closely, and both accounts could give the impression of a rift between Jesus and his family.[23] Luke, on the other hand, treats differently both that narrative (8:19–21), and the rejection of Jesus in Nazareth (4:16–30), reversing the order in which he recounts the stories, and omitting elements that would evoke a negative understanding of the family.[24] Indeed, as Painter has observed, Luke indicates that Jesus' 'true' family—'those who hear the word of God and do it' (8:21 NRSV)—does *not* exclude his *natural* family.[25] A possible example of this is Clopas, Joseph's brother and hence Jesus' uncle,[26] who, if he may be identified with Cleopas of Luke 24:18, became a believer.[27] Nevertheless, since there are no canonical references to any family members being believers during Jesus' ministry, we need to consider how they may have been affected by his words and actions at the Last Supper and after his subsequent crucifixion.

2.3 The Family Connection at the Last Supper

As we have seen, Luke made significant modifications to passages in Mark that were relevant to Jesus' family, and he has done so too in his account of the preparations made for the Passover (Luke 22:7–14). The parallels between Mark's narrative about the entry to Jerusalem (11:1–6) and the arrangements for Passover (14:12–16) are well recognised,[28] and they are evident also in the corresponding accounts in Luke (19:29–35; 22:7–13).[29] While it is therefore clear that the passages are to some extent fictional, several of Luke's changes are noteworthy. Whereas Mark has two anonymous disciples sent into the city, Luke names them as Peter and John (22:8). This is significant, as the two feature together in both the Gospel and Acts.[30] Jesus states that a man with a jar of water will meet the disciples,[31] and they are to follow him into the house he enters, and speak to the owner about the meal arrangements (22:10–11). The term used by Luke for the owner is οἰκοδεσπότῃ τῆς οἰκίας· where Mark's οἰκοδεσπότῃ (14:14) may have sufficed, but I contend that it is a technical term for the overseer *(mebaqqer)* of the household.[32] Luke, like Mark, employs the term κατάλυμα (22:11) which is properly translated here as 'dining room',[33] but the question to be asked is, 'Where is the dining room?' as distinct from Mark's Jesus who wishes to know ποῦ ἐστιν

---

22 Note that the ambiguous expression οἱ παρ' αὐτοῦ in Mark 3:21 is properly understood to refer to Jesus' family. See Guelich, *Mark*, 172.
23 Bauckham, *Jude and the Relatives*, 50.
24 Painter, *Just James*, 38, 41.
25 *Just James*, 41. It is noteworthy that Luke, in his infancy narrative (esp. 1:38,45), has provided such an example in Mary, the mother of Jesus. This is reinforced by the evangelist's modification of Mark's order in his relocation of the teaching concerning 'true kindred', to *after* the Parable of the Sower, so that Jesus' reference in 8:19 to his mother and brothers recalls the 'good soil' of 8:15.
26 Bauckham, *Jude and the Relatives*, 16–17.
27 See Bauckham, *Jude and the Relatives*, 51–52; Painter, *Just James*, 145 n.92.
28 See e.g. Nolland, *Luke*, 1032.
29 Nolland, *Luke*, 1032.
30 See Nolland, *Luke*, 1033; Luke 8:51; 9:28; Acts 1:13; 3:1,3,4; 4:13,19; 8:14.
31 Riesner notes that the water being carried may have been drawn from near the pool of Siloam by the southeast city gate, as a street ran from there to the southwest quarter. He suggests that this might indicate a situation that Jesus could foresee from experience, rather than with miraculous foresight. See Riesner, *Jesus and the Dead Sea Scrolls*, 219.
32 Vermes and Goodman, *The Essenes*, 7. See also Marshall, 'Essenic Influence on Jesus', 60.
33 See 'κατάλυμα', BDAG 521.

τὸ κατάλυμά μου;[34] The upper room in Luke (22:12) is furnished, but not 'ready' as in Mark.[35] Whereas in Mark, Jesus comes with the Twelve, in Luke, since Peter and John are already there, he takes his place at table with the apostles (22:14).

These are minor changes but most make Luke's account a better fit with the surmised circumstances: that James, Jesus' brother, is a key member of this Essene household, the *mebaqqer*, who may have had multiple roles.[36] The point is that Jesus and his disciples, as non-Essenes, would not have had entrée without a resident of the household to facilitate the arrangements.

It will be useful here to mention the findings of some relatively recent research concerning the development of the Passover seder, which has usually been considered as occurring after the destruction of the Temple in 70 C.E.[37] The 'fixed order' of the proceedings ('seder'), and the ritual recitation (haggadah) linking the elements of the meal with the biblical account of the exodus from Egypt, are regarded by most scholars as later additions to the liturgy.[38] However, Marcus notes that *Jubilees*, a work known to be significant to the Essenes,[39] featured the drinking of wine at the paschal meal, indicating that the occasion was being celebrated in a leisurely and joyful manner by the second century B.C.E.[40] Philo's work supports this view, demonstrating (in *de Congressu* 167) that the 'bread of affliction' (Deuteronomy 16:3) is to be associated with joy and festivity, rather than suffering.[41] That perspective is retained in the seder, in the portion termed *Ha Lachma*, the title deriving from the initial two Aramaic words which refer to the bread of affliction,[42] with the translation commencing: 'This is the poor bread which our ancestors ate in the land of Egypt', and continuing with an invitation to the needy and hungry to come to the dwelling where the celebration is taking place, and to *eat* this bread.[43] Elsewhere, Philo provides symbolic interpretations of the paschal elements (*matzah* and herbs), in a manner similar to the haggadah featured in the *Mishnah*.[44] Thus it is feasible that interpretation of the elements of the meal may have occurred during the feast in Jesus' time,[45] though it would presumably have been the role of the host to offer it. These insights will be of value in the assessment of Jesus' actions and words during the Last Supper.

Extensive coverage of the meal is beyond the scope of this essay, so only the main points are mentioned. The number of commensals would have been large—maybe 30 or more—comprising: James and at least nine other Essenes; Jesus and the Twelve; the women who followed from

---

34 See Nolland, *Luke*, 1034. Capper, 'With the oldest monks', 16–17, considers that the narrative may suggest Jesus' familiarity with the house and its head.
35 Nolland, *Luke*, 1034.
36 For details of the various roles of leaders in such a household, see Marshall, 'Essenic Influence on Jesus', 60 nn.72–78. On the κηδεμών, who took care of strangers, see Vermes and Goodman, *The Essenes*, 4, 4 n.32; and Josephus, *J.W.* 2.124–125; and on the ἐπίτροπος, whose permission was required in the case of support being given to relatives, see Vermes and Goodman, *The Essenes*, 4, 4 n.31; and Josephus, *J.W.* 2.134.
37 Marcus, 'Passover and Last Supper', 304–305 n.10.
38 See Marcus, 'Passover and Last Supper', 305–307, for the reasons cited for the opinion.
39 VanderKam, *Dead Sea Scrolls and the Bible*, 76.
40 Jub. 49.6. See the citation in Saulnier, *Calendrical Variations*, 96. Note that Jub. 49.2 describes the beginning of Passover as 'the beginning of joy'. See Saulnier, *Calendrical Variations*, 95 n.15, 96.
41 Marcus, 'Passover and Last Supper', 308. For dating see Marcus, 'Passover and Last Supper', 309; and VanderKam, *Dead Sea Scrolls and the Bible*, 76. For further reference to the joyousness of the paschal celebration see Saulnier, *Calendrical Variations*, 94–95; Marcus, 'Passover and Last Supper', 310.
    See Marcus, 'Passover and Last Supper', 310.
42 Marcus, 'Passover and Last Supper', 310, and n.31.
43 Marcus, 'Passover and Last Supper', 310.
44 The text is from *Quaestiones et Solutiones in Exodum* 1.15. See Marcus, 'Passover and Last Supper', 310.
45 Marcus, 'Passover and Last Supper', 311.

Galilee;[46] and possibly others.[47]

Attendees would have been seated, not reclining.[48] While in Jewish tradition the *wine* was blessed first, some Dead Sea Scrolls indicate that in Essene communities the head of the household—a priest—first blessed the *bread* and then the wine.[49] Hence Jesus' first action, with a cup (Luke 22:17), must have taken place after those benedictions. He has already spoken (vv.15–16) of his eagerness to eat the Passover with his disciples before he suffers, and asserted that he will not eat it (or never eat it again) until it is fulfilled in God's kingdom.[50] I interpret this as meaning that he would abstain from eating, and his statement in v.18 as indicating that he would not drink wine at the meal either. His two-fold reference to the coming of God's kingdom (vv.16,18) is highly significant because for his Essene commensals, it would have brought to mind the text titled *Rule of the Congregation*, which states as its subject 'the end of days' (1:1).[51] They would surely be recalling the passage concerning the coming of the Messiah of Israel among them, which goes on to state that after the priest has blessed the bread and wine, the Messiah will then bless the bread, and then each member of the congregation will utter a blessing.[52]

Hence, Jesus' introductory words will have dramatically set the scene for his interpretative sayings over the bread and wine. Each of the guests would have an individual serving of *matzah*,[53] and I envisage Jesus as taking his own loaf, giving thanks, breaking it, and distributing it among all (22:19). My interpretation is that the bread signifies Jesus' *living* body, and that he is symbolically passing on to his commensals the essence of himself, to equip them for continuing his ministry.[54]

Luke's version of Jesus' words over the cup (22:20), is close to Paul's (1 Corinthians 11:25). It correctly implies that the cup itself has theological significance, foreshadowing Jesus' renewal of the covenant: 'This cup that is poured out for you is the new covenant in my blood' (NRSV).[55] Since the saying refers to the *cup* (not Jesus' blood) being poured out, it would seem to recall Exodus 24:9–11, concerning a mountaintop meal in God's presence, rather than 24:8 as is usually cited.[56]

---

46 See Luke 23:49.
47 In Acts 1:14, Jesus' mother is included among the 'certain women' who had followed Jesus from Galilee (Luke 23:49,55), and according to John 19:25-27 she witnessed the crucifixion, but it is unclear whether she or Jesus' other brothers may have been present at the meal. Nevertheless, the attendance of disciples other than the Twelve can be considered plausible on several grounds. First, it clearly coheres with the above findings concerning *Ha Lachma*. Second, as explicated in my doctoral dissertation, 'Jesus and the Banquets', 156, it was deemed appropriate, according to the hospitality customs of the era, for an invited guest to be accompanied at a meal by one or more relatives or friends, who were termed *umbrae*, or 'shadows'. See also Marshall, 'Glutton and Drunkard?', 50–51. Third, as Capper, 'Judaean Cultural Context', Part III, 34–52, esp. p.46, explains, most villages and towns in the Judaean heartland contained a community house run by celibate male Essenes, with a commitment to care for the poor and needy. James' establishment was not necessarily a community house, but in light of Essenic ethics, Jesus' associates and family members would not have been turned away.
48 See respectively, Marshall, 'Re-examining the Last Supper Sayings', 200 n.42, citing Josephus *J.W.* 2.130; Nolland, *Luke*, 1049.
49 See 1QS VI, 4–6; 1QSa II, 11–22. Regarding the status of James as a priest, see 'Essenic Influence on Jesus', 55–57.
50 Note that the NRSV rightly renders πάσχα as 'Passover' in both Luke 22:11 and 15, pace 'πάσχα', BDAG 784–85, (784), meaning 2 which suggests that in Luke 22:15 the term has the 'specific sense "Passover lamb"'.
51 See VanderKam, *Dead Sea Scrolls and the Bible*, 125.
52 1QSa II, 11–22. For a translation of the passage, see VanderKam, *Dead Sea Scrolls and the Bible*, 126; and for commentary, 120–27, esp. p.125–27.
53 That the Essenes customarily used individual servings is clear from Josephus' statement that 'the baker serves them loaves in order' (*J.W.* 2.130).
54 For discussion on this see Marshall, 'Re-examining the Last Supper Sayings', 209.
55 For a detailed explanation, see Marshall, 'Re-examining the Last Supper Sayings', 209–211, and also Marshall, 'The "New Covenant" Debate Revisited', esp. sections 2, 3, and 8.
56 See Marshall, 'Re-examining the Last Supper Sayings', 211, n.116.

The 'new covenant' reference is mostly linked with Jeremiah 31:31–34, but it correlates too with the writings of other major prophets.[57] The covenant they envisaged involved a transformation of the heart, and a relationship with God to be embraced willingly, rather than being imposed.[58] A 'spiritual trend' of that nature had begun in the First Temple period, and was eventually crystallised in the third or second century as 'the community of the renewed covenant'.[59] The Essenes at Jesus' last meal were all members of that continuing community, each having made a personal commitment to God—a covenant to be confirmed or renewed at the annual Festival of Weeks.[60] For them, the 'new covenant' was already a reality, described in their community's writings.[61] Hence, in view of their belief in the imminent coming of a royal anointed one, and with Jesus' extraordinary saying over the cup, we can surmise that the Essenes at the Last Supper, including James, recognised that the Messiah was there among them. This finding would contradict the traditional view that James was 'converted' by the appearance to him of the risen Jesus, cited by Paul in 1 Corinthians 15:7.[62]

In the next section we will see whether the idea that James and his fellow Essenes came to belief at the Last Supper coheres with relevant passages in Acts.

3. James, Brother of Jesus, in Acts

Following the ascension, Luke depicts the eleven remaining apostles as meeting in the upstairs room where they were staying, and constantly devoting themselves to prayer, together with 'certain women', including Jesus' mother, and also his brothers (Acts 1:13–14). While it is not certain whether these members of Jesus' family were present at the Last Supper, it is considered likely that the unnamed women other than Mary attended. Throughout his Gospel, Luke has already depicted Jesus' mother as a believer,[63] and we may assume that if James' brothers had not been present at the meal, he would have related the events to them.

As for the experience of the apostles at the Last Supper, Luke portrays them as apparently being unmoved by the events, despite Peter's earlier identification of Jesus as 'the Christ of God' (Luke 9:18–21), and three of them (Peter, John, and James) having experienced the transfiguration (Luke 9:28–36). At the meal, a dispute about predominance occurred, seemingly involving all of the Twelve (22:24–30), and afterwards Peter, as predicted, thrice denied knowing Jesus (22:34,54–62).

---

57 See also Jer. 32:37–41; and Isa. 55:3; 59:21; Ezek. 16:60; 37:26; Hos. 2:18 [20]; and Herion, 'Covenant', 291–92.
58 See Herion, 'Covenant', 291.
59 See Saulnier, *Calendrical Variations*, 173 n.47, citing Shemaryahu Talmon.
60 For details of the Essenes' commitment see VanderKam, *Dead Sea Scrolls and the Bible*, 96, 101–104; and on covenant renewal and the Festival of Weeks, see 151–52. See also Green, *Gospel of Luke*, 763, n.73; Vermes and Goodman, *The Essenes*, 10.
61 See e.g. 1QpHab II, 3; CD VIII, 21, 35 (=XIX, 34) as mentioned in Vermes and Goodman, *The Essenes*, 10, and cited in García Martínez, *The Dead Sea Scrolls Translated*, 198, 38, 46, respectively.
62 Bernheim, *James, Brother of Jesus*, 97, asserts that this traditional concept has no basis in the NT or any apostolic writing; and see also Painter, *Just James*, 42. Painter (p.13) surmises that it is John 7:5 that led to the view that Jesus' brothers, in particular, were unbelievers. Luke's depiction of the family relationships does not indicate any such negativity, and as Painter points out, it is possible that the portrayal of the family has been subjected to certain pressures which have skewed the picture (p.14). Note that Saxby's proposal, *James, Brother of Jesus*, 40, that James 'was already leader (even founder) of a Torah-observant renewal movement in Jerusalem' is unconvincing.
63 This notably includes 1:38,45 where, as Balch, 'Luke', 1107, observes, Mary is 'a female example of a believing disciple', in contrast to Zechariah, who in 1:20 is 'an example of unbelief'.

Nevertheless, those described in Acts 1:13–14 are now depicted as disciples of Jesus, and are regarded by Luke as being among the earliest believers.[64] Intriguingly, James is not named at this point, and it appears that the other family members and apostles stayed in a different household from where the Last Supper was held.[65] What is also of particular interest is that in Acts 1:15, when Peter addresses the believers, what had been a group of perhaps twenty at most, has grown to 120.[66] I propose that this has come about as a result of the Essenes present at the Last Supper having become believers,[67] and then sharing their faith within their wider community in the southwest quarter of Jerusalem.[68]

There is nothing in Acts that explains James' rise in a progressive manner. Rather, he suddenly appears in 12:17—without actually being identified as Jesus' brother.[69] The first eleven chapters focus mainly on Peter,[70] but the following chapter reports on the period of persecution by Herod Agrippa I,[71] which results in the martyrdom of James son of Zebedee, and the arrest of Peter (12:2–3). After Peter's miraculous escape from prison, he explains to those in the house of Mary, mother of John Mark, how this occurred, before adding, surprisingly: 'Tell this to James and to the believers' (12:17). The threat to Peter's life causes him to depart to Caesarea (12:19), and it becomes apparent that between 11:1 and 12:17, there has been a shift in the leadership of the church and that it is centred in Jerusalem under James, rather than the Twelve.[72]

The next crucial point is in Acts 15, which describes the Council of Jerusalem, and its outcome. Ostensibly, the meeting is primarily concerned with whether or not Gentile believers need to be circumcised in order to be saved (15:1–2,6), with Paul and Barnabas set against the believers based in Jerusalem. After some debate, Peter is the first to speak, describing his missionary work with Gentiles, and his belief that they will be saved by grace (15:7–11). Barnabas and Paul then report on their work (15:12), before James speaks authoritatively about the issue. He reaches the conclusion that it is not essential for Gentile believers to be circumcised, providing they abstain from certain foods, from blood, and from fornication, and that a letter should be written to the Gentile believers with this advice (15:19–21). What is significant for our purposes is the fact that in v.19 James employs the verb κρίνω, meaning 'I decree, judge, or decide' to express his opinion.[73] Clearly at this point he is preeminent, and it is also noteworthy that Peter and the other apostles cease to feature in Acts following the Council of Jerusalem.[74] It should be mentioned that the placement of the Council in Acts 15 does not cohere with Paul's accounts of his visits to Jerusalem.[75] However, in Galatians 2:9, Paul refers to James, Cephas, and John as the acknowledged 'pillars', and the fact that James is first-named surely underlines his

---

64 Bernheim, *James, Brother of Jesus*, 95; and see Painter, *Just James*, 42.
65 We will return to this point in section 4.
66 According to my proposal, the initial group of believers would have comprised eleven apostles, Mary, her sons (Joses, Judas, and Simon, according to Mark 6:3), and an unknown number of other women, probably including Mary Magdalene, Joanna, and Mary the mother of James, as mentioned in Luke 24:10.
67 See Marshall, 'Essenic Influence on Jesus', 70–71, for a summary concerning identification of Jesus as Messiah.
68 It may probably be assumed that the 'many thousands' of Jews reported in Acts 21:20 to be believers, included many Essenes.
69 Bauckham, *Jude and the Relatives*, 52.
70 Turner, 'James, the Lord's Brother', 51.
71 Bauckham, 'James and the Jerusalem Church', 415.
72 Turner, 'James, the Lord's Brother', 37. See also Bernheim, *James, Brother of Jesus*, 193, 304–305 n.11, 202–204; Bauckham, 'James and the Jerusalem Church', 416.
73 See Bernheim, *James, Brother of Jesus*, 193–94.
74 Bernheim, *James, Brother of Jesus*, 194.
75 See Gal. 1:18–19; 2:1–10; and Nelson, 'Apostolic Council', 79.

prime position.[76] Another interesting point is James' reference to Simeon in his speech (15:14). While this is mostly interpreted as an alternative name for Peter, I support Riesner's suggestion that it may actually refer to the prophet Συμεών who features in Luke 2:25–35, speaking of the Messiah, and of Jesus as 'a light for revelation to the Gentiles' (2:26,32).[77] This possible identification has some bearing on James' background, and we will return to it in section 6.

The third pivotal point concerning James is Acts 21:18 where Paul visits Jerusalem to see him. James obviously has precedence, with the other senior believers now termed 'elders', whereas in Acts 15:22 the leadership group had comprised 'apostles and elders'.[78] The speech in 21:20–25 is not delivered by James personally, but rather is expressed in first person plural, perhaps to indicate that it represents the voice of the whole church, or to remove from James any blame attributed for the consequences. Paul is told to 'Do what we tell you' (v.23), in a tone reminiscent of κρίνω in Acts 15.[79] He obeys, and is arrested as a result.

In the next section we explore other factors, mainly in passages from Acts, that reinforce the hypothesis of a nexus between the first Christians and the Essenes, and that the nucleus of the early church was spawned at the Last Supper.

4. The Early Church and the Essenes

There are many passages in Acts that suggest a link between the nascent Christian community and the Essenes. The reference in 1:13–14 to the apostles and Jesus' family members meeting in the upper room in Jerusalem coheres with evidence of an Essene quarter in the southwest of the city, in the area traditionally associated with the Cenacle.[80] Acts 6:7 mentions that many priests accepted the faith, and these may well have been Essenes from the Mount Zion community.[81] Moreover, the term 'The Way', used several times in reference to the early Christians,[82] is employed also in Qumran texts, particularly *Rule of the Community*,[83] to describe the community's beliefs and culture.[84] Casting lots—the method used for the election of Matthias in Acts 1:15–26—features also in *Rule of the Community*.[85]

Particular attention needs to be given to Luke's account of the coming of the Holy Spirit in Acts 2, because of the immense importance the Festival of Weeks held for the Essenes. In the book of *Jubilees*, *Rule of the Community*, and also in the *Damascus Document*, this occasion—one of the three mandatory pilgrimage festivals in the year—was associated with covenant renewal.[86] For the

---

76 Bernheim, *James, Brother of Jesus*, 199–201.
77 See Riesner, 'James's Speech', esp. 263–65 for his introduction to the notion.
78 See Bauckham, *Jude and the Relatives*, 74–75.
79 Turner, 'James, the Lord's Brother', 87.
80 See Capper, 'Palestinian Cultural Context', esp. 341–50, 355–56; and 'Jesus, Wealth and Poverty', 33; Pixner, 'Mount Zion', 309–22. See also Riesner, 'Jesus, the Primitive Community', 206–221; Bernheim, *James, Brother of Jesus*, 211, citing Riesner, 'Jesus, the Primitive Community', but mistakenly locating the Essene quarter in the southeast instead of southwest of the city, near the Essene Gate.
81 Pixner, 'Mount Zion', 321.
82 See Acts 9:2; 18:25–26; 19:9, 23; 22:4; 24:14, 22. See also Joseph, *Jesus, the Essenes*, 164–65.
83 See Evans, 'Synoptic Gospels and the Dead Sea Scrolls', 91–94. Texts cited are: 1QS VIII, 13–14; IX, 16–22; X, 20–21; XI, 17; 1QH XII, 4; and CD II, 6.
84 Bernheim, *James, Brother of Jesus*, 211.
85 See Bernheim, *James, Brother of Jesus*, 211. The relevant text is 1QS VI, 13–23. Note that MacDonald, *Does the New Testament Imitate Homer?*, 114–15, contends that the text refers to the vote of the community, rather than to drawing lots, but see also p.199 nn.15, 17, for the view of Jaubert and Schmidt that the Qumran ritual was an actual lottery.
86 VanderKam, *Dead Sea Scrolls and the Bible*, 147–56.

Essenes, this was linked not only with the Mount Sinai covenant, but also with the commitment made by each individual member of the community.[87]

The matter of community of goods is complex, requiring careful explication, and is best considered together with the account of the believers' care of the needy. This involves exegesis of Acts 2–6, including the introductory comments in 2:44–45 on having all things 'in common' (κοινός); sharing of possessions and the example of Barnabas (4:32–37); the Ananias and Sapphira narrative (5:1–11); the conflict between Hellenists and Hebrews, and the selection of the seven (6:1–6). It also draws on practices described in both the *Rule of the Community*,[88] and the *Damascus Document*,[89] which differ somewhat,[90] as well as on writings of Plato, Philo, Pliny the Elder, and Josephus.[91] Capper concludes that Acts 2–6 provides a 'historically verifiable' account of the practices of the earliest Christians, which were close in form to those of the Essenes.[92]

Hence there are significant parallels between Acts and the scrolls.[93] The next section considers whether the Epistle of James provides support for the concept that James was associated with the Essenes.

5. The Epistle of James

Scholarly debate continues as to the authenticity or otherwise of the letter attributed to Jesus' brother James. Bauckham asserts that it was written by James, though in view of the quality of the Greek, acknowledges that the author possibly had the assistance of a secretary.[94] The section on justification in 2:14–26 was formerly considered to be an indication that the author was specifically contending against Pauline doctrine,[95] but Bauckham has shown that this is not valid, and that 'the passage is wholly intelligible without reference to Paul'.[96] The letter cannot be dated with certitude, but may have been written in the 60s or 70s, and could plausibly be regarded as an edited version of a text written by James for Jewish Christians.[97] It comprises Wisdom instruction on traditional

---

87 See VanderKam, *Dead Sea Scrolls and the Bible*, 151–52, who also observes that the evangelist 'drew upon exegetical traditions that had accumulated around the festival in some Jewish circles, including especially ones attested in Qumran texts' (p.155).
88 1QS VI, 13–23 on rules concerning communal property, and 24–25 on a rule relating to lying about property matters. See Capper, 'Palestinian Cultural Context', 328.
89 CD XIV, 13 (Capper, 'Palestinian Cultural Context', 332–333, 333 n.27; and Capper, 'Voluntary Economic Association', 3, 4, 15–16, 18 n.4, 20 n.48).
90 Capper, 'Palestinian Cultural Context', 332–333, 355, notes that the regulations in the *Damascus Document* are less stringent, and more suited to married communities.
91 Capper, 'Palestinian Cultural Context', 323–56.
92 Capper, 'Palestinian Cultural Context', 356. See also Capper, 'Essene Community Houses', esp. pp.486, 490; and update in Capper, 'Jesus, Wealth and Poverty', 1–59; VanderKam, *Dead Sea Scrolls and the Bible*, 142–47, citing CD XIV, 12–16 on p.144.
93 With regard to the early chapters of Acts, see esp. VanderKam, *Dead Sea Scrolls and the Bible*, 142.
94 Bauckham, 'James', 1483. See also Bernheim, *James, Brother of Jesus*, 227.
95 Notably Gal. 2:16, and Rom. 3:27–28.
96 Bauckham, 'James', 1483, and see also p.1487, for commentary on James 2:14–26. It is perhaps significant that in the Orthodox canon, James is placed immediately after the Gospels and Acts, before the six other catholic letters, and then the Pauline epistles and Revelation. See Bauckham, *James: Wisdom of James*, 115.
97 Bernheim, *James, Brother of Jesus*, 244. Bibliowicz, *Jewish-Christian Relations*, 73, lists alternative views, including a minority opting for a second-century dating. He himself doubts that James was the author (p.77).

themes that are found especially in Proverbs, Sirach, and several Qumran texts,[98] but which also occur in Matthew and Q.[99] However, an important factor is that many of the traditional topics of Jewish wisdom are *absent* from both the teaching of Jesus and of James.[100] According to Bauckham, the epistle represents a creative development of the Jewish tradition, 'inspired and shaped by the wisdom of Jesus'.[101] What can be surmised then, is that both Jesus and James have been influenced by Essenic beliefs, but have focused attention on only certain topics of the many in the Wisdom tradition, such as attitudes to wealth and poverty.[102]

Regardless of the mystery surrounding the dating and authorship of the epistle, it plays an important part in Bibliowicz's argument, which I support, that the rift among different factions in the nascent church was not between Jews and Christians as has traditionally been held, but between Jewish and Gentile followers of Jesus.[103] Bibliowicz shows that the letter sheds significant light on James' position in the early church, over against that of Peter.[104] Both the concern for the poor—the mark of 'religion that is pure and undefiled before God' (1:27)—and the efficacy of anointing and the prayer of faith for forgiveness of sins (5:15)—without any reference to Jesus' death and resurrection—indicate that the theology is Jewish and early, and fits with a type of belief in Jesus that is consistent with what is found in Q and M.[105] Bibliowicz observes that while James and Peter were both still alive, James' preeminence was self-evident,[106] but to explain the actual scenario, he cites Painter:

> In the light of the emergence of the Gentile mission Peter's position became more important and Acts obscures the leadership of James in order to portray the Jerusalem church in terms closer to Peter than James. The emergence of the leading role of Petrine tradition is imposed in the wake of the destruction of Jerusalem and the dispersal of the Jerusalem church.[107]

6. Conclusion

Acts 1:13–14 is usually read as if Jesus had hired a room for Passover and that after his death, the apostles and his family continued to stay there, forming the nucleus of the Christian community.[108] This is not compatible with my hypothesis, and I suggest that after Passover they arranged accommodation nearby.[109] This would allow for James to have continued in the same celibate household in Jerusalem, with fellow Essenes who had also become believers. Until

---

98 1Q26; 4Q184-85, 298, 415-18, 420-21, 423, 424, 525. Themes from Pseudo-Phocylides are also represented. See Bauckham, 'James,' 1484, and for details of scrolls cited, see García Martínez, *Dead Sea Scrolls Translated*, 469, 487, 497, 504-505, 511.
99 See Painter, *Just James*, 260-64.
100 Bauckham, *James: Wisdom of James*, 95.
101 Bauckham, *James: Wisdom of James*, 111.
102 On the similarity of some of Jesus' teachings to those of the Essenes, e.g. on poverty and divorce, see Broshi, 'What Jesus Learned from the Essenes'.
103 For a summary of Bibliowicz's theory, see *Jewish-Christian Relations*, esp. pp.19, 23, 25-26; and on the epistle's relevance to his argument, see esp. pp.66-80.
104 *Jewish-Christian Relations*, 75-76.
105 Bibliowicz, *Jewish-Christian Relations*, 75.
106 Bibliowicz, *Jewish-Christian Relations*, 75.
107 See Bibliowicz, *Jewish-Christian Relations*, 75, 345 n.245. The quote is from Painter, 'James and Peter', 191.
108 See e.g. Riesner, 'Jesus, the Primitive Community', 204, 225 n.58.
109 On possible accommodation see Capper, 'Essene Community Houses', 491-92 describing care for the 'wandering', which would initially have been applicable to those from Galilee.

Peter's arrest and escape, James would be somewhat cloistered, whereas the apostles were more vulnerable to persecution.

I believe that the above findings have already made a convincing case for the proposal, but will assemble relevant material here for reference. First, regarding the Last Supper, I consider that the proposed date, the associated explanation for the disparity between the Johannine and synoptic accounts, and the supposition that the venue was in the Essene quarter in the southwest of Jerusalem, are well-grounded and solidly researched. The notion that it was a lambless celebration fits with both the Essenes' ethos and the synoptic descriptions of the occasion, and coheres with the subsequent identification of Jesus as the paschal lamb.

Section 2 worked through what we can surmise of Jesus' family from the Gospels, and made sense of the need for the apostles and others to gain entry to the household to be eligible to receive hospitality in accordance with Essenic regulations and the customs of the day. The background concerning the proceedings for the celebration—the joyfulness of the occasion, the ancient meaning of the 'bread of affliction', its connection with the invitation to the poor to come and *eat* this bread, and the likelihood of a tradition of symbolic interpretations—provided a valuable introduction to Jesus' words and actions over the elements, as well as linking closely with the actual circumstances. Jesus' references to the coming kingdom of God, and his bread and cup words, would obviously have profound meaning for the Essenes, who would be very familiar with the relevant scriptures, and particularly mindful of them at Passover, with its eschatological focus. The giving of portions of bread to the Essenes, together with the apostles and others, would have had the effect of binding all together as a group, enjoined to continue Jesus' ministry.

Section 3 demonstrated that there was substantial growth in the number of believers during the forty days after the ascension, and it would be feasible to link this to the Essenes in the vicinity. James' extraordinary rise to fame in the Acts account was explored, but unexplained, at that point. Section 4 provided evidence of many strong links between Essenes and the early church.

The exploration of the Epistle of James in section 5 revealed the similarity of Jesus' and James' theological outlook, and that it was close to that of the Essenes. The lack of reference to or interest in Jesus' death and resurrection showed that the letter expressed a Jewish theology representing the faith of the original followers of Jesus, over against that of the Gentile believers who were influenced by Pauline interpretations. It was asserted that the rift in the infant church was not between Jews and Christians, as is traditionally thought, but was the result of the disparity between the faith of Jewish versus Gentile believers. A succinct quotation concerning the emergence and eventual prevalence of the Gentile mission referred to the rivalry between Peter and James in their leadership roles, and provided a reason for suppression of details about James' leadership in the early chapters of Acts.

Despite the later predominance of the Petrine tradition, James became the first 'bishop' of Jerusalem,[110] and on the basis of my hypothesis, it is easy to see how natural a progression it would be from *mebaqqer* (overseer) of his household to the equivalent Greek term (ἐπίσκοπος) in the infant church.

Returning now to James' speech in Acts 15:14, and the link with Luke 2:25–35, Riesner proposed that both Symeon and James were *ḥasidim*, as distinct from the more rigid Qumran Essenes.[111] This would fit well with my hypothesis and coheres with the findings on the Epistle of

---

110 Painter, *Just James*, 13–14; Bauckham, *Jude and the Relatives*, 70–71.
111 See Riesner, 'James's Speech', 277, 277 n.80, citing Adamson, *James—The Man and His Message*, 20. In support of the concept of an Essenic connection is the fact that Symeon's citation of Amos 9:11 in Acts 15:16 is nearer to the text in CD VII, 16, than to the LXX version (Riesner, 'James's Speech', 271).

James. It is noteworthy that both Symeon and James were characterised as 'righteous and pious'.[112]

Although my proposal is speculative, I believe that it is well-founded. Further support for it may be found in several legends about James the Just.[113] Of particular interest is one in the Gospel of the Hebrews, bearing testimony both to James' presence at the Last Supper and an appearance to him of the risen Jesus.[114]

Mary J. Marshall
Murdoch University

---

[112] For Symeon, see Riesner, 'James's Speech', 277; and on James see the traditions derived from Hegesippus in Bernheim, *James, Brother of Jesus*, 5.

[113] See Marshall, 'Essenic Influence on Jesus', 64–66.

[114] Vielhauer and Strecker, 'The Gospel of the Hebrews', 172, 178. See also Marshall, 'Essenic Influence on Jesus', esp. pp.64–65.

Bibliography

Adamson, J. B.	*James—The Man and His Message* (Grand Rapids, MI: Eerdmans, 1988).
Balch, D. L.	'Luke', in J. D. G. Dunn and J. W. Rogerson (eds.), *Eerdmans Commentary on the Bible* (Grand Rapids, MI: Eerdmans, 2003), 1104–1160.
Bauckham, R.	'James', in J. D. G. Dunn and J. W. Rogerson (eds.), *Eerdmans Commentary on the Bible* (Grand Rapids, MI: Eerdmans, 2003), 1483–92.
Bauckham, R.	'James and the Jerusalem Church', in R. Bauckham (ed.), *The Book of Acts in Its Palestinian Setting* (vol. 4 of The Book of Acts in its First Century Setting; Grand Rapids, MI: Eerdmans, 1995), 415–80.
Bauckham, R.	*James: Wisdom of James, Disciple of Jesus, the Sage* (*New Testament Readings*; London: Routledge, 1999).
Bauckham, R.	*Jude and the Relatives of Jesus in the Early Church* (Edinburgh: T&T Clark, 1990).
Bernheim, P.-A.	*James, Brother of Jesus* (trans. J. Bowden; London: SCM, 1997).
Bibliowicz, A. M.	*Jewish-Christian Relations: The First Centuries* (rev. edn; Coppell, TX; Mascarat, 2019).
Broshi, M.	'What Jesus Learned from the Essenes', *BAR* 30.1 (2004), 32–37, 64.
Capper, B.	'Essene Community Houses and Jesus's Early Community', in J. H. Charlesworth (ed.), *Jesus and Archaeology* (Grand Rapids, MI: Eerdmans, 2006), 472–502.
Capper, B.	'The Judaean Cultural Context of Community of Goods in the Early Jesus Movement, Part II: Jesus, Wealth and Poverty, and the Fully Property-Sharing Religious Life', *Qumran Chronicle* 26 (2018) 1–59.
Capper, B.	'The Judaean Cultural Context of Community of Goods in the Early Jesus Movement, Part III: The Distribution of Essene Community of Goods in Southern Palestine and its Poverty-Relieving Macroeconomic Significance at the Time of Jesus', *Qumran Chronicle* 25 (2019) 1–67.
Capper, B.	'The Judaean Cultural Context of Community of Goods in the Early Jesus Movement, Part V: Voluntary Economic Association and the Creation of Economic Security through Education and Occupational Training in the Essene Fictive Kinship Groups of Ancient Judaea', *Qumran Chronicle* 27 [1–2] (2019) 1–22.
Capper, B.	'The Palestinian Cultural Context of Earliest Christian Community of Goods', in R. Bauckham (ed.), *The Book of Acts in Its Palestinian Setting* (vol. 4 of The Book of Acts in its First Century Setting; Grand Rapids, MI: Eerdmans, 1995), 323–56.
Capper, B.	' "With the oldest monks …" Light from Essene History on the Career of the Beloved Disciple?' *JTS* 49 (1998), 1–55.
Carrigan, H. L.	'Virgin Birth', *EDB*, 1359.

Danker, F. W., W. Bauer, W. F. Arndt, and F. W. Gingrich   *Greek-English Lexicon of the New Testament and Other Early Christian Literature* (3rd edn; Chicago: University of Chicago Press, 2000).

Evans, C. A.   'The Synoptic Gospels and the Dead Sea Scrolls', in J. H. Charlesworth (ed.), *The Bible and the Dead Sea Scrolls: The Second Princeton Symposium on Judaism and Christian Origins* (vol. 3 of The Scrolls and Christian Origins; Waco, TX: Baylor University Press, 2006), 75–95.

García Martínez, F.   *The Dead Sea Scrolls Translated: The Qumran Texts in English* (2nd edn; Leiden: Brill, 1996).

Green, J. B.   *The Gospel of Luke* (Grand Rapids, MI: Eerdmans, 1997).

Guelich, R. A.   *Mark 1–8:26* (WBC 34A; Dallas, TX: Word, 1989).

Herion, G. A.   'Covenant', *EDB*, 288–92.

Holladay, W. L. (ed.)   *A Concise Hebrew and Aramaic Lexicon of the Old Testament* (10th edn; Grand Rapids, MI: Eerdmans, 1988).

Humphreys, C. J.   *The Mystery of the Last Supper: Reconstructing the Final Days of Jesus* (Cambridge: Cambridge University Press, 2011).

Joseph, S. J.   *Jesus, the Essenes, and Christian Origins: New Light on Ancient Texts and Communities* (Waco, TX: Baylor University Press, 2018).

Levine A.-J., and M. Z. Brettler   *The Bible with and without Jesus: How Jews and Christians Read the Same Stories Differently* (New York, NY: HarperCollins, 2020).

MacDonald, D. R.   *Does the New Testament Imitate Homer? Four Cases from the Acts of the Apostles* (New Haven, CT: Yale University Press, 2003).

Maier, J.   *The Temple Scroll: An Introduction, Translation and Commentary* (JSOTSup 34; Sheffield: JSOT Press, 1985).

Marcus, J.   'Passover and Last Supper Revisited', *NTS* 59 (2013), 303–24.

Marshall, M. J.   'Essenic Influence on Jesus, His Brothers, and the Early Church', in P. G. Bolt (ed.), *The Future of Gospels and Acts Research* (CGAR Series, 3; Macquarie Park: SCD Press, 2021), 51–76.

Marshall, M. J.   'Jesus and the Banquets: An Investigation of the Early Christian Tradition concerning Jesus' Presence at Banquets with Toll Collectors and Sinners', unpublished Ph.D. dissertation, Murdoch University, 2002. Accessible online: https://researchrepository.murdoch.edu.au/id/eprint/183/.

Marshall, M. J.   'Jesus: Glutton and Drunkard?' *JSHJ* 3.1 (2005), 47–60.

Marshall, M. J.   'Re-examining the Last Supper Sayings in Light of the Hebrew Scriptures', in T. Hägerland (ed.), *Jesus and the Scriptures: Problems, Passages and Patterns* (Library of Historical Jesus Studies 9; Library of New Testament Studies 552; London: Bloomsbury T&T Clark, 2016), 193–214.

Marshall, M. J.   'Rethinking the Last Supper Again—with Insights from Luke', in W. Kahl and V. Wittkowsky (eds.), *Das lukanische Doppelwerk in neuen*

	internationalen Perspektiven / Luke-Acts in New International Perspectives (Leipzig: Evangelische Verlagsanstalt, 2023, forthcoming).
Marshall, M. J.	'The "New Covenant" Debate Revisited', in P. G. Bolt (ed.), *Jesus: Beginning, Middle, & End of Time? Eschatology in Gospels & Acts Research* (CGAR Series, 4; Macquarie Park, NSW: SCD Press, 2022, forthcoming).
Nelson, P. K.	'Apostolic Council', *EDB*, 79.
Nolland, J.	*Luke 1–9:20* (WBC 35A; Dallas, TX: Word, 1989).
Nolland, J.	*Luke 18:35–24:53* (WBC 35C; Dallas, TX: Word, 1993).
Painter, J.	'James and Peter: Models of Leadership and Mission', in B. D. Chilton and C. A. Evans (eds.), *The Missions of James, Peter, and Paul: Tensions in Early Christianity* (NovT 115; Leiden: Brill, 2005), 143–209.
Painter, J.	*Just James: The Brother of Jesus in History and Tradition* (Minneapolis, MN: Fortress, 1999).
Pixner, B.	'Mount Zion, Jesus, and Archaeology', in J. H. Charlesworth (ed.), *Jesus and Archaeology* (Grand Rapids, MI: Eerdmans, 2006), 309–22.
Riesner, R.	'James's Speech (Acts 15:13-21), Simeon's Hymn (Luke 2:29–32), and Luke's Sources', in J. B. Green and M. Turner (eds.), *Jesus of Nazareth: Lord and Christ: Essays on the Historical Jesus and New Testament Christology* (Grand Rapids, MI: Eerdmans, 1994), 263–78.
Riesner, R.	'Jesus, the Primitive Community, and the Essene Quarter of Jerusalem', in J. H. Charlesworth (ed.), *Jesus and the Dead Sea Scrolls* (ABRL; New York, NY: Doubleday, 1992), 198–234.
Saldarini, A. J.	'Matthew', in J. D. G. Dunn and J. W. Rogerson (eds.), *Eerdmans Commentary on the Bible* (Grand Rapids, MI: Eerdmans, 2003), 1000–1063.
Saulnier, S.	*Calendrical Variations in Second Temple Judaism: New Perspectives on the 'Date of the Last Supper' Debate* (Supplements to the *Journal for the Study of Judaism* 159; Leiden: Brill, 2012).
Saxby, A.	*James, Brother of Jesus, and the Jerusalem Church: A Radical Exploration of Christian Origins* (Eugene, OR: Wipf & Stock, 2015).
Tuckett, C.	'Synoptic Gospels', *EDB*, 1262–63.
Turner, P.	'James, the Lord's Brother: The Figure of James in Earliest Christianity: A Study in History and Theology' (Unpublished Honours thesis, Murdoch University, 1993).
VanderKam, J. C.	*The Dead Sea Scrolls and the Bible* (Grand Rapids, MI: Eerdmans, 2012).
Vermes, G., and M. D. Goodman (eds.)	*The Essenes: According to the Classical Sources* (Sheffield: JSOT Press, 1989).
Vielhauer, P., and G. Strecker	'The Gospel of the Hebrews', in W. Schneemelcher (ed.), *Gospels and Related Writings* (vol. 1 of New Testament Apocrypha; rev. edn; Louisville, KY: Westminster John Knox, 1991), 172–78.

'... at the same time he hoped that money would be given to him by Paul' (Acts 24:26):

Corruption in the Book of Acts and its Implications

CHRISTOPH STENSCHKE

Abstract

Perhaps surprising for a historical monograph that traces the development of the Jesus movement from Judea to Rome, the Book of Acts contains several occurrences of corruption in a broad sense. Some occurrences are directly identified as such. In other cases, corruption is likely in the background. They include the use of funds by Ananias and Sapphira in order to gain status in the community, the use of bribes to secure false witnesses, Simon's intent to pay for spiritual authority to regain his status, the likely bribes given to Blastus, the likely securing of support with money through the opponents of Paul's mission, the admitted payment of bribes to obtain citizenship and office, and a Roman governor's expectations to receive a bribe from Paul. After some definitions and preliminary remarks, this article examines these accounts, places them in the wider context of the misuse of power and greed which often appear hand-in-hand with corruption. This picture is briefly contrasted with the proper Christian use of financial resources as the antidote to corruption as outlined in Acts. In closing, we discuss the implications of this portrayal for the contemporary church and society at large.

1. Introduction

Several passages in the Book of Acts refer to corruption, the misuse of power, and greed and provide some clues for its understanding and overcoming. What is the thing we are looking for? The non-government organisation *Transparency International* defines corruption in broad terms 'as the abuse of entrusted power for private gain'.[1] According to the more narrow definition of the World Bank, corruption

> is a form of dishonesty or criminal offense undertaken by a person or organization entrusted with a position of authority, to acquire illicit benefit or abuse power for one's private gain. Corruption may include many activities including bribery and embezzlement, though it may also involve practices that are legal in many countries. Political corruption occurs when an office-holder or other governmental employee acts in an official capacity for personal gain.
>
> Corruption and crime are endemic sociological occurrences which appear with regular frequency in virtually all countries on a global scale in varying degree and proportion. Individual nations each allocate domestic resources for the control and regulation of corruption and crime. Strategies to counter corruption are often summarized under the umbrella term anti-corruption. Additionally, global initiatives like the United Nations *Sustainable Development Goal* 16 also have a target to substantially reduce corruption of all forms.[2]

We draw on this broader definition (that is, *money or other advantages given or accepted illegally to achieve some goals, usually some private gain*) and focus on instances of bribery and other questionable uses of material resources. However, this form of corruption and corruption in general cannot be understood on its own as it forms part of the *immoral triad* with greed and misuse of power which are closely related to each other and often appear in combination. Bachhiesel and his co-authors (2019) have persuasively argued the case for the close combination of these vices in antiquity and presented fascinating analyses of non-biblical instances.

Why focus on the Book of Acts? The 2019 issue of the *Acts of the Catholic Biblical Association of Nigeria* was devoted to the theme of *Integrity and Corruption in the Bible*.[3] It contains studies on corruption in various parts of the Bible, including three essays on instances in Luke's Gospel: Christopher Naseri examines 'The Anti-Corruption Stance of John the Baptist in Luke 3:12–14'. Teresa Okure writes on 'Integrity and Corruption in the Parable of the Shrewd Manager (Luke 16–18): A Contextual Study'. Cosmas Uzowulu addresses the 'Corrupt but Repented Judge – A Study of Luke 18:1–8: Implications for the Contemporary Society'. As this helpful collection of African voices does not contain essays on instances of corruption in the Book of Acts, this will be our focus in this essay. Perhaps because the modern technical terms referring to this vice do not appear in the standard Bible translations, corruption has not received much attention in biblical studies. There are surely also other reasons for this neglect. While Bible dictionaries usually contain entries on various vices, various coins, and more generally on money, few of them include entries on corruption or bribes. A recent example is the *Encyclopedia of the Bible and Its Reception*. While there are several entries on money[4] and an entry on the corruption of the biblical text as a recurrent theme in Islamic polemic and as a central concept in Islamic self-understanding,[5] there is no entry on corruption as a social reality. Despite this lack of attention in scholarship, the reality of corruption and bribes surely also appears in the Bible. The references to corruption and bribery, misuse of power and greed in the Book of Acts build on the intensive teaching of Jesus regarding the proper use of wealth which is so characteristic of Luke's Gospel, the first part of Luke-Acts.[6] For

---

1   See https://www.transparency.org/en/what-is-corruption, accessed 16/05/2021.
2   https://en.wikipedia.org/wiki/Corruption, accessed 03/05/2021.
3   Available at https://www.cabanalive.org, accessed 17/05/2021.
4   Nam, 'Money I'; Stenschke, 'Money III'; Bühler, 'Moneylending I'; and Stenschke, 'Moneylending II'.
5   Hämeen-Anttila, 'Corruption'.
6   For a survey see Hays, *Luke's Wealth Ethics*.

instance, just prior to telling the parable of the rich fool (Luke 12:16–21) who sought to secure his own life through amassing possessions, Jesus states emphatically that one's life does not consist of the abundance of his possessions (12:15). In addition to the teaching of Jesus, we read of the charge of John the Baptist to the tax collectors not to collect more tax than they are authorised to do. Likewise soldiers are charged not to extort money from anyone by threats or by false accusation, and to be content with their wages (3:12–14). According to Luke 19:1, Zacchaeus is a rich chief tax collector. After encountering Jesus, he readily volunteers to give away half of his possessions and to restore fourfold if he defrauded anyone. The Jewish leaders in Jerusalem readily welcome the offer of Judas to betray Jesus to them: 'And they were glad, and agreed to give him money' (22:5). Their agreement suggests that Judas not only offered to co-operate but also demanded payment in exchange for his betrayal of Jesus (22:2–6). In Luke's Gospel, Jesus warns against those who misuse their power and ruthlessly subdue their people, that is, the kings of the Gentiles, who exercise lordship over them. While doing so, they call themselves 'benefactors' (22:25).

In what follows, we focus on the *literary* presentation of corruption, misuse of power, and greed in Acts. We cannot engage the larger issue and highly nuanced discussion of how this presentation relates to history as far as we can ascertain it.[7] Neither can we relate the portrayal in Acts to the accounts of corruption in Graeco-Roman sources or the larger ancient moral-philosophic discourse on corruption and the proper use of material means.

Admittedly, our focus on this topic does not follow Luke's main concern and does not directly address the message he wanted to convey to the first readers. We examine notes that appear *in passing*, not Luke's major concerns. When this is kept in mind, it is astonishing to what extent corruption, the misuse of power, and greed do appear in the narrative. It is noteworthy that the instances of corruption in Acts are not limited to non-Christians or the opponents of the church. Things are not as clear cut. We *first* look at instances in the account where money, the expectance or offer of bribes/money play a role and instances where money or other favours might have been involved, although they are not explicitly mentioned. We then look for instances of misuse of power and greed. Then we will examine the portrayal of the proper Christian use of material possessions as the antidote to corruption. In a final section we suggest a few trajectories for relating the portrayal of Acts to contemporary concerns.

2. Corruption in the Book of Acts

The Book of Acts contains several occurrences of corruption understood to be actions when *money or other advantages are given or accepted illegally to achieve some goals, usually some private gain* (see above). In few instances, such giving and accepting appear directly (as in the mention of Felix's expectation of a bribe), in other cases it is implied or at least likely to be in the background of the accounts. The first instance appears in the description of the early Christian community in Jerusalem.

Acts 5:1–11: Hypocrisy, money and gaining status in the community?

Immediately after the second reference to the early Christian community of goods in Acts 4:32–35 and the splendid example of Joseph, called Barnabas (4:36–37), Acts tells, by way of contrast and to emphasise the authority of Peter, of the failure and demise of Ananias and Sapphira (5:1–11). They

---

[7] For a summary of the issues see Keener, *Acts*, 1.90–220; and Schnabel, *Acts*, 28–41.

sold a piece of property and kept some of the proceeds of their sale to themselves.[8] This was their free choice. They were neither required to sell the property at all nor to donate the entire sum to the community. However, they agreed to pretend to do so and in the course of the events claim that they had donated the full sum. They may have donated the sum they had agreed on, out of pure, charitable motives or, perhaps from the very beginning, in order to enhance their status and standing in the community or with its leaders,[9] or perhaps it was a combination of both motives. Peter unmasked their lie and hypocrisy and they were severely punished.

Even in the believing community, money (or the pretence of giving all of it in order to appear to be more generous than was actually the case) can be used hypocritically by some to enhance their status. This (mis)use of money in the community is associated on the one hand with Satan who is pictured as behind the couple's plans and purposes ('why has Satan filled your heart to lie to the Holy Spirit', 5:3)[10] and on the other hand with the Holy Spirit (in fact, in their schemes, Ananias and Sapphira were not merely lying to people but to the Spirit) and God ('You have not lied to man but to God', 5:4). Recalling certain aspects of Jesus' teaching on wealth, Acts thus underscores that money and, in particular, what is done or not done with it, is not a purely human commodity and interaction. The use of money has a truly spiritual dimension.

Acts 6:11,13: Bribing False Witnesses Against Stephen?

Once Stephen's fierce Diaspora Jewish opponents realised that they could not withstand the wisdom and the Spirit in which he was speaking, they 'secretly instigated people who claimed: "We have heard Stephen speak blasphemous words against Moses and God"' (Acts 6:11). In addition, Stephen's opponents 'stirred up the people, the elders and the scribes' and 'they set up false witnesses who vehemently accuse Stephen: "This man never ceases to speak words against this holy place and the law, for we have heard him say that this Jesus of Nazareth will destroy this place and will change the customs that Moses delivered to us"' (6:12–14). The narrative does not indicate whether procuring these false witnesses involved the offer and acceptance of money or other benefits, or whether the people did so only out of enmity against Stephen. In his discussion of Acts 6:11, 13, Keener refers to Hellenistic-Roman and early Jewish sources.[11] With regard to the occurrences and role of false witnesses, he observes on Acts 6:11 that 'By succumbing to bribery or personal vendettas, even prosecutors could be corrupted (Pliny, *Ep.* 3.9.29–30)'. Keener also notes that 'Most relevant is that hiring false witnesses to get someone stoned (6:13; 7:58–59) recalls the behaviour of wicked rebels against God such as Ahab and Jezebel (1Kgs 21:8–15) '.[12] Keener apparently assumes that some payment was offered/given to the false witnesses. This may be supported by the note that these witnesses were later involved in the actual stoning of Stephen (7:58: 'And the witnesses laid down their garments at the feet of a young man named Saul').

---

8   There is no indication in the text why they chose to do so. The fact that they voluntarily donated some of the proceeds suggests that they were not greedy.
9   As the money was deposited at the apostles' feet (4:35), probably only the apostles knew who contributed to the common fund and how much was given. While Ananias and Sapphira may have sought to endear themselves to the apostles and gain their attention or approval, there is no indication that they sought to exert power over the apostles through their gift. The couple did not themselves distribute their donation to the needy as they saw fit and in this way create relationships of dependency.
10 This recalls the close connection between Satanic activity and money in the account of the betrayal of Jesus by Judas Iscariot in Luke 22:3-6.
11 Keener, *Acts*, II. 1314–1315.
12 Keener, *Acts*, II. 1315.

Being convicted of false witness would have involved serious consequences.[13] This supports the assumption that these witnesses would not have made false claims out of mere shared religious concern but in return for favours received.

Acts 8:18–24: Simon's Offer to Pay for Spiritual Authority

The second instance of Christians giving or accepting money or other advantages to achieve some goals, usually some private gain, occurs in Acts 8. Among the many Samarians who came to faith in Jesus of Nazareth as God's Christ (8:5) was Simon, the magician. Before Philip's arrival, he held a prominent position in the city. With his magic he managed to amaze the people of Samaria and claimed, 'that he himself was somebody great'. All the inhabitants paid attention to him, convinced that 'This man is the power of God that is called great' (8:10; see also v.11).[14] Probably this status also involved considerable financial benefits.

Upon the preaching of Philip, the people of Samaria and Simon came to faith and were baptised. Nothing in the text indicates that Simon's conversion was not genuine, or that it was deficient.[15] Simon adhered to Philip and was amazed by the signs and great miracles performed by Philip. In the wake of the ministry of Philip and his own conversion, Simon lost his power and influence in the Samaritan community and probably also the income that he derived from it.

Later the apostles Peter and John came from Jerusalem (Acts 8:14) and through their prayer and the laying on of hands they bestowed the Holy Spirit on the Samaritans, which they had not received previously.[16] All this was observed by Simon and triggered his plan to regain his former status (power) in the community, his income and a status superior to that of Philip who, despite all the impressive signs that he did (8:6–7), apparently could not himself bestow the Spirit. Simon urgently wanted the apostles' ability for himself. Following his still deeply ingrained pre-Christian strategies and means of reaching such goals, he approached the apostles and *offered them money*, saying: 'Give me this power also, so that anyone on whom I lay my hands may receive the Holy Spirit' (8:19). 'Simon still seeks personal advantage in a conventional way, following the traditional magical worldview. [...] The attempt to buy spiritual power fits the milieu of magicians who traded in magic formulas (cf. 19:9); magicians sought to buy power'.[17]

> The offer of money is motivated by Simon's observation of the manifestations caused by the Holy Spirit, whom the Samaritans receive as Peter and John lay their hands on them. [...] the verb translated 'offered' [...] implies that Simon brought money to the apostles for them to grant his request to receive 'the power' [...] to confer the gift of the Holy Spirit by the laying on of hands.[18]

According to Barrett,[19] Simon's readiness to pay for the right to confer the Spirit presumably implies that he would charge for the gift as he bestowed it. Simon's offer indicates a fourfold total misunderstanding of what happened, of the nature of God and his gifts, and of how money can and should be used.[20] In this incident, corruption (that is, 'money or other advantages given or accepted illegally to achieve some goals, usually some private gain') and the desire to regain and maintain power in the community are closely linked.

---

13   See the treatment of 'Investigating and punishing false witnesses' in Keener, *Acts*, II. 1312–1313.
14   See Keener, *Acts*, II.1499–1517.
15   Keener, *Acts*, II.1517–1520; Stenschke, *Luke's Portrait*, 361–362.
16   Keener, *Acts*, II.1520–1529.
17   Keener, *Acts*, II.1529.
18   Schnabel, *Acts*, 412.
19   Barrett, *Acts*, I. 413.
20   See Stenschke, *Luke's Portrait*, 362–363.

Peter's response is trenchant: 'May your silver perish with you, because you thought you could obtain the gift of God (that is, the ability to bestow the Spirit and the Spirit itself) with money! You have neither part nor lot in this matter, for your heart is not right before God' (8:21–22).[21] This is a clear rejection of the notion that spiritual gifts can be obtained with money. People who so thoroughly misunderstand God and the Spirit will perish, together with their money. The intention to use money in this way excludes people from the Spirit and its bestowal, as well as indicating a deficient relationship with God.

In the wake of this account, the sale or purchase of church offices came to be called *simony*. The practice and sin of simony was rife in the early Middle Ages and discussed and condemned at many church councils.[22] There was agreement that procuring offices in this way would not bring people into ecclesial offices qualified by their spiritual gifts, their personal integrity and willingness to serve the body of Christ. In particular, when church office involved generous reimbursement, other privileges, power, or public honour, many succumbed to procuring such offices through illicit payments, be they donations to the churches of higher office bearers or their private pockets.

Both cases of corruption by believers, Ananias and Sapphira's use of money and lies to enhance their status in the Jerusalem community (5:1–11), and Simon's offer in a non-Jewish context, point to deeply entrenched ways of using financial means to further one's own interests and status. In contrast, the apostles, Philip and Paul, give freely what they have freely received (Matt 10:8; Acts 3:6).[23] This indicates to what extent Christians need instruction and admonishment and may explain the ethical emphasis in Luke's Gospel on the proper use of material possessions.[24]

In view of the few other and 'mild' instances of failure of Christians in Acts, such as the murmuring of the Hellenist Jewish Christians of Jerusalem (6:1) or the sharp dissension between Paul and Barnabas (15:39) and their consequences, these two incidents are noteworthy, in particular, as their occurrence in the narrative is not crucial for moving the plot forward.[25] Why do these two accounts appear? Were they included to warn upper-class Theophilus[26] and other readers, that embracing the Christian message (the *certainty* of which Luke-Acts seek to demonstrate, Luke 1:4) has and must have consequences regarding corruption, (mis)use of power, and greed? Is the brief summary of the content of Paul's conversations with Felix in Acts 24:24–25 not only a report about Paul's faithful ministry as a prisoner and bold prophetic stance,[27] but also a reminder addressed to the readers: 'and heard him speak about faith in Christ Jesus. And as he reasoned about righteousness and self-control and the coming judgement'? Faith in Christ Jesus will and must manifest itself in righteous behaviour, self-control regarding sexual, material, and

---

21 See Stenschke, *Luke's Portrait*, 363–366.
22 Patte, 'Simony', 1159: 'The sale of offices was prohibited by some early councils and popes, but it became a crucial issue in the age of feudalism, when lay appointment to office and investiture with the symbols of office was widespread'.
23 See Keener, *Acts*, II.1531.
24 For a survey see Hays, *Luke's Wealth Ethics*, and Coleman, *Lukan Lens*. It is not clear whether and how this emphasis is related to Paul's collection for the saints of Jerusalem.
25 Acts 5:1–11 serves to show the authority and divine affirmation of Peter in the believing community and beyond (5:11) in the midst of conflict with the established religious leaders (which is also evident in 5:12–16!) and constitutes a parallel to Paul's only punitive miracle in Acts 13:6–11 (Paul had no less authority than Peter). Other than indicating the failure of believers in both Jerusalem and Samaria and describing the encounter of the Christian mission with magic thinking and practices like in Acts 19:11–19, Acts 8:9–24 could be omitted from the narrative.
26 Luke 1:3 addresses Theophilus with the adjective *kratistos*, as are the Roman governors Felix and Festus in Acts 23:26; 24:3 and 26:25. On Theophilus' standing in society and the opportunities and challenges associated with it, see Keener, Acts, I.423–426.
27 See Stenschke, 'Saint Paul as Prisoner'.

other desires and in view of responsibility before God in the final judgement. The model to be emulated is Paul, who could claim that he coveted no one's silver or gold or apparel but rather worked with his own hands and in this way followed the instructions of Jesus that 'it is more blessed to give than to receive' (20:32–35).

Acts 12:20: Bribing Blastus?

The people of Tyre and Sidon had to reconcile themselves to King Herod Agrippa I as they depended on the king's country for their food supplies (Acts 12:21).[28] Their envoys approached Blastus, the king's chamberlain and *persuaded* him to either get access to the king[29] to plead their case themselves or that Blastus would do so in their stead. Watson Ford has suggested that their 'persuasion' of Blastus involved the payment of a bribe: 'Probably through a bribe, a Phoenician delegation persuaded Blastus to intervene on their behalf'.[30] In his *Jewish Antiquities*, the Jewish historian Josephus (18.153) reports of a boundary conflict between the cities of *Sidon* and Damascus, which included the prospect of a large bribe by the Damascenes to *Herod* in return for his support. While Luke's account is placed in a socio-cultural context in which such bribes were rife, Keener rightly cautions that 'while this would not be surprising and is not unlikely, … this meaning is not clear here'.[31] The people of Tyre and Sidon were successful and could officially meet the king on the appointed day. If there was money involved, its payment served as a 'door opener' and led to the intended effect of reconciliation with the king and securing food supplies for the population of these cities. This is the way in which things were 'done'.

Acts 13:50; 14:2,5, 17:5,13: Securing Support by Money?

In several passages of Acts, the Jewish opponents of the Christian mission get support for their case against the missionaries by enlisting the help of others:

- 'But the Jews incited devout women of high standing and the leading men of the city, stirred up persecution against Paul and Barnabas …' (13:50).[32]

- 'But the unbelieving Jews stirred up the Gentiles and poisoned their minds against the brothers. […] But the people of the city were divided; some sided with the Jews and some with the apostles. When an attempt was made by both Gentiles and Jews, with their rulers, to mistreat them' (14:2,5).

- 'The Jews came from Antioch and Iconium, and having persuaded the crowds, they stoned Paul … (14:19).[33]

- 'But the Jews were jealous and taking some wicked men from the rabble, they formed a mob, set the city in uproar, and attacked the house of Jason' (17:5).

---

28 For the historical background see Keener, *Acts*, II.1958–1961.
29 Blastus was 'an important official who controlled access to the king', Keener, *Acts*, II.1960.
30 Watson Ford, 'Blastus'.
31 Keener, *Acts*, II. 1960.
32 See Keener, *Acts*, II. 2103–2105.
33 Keener, *Acts*, II. 2175–2176 notes that: 'If any of the apostles' adversaries were familiar with local language […] or at least local customs […] they would have an advantage over Paul and Barnabas, who were clearly foreigners. Certainly, they could pose as locals better than Paul, in any case'.

- 'They came there [Berea] too, agitating and stirring up the crowds' (17:13). Schnabel notes that: 'The present tense of the participles here indicates that their efforts to disrupt and terminate the preaching of Paul in Berea took some time to be successful'.[34]

We do not know why those non-Jewish people supported the Jewish opponents of Paul and his companions. Was it out of sympathy, political expediency,[35] or because of how they were influenced and the lies they were told?[36] As there is no direct mention of money, we can, on the basis of what is known of the economic situation (for instance, idle people on Thessalonica's marketplace who had not found work as day labourers),[37] only assume that something was promised or given to them to secure their support.

Likewise, there is no direct reference to money in Acts 21:27, when some Jews from the greater Ephesus area recognised Paul's Gentile Christian travel companion Epaphroditus in Jerusalem and charged Paul with bringing a Gentile into the temple precincts reserved for Jews.

Acts 17:9: Money as a Security

The city authorities of Thessalonica accepted money as a security from Jason and other Christ believers of Thessalonica.[38] As a consequence, Jason and the other believers were released from prison. Nothing is reported of further legal consequences. In the Lukan portrayal, this was a legal option and did not involve the payment of bribes.

Acts 22:28: Paying Bribes to Obtain Roman Citizenship and Office?

While Paul's letters do not mention his Roman citizenship, it is a recurring theme in Acts (16:37–39; 25:10–12; 26:31–32). In the context of Paul's claim to Roman citizenship following his arrest in Jerusalem and the impending interrogation with scourges by Roman soldiers,[39] Acts 22 notes the reaction of the Roman tribune in Jerusalem.[40] Once he hears of Paul's Roman citizenship, the tribune directly questions him: 'Tell me, are you a Roman citizen?' (22:27). On the affirmation by Paul that this is indeed the case, the tribune answers: 'I bought (ἐκτησάμην) this citizenship for a large sum of money (πολλοῦ κεφαλαίου)' (22:28). Paul, in contrast, can claim this privilege from birth and thus his superior status over the tribune who acted carelessly with regard to Paul.

A number of scholars have suggested that the tribune refers to and admits to an illegal practice: 'this tribune [...] had sufficient wealth to achieve Roman citizenship and may have used the same to achieve his office, even if he was, as many scholars suggest, promoted through the ranks'.[41] Keener suggests that the tribune would have 'probably bribed imperial agents to add his

---

34 Schnabel, *Acts*, 711.
35 Keener, *Acts*, II.2122: 'many elites in the empire were sympathetic toward their Jewish populations'.
36 See Keener, *Acts*, II.2176, for Lystra, 'Counteracting the benevolent appearance of a public miracle would not necessarily prove difficult, since supernatural power could derive from various sources'.
37 Keener, *Acts*, III.2546–2548, speaks of 'idlers [...] who spent most of the day in the marketplace; usually these people were marginalized, unemployed day labourers'.
38 See the detailed discussion Keener, *Acts*, III.2557–2558.
39 See Rapske, *Paul*, 136–145.
40 On the Roman army in Judea see Kyrychenko, *Roman Army*, 34–44.
41 Keener, *Acts*, III.3253, who mentions Fitzmyer, Conzelmann and Witherington as proponents of this view. According to Witherington, *Acts*, 681, the tribune's 'buying' of his citizenship was 'of course not actually the case, because it was not legal to do so. What this meant is that through the paying of a bribe, citizenship had illegally been obtained'. Witherington suggests that probably Lysias 'had worked up his way through the military ranks but would have been barred from the rank of tribune because he was not already a citizen of equestrian rank. He solved this problem through a bribe' (p.681).

name to the list of new citizens, a practice that Claudius ignored'.[42]

Keener indicates that bribes may also have been involved in how Claudius Lysias received the military rank of a tribune:

> According to the traditional rules, one could not become a tribune unless one was an equestrian (The minimum qualifications for achieving equestrian status were Roman citizenship, free birth, and holding four hundred thousand sesterces; scholars debate whether additional qualifications were necessary). By the time of Claudius, however, it was possible to be promoted through the ranks, an accepted practice in this period; bribes could buy both citizenship and the tribune office.[43]

Thus, 'Lysias comes from a wealthy family with good Greek education; he could have advanced in his position quickly with financial help'.[44] In contrast to Claudius Lysias, Paul was a Roman citizen by birth and also a member of the people of God and a 'Pharisee of Pharisees'. He obtained his status as 'chosen instrument' by the risen Christ (9:15).[45]

It is not immediately clear why Claudius Lysias would in this context disclose that he had acquired Roman citizenship for a large sum.[46] Is this an admission to having paid bribes? If this is the case, it is unlikely that he was not aware that the practice was illegal. However, if the practice was common under Claudius and not prosecuted (as indicated above), the tribune might not have made much of it and readily admitted to it in a conversation between two people from the Roman East[47] on ways to obtaining Roman citizenship and claiming superior status.

Acts 24:26: Illicit expectations of a Roman governor

The most explicit case of corruption in Acts concerns the Roman governor Felix, before whom Paul appeared in Caesarea for his first Roman trial (Acts 24). After the hearing of the opponents of Paul and of Paul's own defence speech, Felix orders light custody for Paul and that his friends should not be prevented from attending to his needs (24:23).[48]

Later Felix called for Paul and heard him speak about faith in Christ Jesus.[49] Reminiscent

---

42. Keener, *Acts*, III.3253, who further notes: 'Dio Cassius indicates that Claudius bestowed citizenship freely and almost indiscriminately (Dio Cass. 60.17.5). The privilege was originally sold "only for large sums," but "it later became so cheapened by the facility with which it could be obtained that it came to be a common saying, that a man could become a citizen by giving the right person some pieces of broken glass" (60.17.6). Claudius's successor, Nero, cracked down on cases of corruption with the previous administration's imperial favours (e.g., *Tac. Ann.* 14.50), suggesting that Luke's portrayal fits the narrow window of time during Claudius's rule (41–54 C.E.) or shortly thereafter. That is, even this element of the conversation may reflect genuine memories of a period before Luke composed the work.'
43. Keener, *Acts*, III.3254.
44. Keener, *Acts*, III.3255. Claudius Lysias' letter to Felix in Acts 23:26–30 provides a number of clues as to Lysias' character, in particular his stance on reporting the truth; see the meticulous analysis by Yoder, *Representatives*, 277–282.
45. Despite this likelihood of bribes for citizenship and rank, the portrayal of Paul in protective Roman custody in Acts 21–23 is positive. Says Kyrychenko, *Roman Army*, 151: 'this section portrays Roman soldiers providing order, justice, and protection in striking contrast to the mob rule and the murderous plotting of the Jews. Additionally, by safely delivering Paul to Caesarea, the Roman army serves as God's instrument in advancing the divine messenger on his way to Rome'.
46. Rapske, *Paul*, 144, suggests that Luke's note of this 'should hardly be construed as a cynical jibe or irrelevant small talk. It is much more appropriately read as a study in social/juridical damage assessment. The tribune is drawing Paul into disclosing more personal information for the purpose of comparison. [...] Lysias may have hoped that Paul's was an even more recently-granted citizenship under less auspicious circumstances than his own, rightly thinking that one might only lightly punish or even forgive the mistreatment by a superior of his social inferior'.
47. See Keener, *Acts*, III.3253, for the tribune's Eastern background.
48. See Rapske, *Paul*.
49. For the evaluation of such private meetings of provincial officials in legal contexts, see Keener, *Acts*, IV.3430.

of the Old Testament prophets, Paul also boldly spoke about Felix's ethical failures when he addressed righteousness and self-control.[50] Paul also announced coming divine judgement.[51] For Paul, pointing out ethical failures (and the need to change such behaviour), the required virtues of people in power, and what will be required one day before the heavenly judge were apparently part and parcel of 'faith in Jesus Christ'. It is noteworthy that this happens in conversations of a private nature, not during official trials. Because of the coming resurrection and his own accountability before God, Paul always sought to have a clear conscience before God and people (24:16).

Being alarmed, Felix sent Paul away. 'At the same time he hoped that money would be given him by Paul. So he sent for him often and conversed with him' (24:26). From then on, Felix's pretended interest (sending for Paul and conversing with him) is not motivated by interest in the man and his message or in moving the trial forward, but by Felix's hope for a bribe.

Keener wonders: 'Perhaps Felix is aware that the "alms" mentioned in 24:17 are substantial and assumes that the movement that provided them can also provide the bribe'.[52] He summarises that:

> Bribery occurred in many settings, but the exercise of bribery and corruption was perhaps nowhere so rampant as in the judicial system. Some bribed others to induce them to make false accusations, or to corrupt their perspectives as members of the jury or judges. In some periods of antiquity, the innocent had to pay bribes to spare their lives; on other occasions the guilty either secured or attempted to secure acquittal through bribing jurors. Shameful leaders might release prisoners if they were given sufficient bribes. As in Paul's case, matters could be delayed over money; one praetor kept guilty captives in prison to secure their money, promising to consider their case when he had time.[53]

While Paul certainly longed for release from prison to continue his mission (he mentioned his plans to travel to Spain via Rome in his letter to the Roman Christians just before setting out for Jerusalem in Romans 15:22–32), he refused to employ illegitimate means by fulfilling Felix's expectation of a bribe[54] in order to release him or bring the trial to a conclusion (24:26). After a survey of Paul's financial means and those of the Christian communities in Judea and in the Diaspora, Keener emphasises that 'it appears to be not lack of funds but conviction that prevents the payments'.[55] Because of his unwavering stance over and against these expectations, Paul eventually spent two long years in Felix's custody in Caesarea. When he was succeeded by Porcius Festus (24:27), Felix continues his course of action by leaving Paul in prison with the explicit aim of 'doing the Jews a favour'. In this case, Paul was 'given illegally to achieve some goals, usually some private gain', that is Jewish support for Felix's impending statement of account in Rome.[56]

Paul stood for the righteousness he had demanded from Felix as part of faith in Christ Jesus (24:25). Keener writes:

---

50 According to the extant ancient sources, Felix had a poor record regarding the misuse of power and greed, even if Josephus's evaluation of him may be exaggerated; 'Justice and self-control were vitally important to good governance, especially in its judicial aspect; lack of self-control and commitment to justice led to the perverted judgements for personal gain that were notorious at least since Verres', Yoder, *Representatives*, 297.
51 Acts 24:24-25; see Schnabel, *Acts*, 966-967, and Keener, *Acts*, IV.3433-3436.
52 Keener, *Acts*, IV.3437; see his detailed discussion of corruption in ancient legal contexts and of the corruption of governors on pp. 3437-3442.
53 For attempts to prosecute bribery in legal context see Keener, *Acts*, IV.3438-3439; for ancient sources on the corruption of governors in general, see pp. 3439-3440; for corrupt Roman governors in Judea, see pp. 3440-3442.
54 See Keener, *Acts*, IV.3437-3442.
55 Keener, *Acts*, IV.3442.
56 See Keener, *Acts*, IV.3443-3445.

Paul's noncompliance with the expectation of a bribe appears courageous. It would also stir sentiments of justice on his behalf, whether in a Roman court or among the ideal Greek audience of Luke's finished work. It would normally be indiscreet to challenge the corruption of a governor (who held more credibility with Rome than did Paul), but after Felix's humiliating recall, Luke's credibility might be the greater for challenging him (especially with those who knew anything about Felix). On discovering a person's innocence, a good governor would free the person and possibly even reward him or her.[57]

In all this, Paul, the Jewish envoy of Israel's Messiah, appears as the embodiment of a Roman *vir bonus et honestus*, a good and honourable man.[58]

3. Misuse of Power and Greed in Acts

Following several cases of misuse of power in Luke's Gospel, Acts also contains several instances, although these are not directly related to corruption. Acting out of zeal/envy (Acts 5:17), the religious leaders of Jerusalem use all means at their disposal to curb the apostles' influence and the growth of the Christian community. Rather than following proper legal procedure, the members of the Council in Jerusalem lynch Stephen (6:15; 7:54–59). The Jewish high priest issues letters to Paul so that he can persecute the Christians in Damascus (9:2). Later, Paul's opponents are seeking to kill him (9:23–24,29 and elsewhere). Herod Antipas executes James and imprisons Peter (12:1–4). The Jewish opponents of Paul use the influence they have (possibly also their financial means; see above) to hinder Paul's mission.

The owners of a slave girl in Philippi seize Paul and Silas and drag them into the marketplace (Acts 16:19). The city's officials misuse their powers by ordering severe punishment for Paul and Silas without proper legal proceedings.[59]

With blameworthy and flagrant lack of concern, the Roman governor Gallio, characterised as 'high-handed and indifferent',[60] does not intervene when the Jewish accusers of Paul seize Sosthenes, most likely a local Christian, and beat him up in front of the tribunal.[61] 'Gallio should not allow such a prominent individual to be mistreated in his presence'.[62]

While appearing neutral and correct in the trial itself, Felix's suspension of the trial of Paul (24:22) raises suspicions about his character:

> Faced with the moral choice offered by the two speeches, he has temporized. [...] In not releasing Paul, Felix has taken the charges more seriously than his predecessors had done. The reader may have doubts about Felix's purported reason for delay – hadn't the tribune given a full report and made his own assessment of the situation clear? What further need should Felix have had for an interview? And if he was dissatisfied with Lysias' report, why hadn't he had him on hand for the hearing? Felix's stated reason for the delay seems arbitrary, introducing a degree of suspicion about his real motives.[63]

---

57   Keener, *Acts*, IV.3442.
58   For the characterisation of Paul the prisoner in this chapter see Stenschke, 'Paul as Prisoner'.
59   Acts 16:19-24, 37: 'They have beaten us publicly, uncondemned men who are Roman citizens'.
60   Yoder, *Representatives*, 274.
61   Acts 18:16-17; see Yoder, *Representatives*, 270-274, 'Gallio did not intervene because he did not care', 270.
62   Yoder, *Representatives*, 274.
63   Yoder, *Representatives*, 294-295.

In the subsequent events, Felix, 'shows respect for and interest in Paul's "Way" and treats him as a spiritual advisor, all the while holding him in indefinite detention under charges of being an impious troublemaker'.[64] Rather than seeking to administer justice, both Felix and Festus wish to please the Jews (24:27; 25:9). Felix does not release a prisoner whom he deems innocent (24:27).

> The governor is not motivated by considerations of justice, but by a self-serving desire to ensure favour of the local population as he departs his province and prepares to render accounts in Rome. [...] Luke's language emphasises the perfidy of Felix's act: he 'abandons' [...] Paul, trussed up [...] and at the mercy of the next governor (Acts 24:27). Furthermore, Luke's syntax suggests Paul is only a passing concern to Felix.[65]

There are only a few instances of *greed* in Acts. The religious leaders in Jerusalem seek to defend their status as the leaders of Israel over and against the apostles, as their status also secured their livelihood and financial privileges which they were unwilling to surrender. The same probably applies to Simon in Acts 8. Rather than rejoicing that their female slave was delivered from a demon, the slave owners of Philippi, 'seeing that their hope of gain was gone', instigate against Paul and Silas and present false charges (16:19). Demetrius, representative of a trade that 'brought no little business to the craftsmen', becomes active against Paul when his financial interests are threatened (19:23–27).[66]

4. The Proper Christian Use of Financial Resources as the Antidote to Corruption

Acts offers a nuanced portrayal of the Christian use of financial resources. While this does include the account of Ananias and Sapphira and their attempt to use their resources to enhance their status in the community and of Simon who sought to regain through money his former status in Samaria, Acts also reports the genuine generosity of Christians and their responsible handling of money and other resources in support of each other and the gospel.

In the early chapters of Acts, the apostles refer to the resources available to them: they do not have silver or gold at their disposal, but are called to draw on the power of the risen Jesus (3:6), in whose name they act when they heal a lame man on the temple precincts free of charge.

Those who donate generously to the community in the sharing of goods, place their donations at the apostles' (plural!) feet (2:45; 4:32–37). They do not give the money to individuals with the intention of forging relationships of dependency and influence. In Joppa, a female disciple named Tabitha/Dorcas apparently shared her resources by making tunics and garments for the widows in the Christian community (9:39).

---

64 Yoder, *Representatives*, 296, who also notes that 'At the mention of the two years Paul languishes in prison, it becomes clear that Felix's promise of a further interview with Lysias was also disingenuous. Once the trial is adjourned Lysias' name never comes up again', (p.297).

65 Yoder, *Representatives*, 298, also notes: 'Felix is also a governor who fails to command the respect of his inferiors. Lysias does not expect him to inquire closely into the events in Jerusalem, and feels free to misrepresent the course of events. The continuation of the narrative bears witness that the tribune's evaluation of his superior was correct. Tertullus' rhetoric suggests that he expects Felix to respond to flattery and the influence of his powerful clients. The rhetor too proves to be correct, at least on Felix's responsiveness to influence' (p.300).

66 There are a few references to the misuse of power and greed in Stephen's historical survey in Acts 7: The Egyptians enslave and afflict the Israelites for four centuries (7:6; see also v. 19, 34). The patriarchs, jealous of Joseph sell him into Egypt (7:9). Moses slays an Egyptian (7:24). The ancestors persecuted and killed the prophets (7:52); see also Acts 5:36–37.

According to Acts 11:27–30, the Christians of Antioch gather funds as a famine relief for the poor believers in Jerusalem. They do so, 'every one according to his ability'. When Christians put money together, it is for famine relief for the church in Jerusalem,[67] not for securing their own purposes. Christian sharing includes the provision of generous hospitality (10:48; 16:15, 34).

Paul is portrayed as working in his trade as a tent-maker in Corinth (18:2) and emphasises in his statement of account of his ministry to the Ephesian elders that he did not covet any one's silver or gold or apparel. Rather, he worked with his own hands to support himself.[68]

In addition to the portrayal of how Christians use their material resources and how they 'solve' problems, there is also the, admittedly weaker, argument from silence of what Christians are *not* portrayed as doing in Acts. In the conflict of Acts 4—5, the apostles and other Christ-followers do not resort to bribes to be released from prison or to incite the crowds against the religious leaders. Rather than *paying*, the Christians are portrayed as *praying* to God (5:23, 29). The apostles are released from prison by divine intervention, not because they use money. The conflict in Acts 6:1–7 is resolved in full transparency and without any resort to bribes. Throughout Acts, the Christ-believers do not resort to bribery against their opponents. While Felix expects bribes, Paul does not pay his way out.

5. The Challenge of Acts Today

What are we to make of this portrayal consisting of a few references 'in passing'? As is the case with other vices and failures, Acts does not directly condemn corruption, the paying or receiving of bribes, the misuse of power, or greed. When corruption occurs on its pages, it appears simply as how things are done in the world of the narrative by those who have the resources and the power to do so and readily and cunningly know how to employ them to further their own interests—much like in today's world.

The portrayal of Acts is not as clearly cut as Christian readers might wish it to be in their canonical writings. Both cases involving believers reveal the close connection between money and status in the community or before its leaders. Ananias and Sapphira's agreement and behaviour indicate that the concern for status can lead to questionable use of money, be it in donating it or in holding back some of it.

Still entangled in his pre-Christian value system and entrenched way of gaining and keeping status in the community, Simon, the former magician, offers money to the apostles and is severely reprimanded for doing so. These incidents link such intentions to the Devil and underline that one cannot serve God and Mammon, as Jesus emphasised (Luke 16:13). Within the Christian community, money is to be used accountably and with great care before the Holy Spirit and God. The proper use of material possessions remains challenging and requires spiritual discipline and generous and systematic instruction.[69] It is not surprising that the proper use of wealth is one major emphasis in Luke's ethical instruction.

---

67   Curiously, Acts does not directly mention Paul's collection enterprise for the saints of Jerusalem which would have served as a stunning example of the proper use of resources.
68   Acts 20:33–35; for a survey of the Christian use of material means see Beck, *Christian Character*, 28–54. Acts also contains references to the hospitality and provisions provided by non-Christians (Acts 28:7, 10). Leading officials of the province of Asia were friendly with Paul and urged him not to venture into the theatre (19:31)—for his own safety and not to escalate the conflict further.
69   For its need and extent in Acts see Stenschke, *Luke's Portrait*, 335–347.

In the narrative of Acts, corruption and bribes are characteristic of the opponents of the gospel or of office bearers who pursue their own interests, be they financial or otherwise, rather than justice. Acts underlines that corruption is by no means harmless: people most likely bought with money bring Stephen to his death, stone Paul, and hinder the proclamation of the gospel. Because Paul refuses to meet Felix's expectations, justice is denied to him and he remains imprisoned for two years rather than travelling to Spain as he had intended. Recourse to such means of influence characterises the opponents of Jesus.

At the same time, it is comforting to note that on the pages of Acts, despite its prevalence and severe consequences, corruption cannot permanently hinder the course of the gospel:

- Following Stephen's death, the gospel ventures beyond Jerusalem.

- The opponents of Paul and their instigations in their own way propel the proclamation of the gospel forward to ever new places.

- During his long stay in Caesarea, Paul was protected from his militant opponents and perhaps wrote some of his prison letters.

- During this time the author of Luke-Acts[70] who had come with Paul to Jerusalem (Acts 20:5–21:16)[71] may have used the opportunity to investigate in Judea 'the things that have come to fulfilment among us', as indicated in the prologue to Luke-Acts.[72] Felix's corrupt intentions may thus have impacted on the production of Luke-Acts in its present form.

In the world to which Acts invites its readers, believers rely on God, rather than on corrupt schemes. They do not give or accept money or other advantages illegally to achieve some goals, usually some private gain. Their interest is not private gain but the kingdom of God. Believers willingly serve God and each other, share their resources without intention to gain status or influence and in this way, they provide hospitality and do not burden each other. There is to be no place for greed which is rife in our societies (at times celebrated as a virtue which drives a neoliberal capitalist economy) and 'a root of all evil' (1Tim. 6:10), including being the occasion for corruption and misuse of power. Jesus' radical teaching on wealth is a much-needed antidote to what we find in Acts and today. It urgently needs fresh attention and obedient responses.

The portrayal of Acts also urges Christians to use their influence and take a stance in society against corruption, the misuse of power, and greed. To the extent that they themselves exemplify and display the opposing virtues of personal integrity, legal and beneficial use of power, and generosity, there is a chance that their voice will be heard. Paul's demand of those in power for self-control, commitment to justice, and accountability (Acts 24:25) is as relevant here and now as it was then and there.

Christoph W. Stenschke
Biblisch-Theologische Akademie Forum Wiedenest, Bergneustadt, Germany.
Department of Biblical and Ancient Studies, College of Human Sciences, University of South Africa, Pretoria, South Africa.
CStenschke@t-online.de

---

70 Acts 24 occurs between the second and third 'we-passage' of Acts.
71 see Thornton, *Der Zeuge*, 229–267.
72 Luke 1:1–4; for discussion of the identity of the author see Keener, *Acts*, I.402–422.

Bibliography

Bachhiesl, C., M. Handy, P. Mauritsch, W. Petermandl (eds.) *Gier, Korruption und Machtmissbrauch in der Antike* (Antike Kultur und Geschichte 20. Vienna: LIT, 2019).

Barrett, C. K. *A Critical and Exegetical Commentary on the Acts of the Apostles I: Preliminary Introduction and Commentary on Acts I–XIV* (ICC; Edinburgh: T. & T. Clark, 1994).

Beck, B. E. *Christian Character in the Gospel of Luke* (London: Epworth, 1989).

Bühler, A. 'Moneylending I. Ancient Near East and Hebrew Bible/Old Testament', *EBR* 19 (2021), 768–770.

Catholic Biblical Association of Nigeria (ed.) *Integrity and Corruption in the Bible* (Port Harcourt: CABAN Publications, 2019). https://www.cabanalive.org/publications/vol-12-2019 (16/05/2021).

Coleman, R. L. *The Lukan Lens on Wealth and Possessions: Perspectives Shaped by the Themes of Reversal and Right Response* (B.I.S. 180; Leiden, Boston: Brill, 2020).

Hämeen-Anttila, J. 'Corruption of Scripture', *EBR* 5 (2012), Cols. 826–828.

Hays, C. M. *Luke's Wealth Ethics: A Study of Their Coherence and Character* (WUNT II.275. Tübingen: Mohr Siebeck, 2010).

Keener, C. S. *Acts: An Exegetical Commentary.* Vol. I: *Introduction and 1:1–2:47* (Grand Rapids, MI: Baker, 2012).

Keener, C. S. *Acts: An Exegetical Commentary.* Vol. II: *3:1–14:28* (Grand Rapids, MI: Baker, 2013).

Keener, C. S. *Acts: An Exegetical Commentary.* Vol. III: *15:1–23:35* (Grand Rapids, MI: Baker, 2014).

Keener, C. S. *Acts: An Exegetical Commentary.* Vol. IV: *24:1–28:31* (Grand Rapids, MI: Baker, 2015).

Kyrychenko, A. *The Roman Army and the Expansion of the Gospel: The Role of the Centurion in Luke-Acts* (BZNW 203; Berlin, Boston: De Gruyter, 2014).

Nam, R. 'Money I. Ancient Near East and Hebrew Bible/Old Testament', *EBR* 19 (2021), 714–743.

Patte, D. 'Simony', in D. Patte (ed.), *The Cambridge Dictionary of Christianity* (Cambridge: Cambridge University Press, 2010), 1158–1159.

Rapske, B. *Paul in Roman Custody* (AFCS 3; Grand Rapids, MI: Eerdmans, 1994).

Schnabel, E. J. *Acts* (ECNT; Grand Rapids, MI: Zondervan, 2012).

Stenschke, C. W. *Luke's Portrait of Gentiles Prior to Their Coming to Faith* (WUNT II.108; Tübingen: Mohr Siebeck, 1999).

Stenschke, C. W.	'"So I always take pains to have a clear conscience toward both God and man" (Acts 24:16): Saint Paul as Prisoner and Ethical Societies', *Journal of Dharma: Dharmaram Journal of Philosophies and Religions* 45.3 (2020), 391–406.
Stenschke, C. W.	'Money III. New Testament', *EBR* 19 (2021), 744–746.
Stenschke, C. W.	'Moneylending II. New Testament', *EBR* 19 (2021), 771–772.
Thornton, C.-J.	*Der Zeuge des Zeugen: Lukas als Historiker der Paulusreisen* (WUNT 56. Tübingen: Mohr Siebeck, 1991).
Watson Ford, J.	'Blastus', *ABD* (1992), I.753.
Witherington, B.	*The Acts of the Apostles* (Carlisle: Paternoster; Grand Rapids, MI: Cambridge: Eerdmans, 1998).
Yoder, J.	*Representatives of Roman Rule: Roman Provincial Governors in Luke-Acts* (BZNW 209; Berlin, Boston: De Gruyter, 2014).

Book reviews

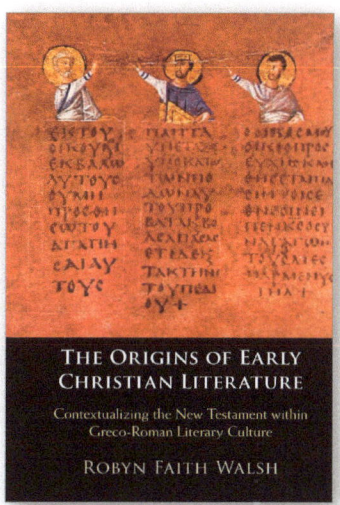

Robyn Faith Walsh. *The Origins of Early Christian Literature: Contextualizing the New Testament within Greco-Roman Literary Culture.* Cambridge: Cambridge University Press, 2021. xix + 225. Hardcover. ISBN: 9781108835305. $99.99.

This new monograph by Robyn Faith Walsh is a watershed moment in the history of New Testament scholarship. By probing the origins of several fundamental assumptions about the New Testament authors, their social and literary milieux, and the nature of their contribution to the literary culture, Walsh offers an original reading of the Gospels, which begins to break down the longstanding barriers between the fields of New Testament studies and Classics. It is safe to say at the outset that Walsh accomplishes her task by convincingly identifying the more realistic social setting for the writers of the Gospels as a relatively small circle of elite Graeco-Roman cultural and artistic producers.

After an introduction laying out the problem, solution, and argument to follow, Walsh's contribution unfolds in five chapters. Chapter 1 reexamines the pervasive framework in New Testament scholarship which looks for the 'communities' of Gospel writers. These supposed 'Gospel communities' are typically regarded as the most significant and formative social group for the canonical evangelists. Instead, given what we know about writing practices and literary production in the Graeco-Roman world, we should look for the Gospel writers' primary and most formative social context in the Graeco-Roman literary elite, who shared, borrowed, adapted, criticized, and helped revise each other's work in their processes of composition.

Walsh's proposal leads her to seek out the intellectual origins of, and to reevaluate the foundations for, hypothetical Gospel communities (chapter 2). Readers of this journal will undoubtedly think of the work of Richard Bauckham which questions the existence and relevance of Gospel communities, but Bauckham later becomes a recipient of much of the same criticisms offered towards form and redaction critics who continue to argue about these hypothetical communities. Walsh's intellectual history probes much deeper than Bauckham's (who begins with B.H. Streeter) by tracing the foundations of hypothetical Gospel communities to the German romantic idealists of the eighteenth century. Walsh's fascinating historical narrative implicates such (relatively) familiar names as Johann Gottfried Herder and Johann Adam Möhler, as well as some surprising figures like the brothers Grimm, as originators of the search for communities behind the composition of the Gospels. Twentieth-century form and redaction critics later became heirs to the German romantic idealist notion of 'the author-genius' who worked as little more than a mouthpiece expressing the 'spirit' (*Geist*) of the community (*Völker*), which passed along through 'oral tradition'. The degree to which Walsh identifies German nationalistic tendencies in this manner of thinking is surprising but entirely convincing. She concludes that, at best, the search for Gospel communities is misguided and anachronistic, and we should search instead for new and different social contexts for the evangelists.

In chapter 3, Walsh redescribes first-century Christian literature by identifying its authors as elite cultural producers. Here, Walsh argues that writing in Graeco-Roman antiquity was at once a product of Greek rhetorical education/*paideia* as well as the result of feedback from relative peers—that is, other elite cultural producers. Walsh identifies this circle of elite Graeco-Roman writers and literary critics as the 'most immediate and formative social network' of the Gospel authors (pp. 109–110). Scholars should imagine the composition of the Gospel taking place among the literary elite, in the manner of the depiction in Athenaeus Naucratita's *Deipnosophistae*, which portrays various elite authors and critics reading, conversing, debating, and offering revisions for one another's work.

Walsh offers an original reading of the Gospel

Given this reimagined social setting of the Gospel writers as among the literary elite, Walsh's reading of the Gospels opens up a world of *comparanda* that have often been overlooked. In chapter 4, Walsh draws attention to numerous *topoi* employed by the evangelists that were often thought unique but that have a corollary in a variety of Graeco-Roman genres, including epic, philosophy, *bioi*, historiography, satire, and paradoxography. For Walsh, the social location that best explains this sort of 'literary borrowing' should be identified as the material exchange known to occur among the Graeco-Roman literary elite. Consequently, Walsh identifies many of these supposedly unique features of the Gospels (e.g. anonymous writing, divine genealogies, healings, teachings, and fellowship meals) with common literary *topoi* and rhetorical strategies. The immediate payoff is the ability to identify a rather precise rhetorical purpose for the inclusion of such material.

In the final chapter, Walsh applies her reading to the Gospels. She identifies the Gospels as an innovation on the genre *bios* dubbed 'subversive biography'. The Gospels therefore fit alongside works like the *Life of Aesop*, Xenophon's *Memorabilia*, or the *Alexander Romance* by portraying their subject as a sort of laudable 'antihero' (p. 171), whose life and teachings subvert contemporary structures of power. Walsh's generic proposal makes good sense of several strange elements in the Gospel as, for example, Mark's characterization of Jesus as temperamental (1:41), Matthew's portrait of Jesus offering witty remarks or jokes that subvert established leadership (19:24), or Luke's depiction of Jesus' precocious behavior as a child (2:41–42). The result of this reading: 'the gospels [sic] are situated in conversation with the literary tradition of biography, demonstrating that certain details of Jesus' life may have been the product of an author's engagement with an established genre of writing lives, and not necessarily the reflection of an "oral tradition"' (p. 194).

In conclusion, Walsh's work represents a profound and compelling response to more than a century of research on the Gospels and paves many new directions for Gospels and Acts research. It should be read closely by every specialist in the Gospels and Acts, who undoubtedly have much to learn from Walsh, as I did. This work, though generally convincing in its major proposals, left me with several unaddressed questions or avenues for further inquiry. How does the model of the *yaḥad* ('community') at Qumran figure into her analysis? Given that the Gospels are Jewish compositions, and each of them display at least some influence by apocalyptic Judaism, it is not unreasonable to look to the Qumran context for illumination of the evangelists' compositional practices, as well as their relation of literary, social, and religious contexts. Second, given the radical nature of authorial freedom in Walsh's model, I wondered why the Synoptic evangelists were so conservative with their use of material. Were they simply imitating their sources, or were they, to some extent, also beholden to the historical tradition that they may (or, according to Walsh, may not) have personally investigated (cf. Luke 1:1–4)? Finally, I would like to see how Walsh would respond to the work of Charles Talbert on the nature of religious language in the Lukan corpus. According to Talbert, Luke does indeed use the motifs and topoi commonly found in the kinds of biographical, novelistic, and paradoxographical works that Walsh discusses, but, according to Talbert, such use does not imply complete literary freedom but, instead, a language to communicate or express religious convictions held in common with other Christians. However Walsh may respond to these and other questions, it is clear that this book will repay careful study (with interest). Let us hope that Walsh's study is able, like the Gospels, to find a much wider audience beyond a cultured few.

Daniel B. Glover
Lee University

Benjamin L. Gladd. *Handbook on the Gospels.* Grand Rapids: Baker Academic, 2021. 464pp. ISBN: 9781540960160. $39.99.

This volume, the third in Baker Academic's series of New Testament handbooks, intends to accomplish two stated goals. First, Gladd sets out to read the Gospels as narratives and place them within a canonical and redemptive-historical theological context. Second, he intends to situate the Gospels within their Jewish and Graeco-Roman cultural settings. This project, then, aims to be a thorough, but not exhaustive, evangelical biblical-theological summary of the content of the four canonical Gospels. This volume is primarily oriented towards students, pastors, and other Bible teachers. As such, Gladd's focus is on presenting material that is accessible and clear for readers who may not be engaged with the Gospels at an academic or technical level. His focus is consistently on engaging with the stories that the Gospels present and their biblical-theological context. Gladd's centering of the narrative material of the Gospels is evident in the structure of the book itself. This volume is composed of only four chapters, one devoted to each of the four Gospels. This text forgoes typical prolegomenous topics such as issues of genre, source criticism, textual transmission, and the historical Jesus. Each chapter features a minimal treatment of authorship and dating for the corresponding Gospel; Gladd does not attempt to significantly describe the various historical-critical perspectives on these issues, preferring to move directly into a summary of the content of each Gospel. These narrative-theological descriptions comprise the majority of each chapter.

Gladd moves steadily through the story of each Gospel, providing a description of each narrative section. Particular attention is paid to a given passage's canonical connections, both to the Old Testament and to the rest of the New Testament canon. While Gladd's presentation hovers well above the level of a detailed commentary or exegetical study, readers are given enough information about the relevant canonical allusions and biblical-theological connections to assemble an accurate picture of the text's main ideas as understood by Gladd. Citations are sparse and synthesis of secondary literature is largely left behind in favor of centering the narrative content of each Gospel. Gladd's treatment moves through each Gospel sequentially at a consistent pace and avoids getting thrown off course by interpretive issues. His discussion of, for example, the notoriously thorny Olivet Discourse (Matthew 24:1–25:46; Mark 13:1–37; Luke 21:5–36) is relatively restrained in all three synoptic chapters; Gladd brings up various interpretive issues, but seems content to mention the difficulty, present a position, and move on, maintaining focus on the narrative and theological content. Each chapter concludes with a bibliography for the corresponding Gospel.

Gladd's priorities in this volume are to be commended. The lack of the usual prolegomenon is refreshing; many existing introductory textbooks handle the basic historical-critical issues sufficiently and Gladd's move straight into the biblical text is a welcome change of pace. This well-trodden ground is left unvisited. Additionally, the disciplined progression of each chapter makes this an accessible and manageable reference text for students and pastors who need a fulsome yet concise summary of a particular passage or section. The discrete structuring and independent nature of each chapter contributes an inherent utility to this volume. This work would be well-situated in the seminary setting as a survey text alongside a historical-critically oriented introduction to the Gospels. Two cautions should be noted. First, for readers who want to engage further with the secondary literature, Gladd's work may be of limited use, since the infrequent citations give readers little to go on in terms of continued investigation. This is perhaps understandable given Gladd's stated aims for this work, but it should simply be observed that some readers may have to look elsewhere to supplement what they find in Gladd's treatment. Second, Gladd offers little explanation or justification for his method, other than a few brief paragraphs in the preface. This may cause difficulty for readers who are not already familiar with or otherwise amenable to an evangelical biblical-theological or canonical-critical approach to the New Testament. The lack of explicit hermeneutical framing is congruent with the corresponding lack of introductory material for the Gospels themselves, but also leaves key interpretive priorities unstated and potentially unobvious to those who are unfamiliar.

Andrew H. Waller
Ridley College

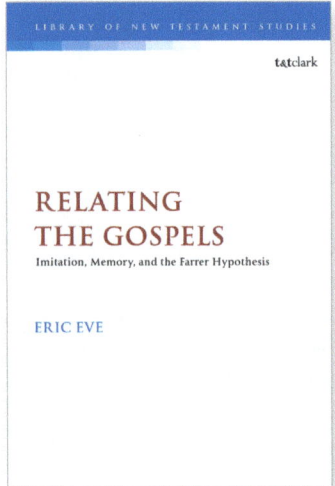

Eric Eve. *Relating the Gospels: Memory, Imitation and the Farrer Hypothesis.* LNTS 592. London: T&T Clark, 2021. vii + 247 pp. ISBN 978-0-567-68110-2 (hardcover). $170.00.

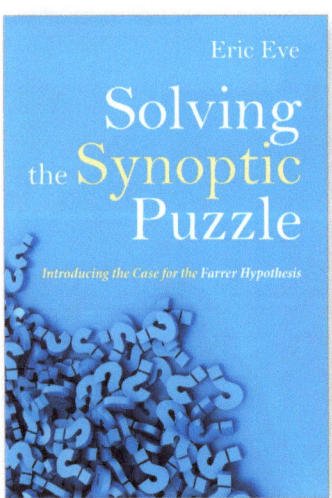

Eric Eve. *Solving the Synoptic Puzzle: Introducing the Case for the Farrer Hypothesis.* Eugene, OR: Cascade Books, 2021. ix + 126 pp. ISBN 978-1-7252-8386-2 (paperback). $AU26.00.

Eric Eve is Fellow and Tutor in Theology at Harris Manchester College, Oxford, and his research interests include the miracles of Jesus in their historical Jewish context, media and memory studies in relation to the composition of the Gospels, and the synoptic problem. A longstanding Q-sceptic, Eve belongs to a group of scholars that advocates the Farrer hypothesis (FH), a source theory that explains the interrelations of the synoptic gospels without reference to the hypothetical sayings source, Q. Focusing on how best to explain the relations between the extant Gospels according to Matthew, Mark, and Luke, the FH endorses Markan priority, accepts Matthew's dependence upon Mark, but explains the material shared between Matthew and Luke but absent from Mark by Luke's dependence on Matthew as well as on Mark, hence dispensing with Q. The two books here under review follow several important shorter studies and two significant monographs by Eve: *Behind the Gospels: Understanding the Oral Tradition* (SPCK, 2013) and *Writing the Gospels: Composition and Memory* (SPCK, 2016). With this body of work, Eve joins Michael Goulder, Mark Goodacre, and Francis Watson as principal proponents of the FH.

Although *Relating the Gospels* and *Solving the Synoptic Puzzle* cover similar ground, the former focuses on defending the viability of the FH by comparison with the two-document hypothesis (2DH), whereas the latter, though written to introduce the case for the FH, nevertheless provides both an even-handed introduction to the complex data that constitute the synoptic problem and a fair-minded overview of various solutions to this intricate problem. Thus, chapter 1 of *Solving the Synoptic Puzzle* on the nature of the synoptic problem is as valuable for seasoned scholars as for students, if only to be reminded that no source theory explains all the data, that all source theories rely on assumptions of various kinds, and that supposedly simple models of how the first three Gospels are related to one another are but partial and provisional approximations to the actual composition of, and historical relations between, these texts. Aware that gaps in our historical knowledge preclude 'assured results' of scholarship, Eve aims to demonstrate that his preferred FH is no less historically plausible than any other source theory, especially the 2DH, and that the FH is able to account for textual data that advocates of the 2DH consider to be inexplicable by Luke's reliance on Matthew (as well as on Mark) and therefore necessitates Matthew and Luke's independent use of Q. In short, Eve argues on the basis of contextual and comparative plausibility.

'A solution to the Synoptic Problem is more likely to command respect if it fits ancient compositional methods' (p. 5). So begins chapter 2 of *Relating the Gospels*, in which Eve both distils and builds upon his earlier books, *Behind the Gospels* and *Writing the Gospels*. Here he surveys compositional practices contemporaneous with the evangelists, discusses the role memory is likely to have played in the composition of the Gospels, and considers the purpose(s) of the respective Gospel writers. In a similar vein, chapter 3 of *Relating the Gospels* probes what can be known from antiquity about how ancient authors made use of sources in their own compositions. This chapter, titled 'Transformational techniques', engages with the significant work of F. Gerald Downing, Robert Derrenbacker, and Alan Kirk, and it also makes a significant contribution to scholarship on potential precedents for rearranging the sequence of source material used as well as for literary imitation. Similar content is covered more briefly in chapter 2 of *Solving the Synoptic Puzzle*, which presents a contextually informed and lucid description of 'Gospel Writing in the First Century'.

As an advocate of the FH, Eve accepts and defends the priority of Mark's Gospel. Cognizant that several previous arguments advanced in favour of Markan priority are inconclusive or question-begging, Eve proffers various alternative or refined arguments in support of Mark's priority. But at least part of his case for the priority of Mark is that arguments put forward by proponents of Markan posteriority or of some version of Proto-Mark fail to compel, especially by comparison with what seems plausible on the assumption of Matthew and Luke's use of Mark. In an otherwise sure-footed discussion, however, Eve's discussion of problems associated with Delbert Burkett's advocacy of Proto-Mark overlooks his most recent book on the subject, *The Case for Proto-Mark* (Mohr Siebeck, 2018), which presents a wealth of data difficult to explain by the priority of canonical Mark and which has been positively reviewed by proponents of both the 2DH (Craig Evans) and the FH (Mark Goodacre).

Although both of Eve's recent books aim to convince readers to follow Austin Farrer by dispensing with the hypothetical Q source, he understands why advocates of Q think as they do. Indeed, in chapter 3 of *Solving the Synoptic Puzzle*, he provides a balanced summary of reasons for upholding Q (pp. 41–44). From this point forward, however, Eve's objective in both books is to persuade readers that Q is indeed dispensable. In *Solving the Synoptic Puzzle*, he proceeds to contest the various reasons given for Q with a view to showing Luke's familiarity with Matthew's Gospel, reserving the final chapter of the body of the book for arguments associated with significant differences in the relative sequence of non-Markan material shared between Matthew and Luke. In *Relating the Gospels*, chapter 4 surveys 'significant similarities' between Matthew and Luke, chapter 5 addresses 'difficult differences' between Matthew and Luke, and chapter 6 wrestles with 'the order objection'.

In chapter 4 of *Relating the Gospels*, Eve sets out to show that Luke's Gospel resembles Matthew's more than these two Gospels differ. To this end, he discusses agreements between Matthew and Luke against Mark in material shared between all three Synoptic Gospels (the triple tradition), instances of high verbatim agreement in material shared between Matthew

> **Farrer Hypothesis is able to account for textual data.**

and Luke alone, and significant similarities between the opening chapters of the Gospels of Matthew and Luke. Although conceivably explicable by Matthew's dependence on Luke as well as on Mark, as advocated by a minority of scholars, Eve contends that all such similarities point to the conclusion that Luke's dependence on Matthew alongside Mark is more plausible than Matthew and Luke's independent use of Mark and Q. There is much of value in this chapter, but readers need to be especially alert and attentive while reading Eve's discussion of major and minor agreements between Matthew and Luke against Mark in the triple tradition, especially since, for the purpose of greater precision, Eve adopts Werner Kahl's distinction between inclusive and exclusive agreements, the former referring to agreements shared between all three Synoptic Gospels and the latter referring to agreements shared between any two of these Gospels against the third. One therefore finds oneself having to differentiate between $EA^{Mk\text{-}Mt}$ (agreements between Mark and Matthew against Luke), $EA^{Mk\text{-}Lk}$ (agreements between Mark and Luke against Matthew), and $EA^{Mt\text{-}Lk}$ (agreements between Matthew and Luke against Mark). Once again, although proponents of the FH have long considered the more minor agreements between Matthew and Luke against Mark to be more readily explicable by Luke's familiarity with Matthew than by Matthew and Luke's independent reliance on Mark and Q, Burkett's *Case for Proto-Mark* shows that such minor (or exclusive) agreements between any two Synoptic Gospels against the third comprise a body of evidence difficult to account for on the standard hypothesis of canonical Markan priority.

After arguing that various significant similarities between the Gospels of Matthew and Luke are best explained by Luke's creative use of Matthew, Eve discusses various arguments based on differences between these Gospels that are often appealed to in support of their independence. These include: (1) the view that Matthew and Luke's respective infancy and resurrection narratives are too different to be directly related; (2) the contention that Luke sometimes records more primitive versions of traditions found in both Matthew and Luke (the argument from alternating primitivity); (3) the objection that, on the FH, Luke incorporated fewer Matthean alterations to Mark than one would expect, especially additions that appear congenial to Luke; and (4) the somewhat similar protestation that, relatively often on the FH, where Matthew has either amended or added to Mark, Luke apparently follows Matthew's adaptations of Mark more closely than Matthew's close parallels with Mark (the argument from apparent 'unpicking'). Whether by appealing to earlier rebuttals or by careful source-critical argumentation, Eve demonstrates that the most common arguments against Luke's use of Matthew's Gospel are inconclusive. 'Even in combination', he concludes, 'these four arguments do not constitute a convincing demonstration that Luke's use of Matthew is so improbable as to outweigh the evidence of significant similarities between Matthew and Luke identified in Chapter 4. On the contrary, closer examination of these arguments has revealed some further significant similarities' (p. 143).

In both books, the final substantive chapter is devoted to what many consider to be the principal problem for proponents of any source theory that envisages Luke as dependent on Matthew's Gospel. In Eve's words, 'The main objection to Luke's use of Matthew is the difference between the context and order of so much of the double tradition in these two gospels' (p. 143). Although the 'objection of order' is often levelled against advocates of Luke's use of Matthew, Eve begins chapter 6 of *Relating the Gospels* by closely investigating Alan Kirk's tracking of Matthew's use of Mark and Q on the 2DH. In this chapter, one needs to be especially cognizant of the following shorthand: 'FH Luke' = Luke's source utilization of Mark and Matthew as assumed by the FH; and '2DH Matthew' = Matthew's use of Mark and Q on the 2DH. Important features of Kirk's case for Matthew's use of Mark and Q are: (1) Matthew can be assumed to have had good memory command of both Mark and Q; and (2) on the 2DH, Matthew can usually be shown to have worked forward through his two main sources. Assuming the FH, Eve likewise contends that Luke can be assumed to have had equally good memory command of his two related sources, Mark and Matthew, and that, for the most part, FH Luke can be shown to have progressed forward through his two written sources. Regarding Matthew's alleged use of Q in Matthew 5–7 (the Sermon on the Mount), Eve poses pertinent questions of Kirk's proposed index and search strategy for locating and recontextualizing Q materials. As for Matthew's apparent rearrangement of Markan materials in Matthew 8–13, Eve proposes a compositional procedure that ostensibly accounts for such rearrangements as well as, if not better than, Kirk's envisaged redactional scenario. As Eve himself recognizes, however, his explanation here works as well for 2DH Matthew as for FH Matthew, since both source theories accept Matthew's dependence on Mark.

The remainder of Eve's chapter on Luke's narrative order relative to the respective pericope sequences of his two principal sources on the FH (Mark and Matthew) proceeds in four stages. First, Eve argues (against Kirk) that FH Luke's memory-activated use of Matthew in particular is no less capable of explaining Luke's overall sequence of material than 2DH Matthew's memory-activated use of his principal sources (Mark and Q). He then addresses Luke's use of Matthew in Luke 6:20–8:1, focusing especially on Luke's construction of his 'Sermon on the Plain' by essentially distilling Matthew's Sermon on the Mount, while also postulating how Luke drew materials from Matthew and his own special material when composing Luke 7.

Stage 3 in Eve's reconstruction of FH Luke's narrative sequence addresses Luke's central section, beginning at 9:51 and extending to 18:15, at which point Luke can be seen to resume following Mark's narrative order. This block of material is the most challenging to explain on the assumption of Luke's use of Matthew alongside Mark, so this is naturally the longest subsection of chapter 6 in *Relating the Gospels* (over twenty-five pages). As Eve concedes concerning Luke's central section, 'some account needs to be given of FH Luke's method of working' (p. 169). Thus, after identifying several governing concerns and themes operative in the composition of Luke's central section, Eve's detailed discussion focuses mainly on seeking to demonstrate that Luke basically follows Matthew by making his way forward through Matthew's narrative, 'albeit often block by block rather than verse by verse or pericope by pericope' (p. 171). What Eve means by this rather important qualification is that Luke is to be envisaged as having read or recollected Matthean material in pericope blocks or chunks before composing each successive subsection of his own, within which he occasionally rearranged the sequence of material borrowed from Matthew. Even so, Eve concedes that Luke must have sometimes either recalled material from Matthew passed over earlier, as when abbreviating Matthew's Sermon on the Mount, or brought forward material from later Matthean contexts, presumably facilitated by Luke's close familiarity or 'good memory command' (p. 172) of Matthew's Gospel. Eve also posits substantial 'indirect use' of Matthew by Luke in his central section, especially in its second half (pp. 173–74). By Luke's 'indirect use of Matthew' Eve means that the contextualization of some special Lukan material, which by definition is not derived from Matthew, is nevertheless triggered by Matthean cues. According to Eve in *Solving*

Eve poses pertinent questions.

the Synoptic Puzzle, 'We may term this kind of oblique influence a *hidden parallel*, meaning a passage in Luke that has been influenced by Matthew without being a straightforward copy or paraphrase' (p. 89). For example, Eve suggests that Luke 9:52–56 (Jesus' rejection by Samaritans) may have been triggered by the command of Jesus in Matthew 10:5 not to enter any Samaritan town. Aware that what he proposes for Luke's indirect use of Matthew in Luke 9:51–18:14 is difficult to reconcile with what is known of source utilization by ancient authors, Eve nevertheless offers reasons for thinking that his tracing of FH Luke's indirect use of Matthew is not only plausible but also probable. Indeed, the final of his four stages of argumentation in chapter 6 of *Relating the Gospels* is to argue that in antiquity there was no single formula for emulating predecessors and that FH Luke's emulation of Matthew in his central section falls within ancient parameters of compositional emulation. 'Emulation is competitive imitation', he writes, 'and there were no set rules on how to imitate. Luke's emulation of Matthew is an attempt to produce a gospel more suitable for his Gentile church' (p. 195). Whether or not one ultimately finds Eve's argumentation compelling, his mode and manner of argument are admirable. A table at the end of chapter 6 of *Relating the Gospels* displays FH Luke's use of pre-existing materials, with various columns showing Luke's direct use of non-Markan Matthean material largely in Matthean sequence, his indirect use of Matthean materials, his relatively infrequent use of Matthean materials out of sequence, his direct use of Mark, and finally a column that identifies potential intertexts for some of Luke's special material.

No brief review of Eve's two books is able to do justice to their respective contents. What may be said about both books, however, is that they are lucid, even when addressing complex data and arguments, balanced, especially when discussing the views of proponents of alternative source theories, and judicious. Anyone who reads one or other or both of these books will be led into the complex data that comprises the synoptic problem by a dependable guide, and s/he will also learn much that is eye-opening about the synoptic gospels themselves. Even so, it is difficult to envisage many defenders of Q being convinced by Eve to abandon their advocacy of Q as a necessary adjunct to Markan priority. But in view of increasing disquiet over Q discernible especially since the turn of the millennium, Eve's two most recent books are likely to reinforce doubts about Q, especially among those either new to Gospel studies or as yet uncommitted to any particular solution to the synoptic problem. In this connection, it is noteworthy that the two best introductions to the synoptic problem thus far this century have been written by advocates of the FH: Mark Goodacre's *The Synoptic Problem: A Way Through the Maze* (Sheffield Academic Press, 2001) and Eric Eve's *Solving the Synoptic Puzzle*, which contains a helpful appendix offering suggestions for further reading that is not limited to the work of fellow advocates of the FH. Synoptic source specialists cannot afford to ignore *Relating the Gospels*, and *Solving the Synoptic Puzzle* belongs on the reading list of any subject in which students are introduced to the synoptic problem.

David Neville
St Mark's National Theological Centre
Charles Sturt University, Canberra

BOOK REVIEWS

Daniel Daley. *God's Will and Testament: Inheritance in the Gospel of Matthew and Jewish Tradition.* Waco: Baylor University Press, 2021. 413pp. ISBN 978-1481315524. $69.99.

This volume is the author's PhD dissertation completed under Benjamin Wold at Trinity College (Dublin). In his Introduction ("Matthew and Jewish Tradition," ch. 1; pp. 1–43), Daley surveys the surprisingly sparse attention given to the notion of inheritance in Matthew. Daley's work aims to broach the subject in a pervasive manner, bridging gaps between the Hebrew Bible, Second Temple Jewish literature, and the New Testament (p. 3). In doing so he intends to present a 'fairly comprehensive picture of inheritance' in the Apocrypha, Pseudepigrapha, and Dead Sea Scrolls (p. 4) but regards Matthew as 'the climax of this study' because its notion of inheritance is important to understanding the work in its Jewish context. In his methodological discussion (pp. 37–43), the author helpfully articulates his intent to allow for the fluidity of language while avoiding pigeon-holing specific terms into singular meanings or reducing inheritance concepts to a pre-conceived set of lexemes (p. 39). In this respect, the book is 'focused on concepts and themes' rather than particular words, per se, though he rightly acknowledges the need for considerable attention on the uses of words (p. 39).

In Daley's second chapter, 'Inheritance in the Hebrew Bible' (pp. 45–108), he finds that God himself is the primary provider of inheritances (נחל), even where it is mediated through ancestry. This applies to land and property through tribes, clans, and family. He finds that in the Hexateuch priority is given to land, while in the Former Prophets the people, the land, and all that is God's are entrusted to the king as an inheritance. In the Latter Prophets the exile and subsequent loss of land accentuate the notion that inheritance transcends land, and inheritance is cast in terms of eschatological hope and includes non-Israelites (e.g., Ezek. 47:21–23). In all instances, Daley remarks, a relational component with respect to God himself is foundational.

The Second Temple Jewish material is devoted to selections from the Apocrypha and Pseudepigrapha (ch. 3) and the Qumran literature (ch. 4). Inheritance in the former works sometimes reflects the land priority of the Hebrew Bible (Judith), but at other times focuses more closely on Jerusalem or the temple (1 Maccabees and Psalms of Solomon). The books also differ over whether the inheritance is 'this-worldly' (1 Enoch, Tobit, 1 Maccabees) or 'other-worldly' (Psalms of Solomon; p. 149). Why these Second Temple texts were chosen and others excluded is not entirely clear. In the Qumran literature (ch. 4, pp. 153–237) Daley finds inheritance terms more theological than material, rooted in identity and bestowed by God upon his covenant people. In this respect inheritance serves a rhetorical role, and 'the primary focus of inheritance in the Scrolls (esp. Instruction, 4QMysteries, the Community Rule) is on the ability of those who pursue God and his wisdom and righteousness to become members of the heavenly community and have a share in a reconstituted earth' (p. 237).

Chapter 5, 'Inheritance in the Gospel of

Matthew' (pp. 239–356), is the climax of this book. Here the author delves into the key 'inheritance' texts of Matthew, richly informed by his previous discussions. For Matthew 5:5 (pp. 239–302) Daley explores makarisms in Matthew and 'antecedent traditions' (p. 302). For him, those 'meek' who 'inherit the earth' (Matt. 5:5) are those presently participating in the heavenly kingdom, who will receive their inheritance from God himself, as a gift, through Jesus. In short, the 'inheritance is promised to those who follow God and live in an ethical way' (p. 305). The inheritance of eternal life (Matt. 19:29) is to be equated with a kingdom inheritance acquired by following Jesus (pp. 320–321). The inheritance sought by the wicked tenants (Matt. 21:38) is regarded as 'all that is owned by God' (the Kingdom of God, pp. 321–337). The violent usurpers of this inheritance stand in sharp contrast with the meek disciples, who humbly rely on Jesus whose inheritance they hope to share (p. 337).

Delves into 'inheritance' texts of Matthew

In the sheep-and-goats pericope (Matt. 25:31–46) those on the king's right hand inherit the kingdom prepared for them (Matt. 25:34). Here Daley sees 'inheriting the kingdom' (25:34) as synonymous with 'eternal life' (Matt. 27:46), which also 'implies a special aspect of the kingdom of God' (p. 353). The passage, therefore, looks forward to a life in a reconstituted world 'in relationship to God, as Father, who gifts his children with an inheritance in the age to come' (p. 353). In his conclusion to this chapter (pp. 353–356) Daley argues that inheritance language represents 'a single theological purpose' in Matthew, where it consistently refers to the kingdom of God/heaven, with various aspects elucidated in each. Primarily this entails the fact that the kingdom is a gift given by God to his people as a result of his unique relationship with them. Inheritance rightly belongs to Jesus, but he shares it with his followers as a 'reward for their commitment to him and their pursuit of his ideal, which is true discipleship and "greater righteousness"' (p. 354).

The conclusion (ch. 6) is called 'Matthew and the Promise of Discipleship' (pp. 357–363). In it the author rehearses the importance of the respective Judaic contexts from which Matthew's inheritance conceptions emerge and against which they may be compared. He underscores the importance of inheritance not for identifying an alleged community for which the evangelist writes but to contribute to Matthew's ideal of discipleship, which envisions an expansion of Judaism rather than a break from it. He concludes that inheritance in Matthew is an aid for identifying 'ideal disciples' and underscores the relational nature of one's status as a member of a particular community and child of God (pp. 360–363). The book ends with a complete bibliography (pp. 365–386) and indices (pp. 387–403).

This is a fine volume; well-written and compelling. The reader encounters familiar and well-established themes such as the kingdom and discipleship, and Daley successfully demonstrates how inheritance fits into these categories. Moreover, he surveys the breadth of disparate traditions from the Hebrew Bible and select Second Temple Jewish material. The majority of the book deals with inheritance outside of Matthew (pp. 45–237) which may not all be necessary for Daley's treatment of Matthew itself (pp. 1–43, 239–363). However, this material tills soil outside specialized Matthean studies and will serve as a valuable resource for research in these fields. This is a most welcome contribution to Matthean scholarship.

Daniel M. Gurtner
Gateway Seminary

BOOK REVIEWS

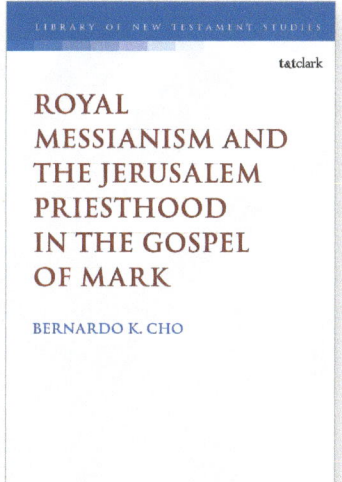

Bernardo K. Cho. *Royal Messianism and the Jerusalem Priesthood in the Gospel of Mark*. LNTS 607. London: T&T Clark, 2019. 256pp. ISBN 978-0-567-69639-7. Hardback, $130.00. Paperback, $40.95.

Royal Messianism and the Jerusalem Priesthood in the Gospel of Mark, a revised version of Cho's doctoral thesis at the University of Edinburgh, considers how Mark 'presents Jesus the messiah in relation to the priestly establishment' (p. 5). Cho's thesis is two-fold. First, royal messianism in the late Second Temple period held that the messiah would help the temple and priesthood achieve its ideal. Second, Mark expects this, but ends up blaming the rejection of Jesus by the priesthood for the temple's destruction.

Chapter one examines the Dead Sea Scrolls. Cho argues against the claim that the Qumran community has completely subordinated the royal messiah under the high priest. 4Q252, 4Q174, 4Q285, 4Q161, 1QSb, 1QS, CD, and 1QSa show that even though the community emphasizes the eschatological high priest, a diminished hope for a royal messiah does not follow. Furthermore, the community anticipated the eschatological high priest would come from their community while the royal messiah would be unknown until his coming.

The messianic king was expected to come and install the Qumran high priest as the head of ceremonial and sacrificial occasions. There would be no rivalry as the king and high priest exercise complementary functions.

Chapter two is on the Pseudepigrapha. The Psalms of Solomon 17 picture a Davidic messiah who would cleanse Jerusalem from both outside oppressors and immoral insiders. While there are no explicit references to priests, the psalm reflects traditions of temple-builder Solomon (17:31). It implicitly envisions the royal messiah would purge Jerusalem and install a pure priesthood. The Similitudes of Enoch are considered but dismissed as irrelevant. 4 Ezra and 2 Baruch contain a tradition that envisions a new Jerusalem and a new temple, complete with new paraphernalia (2 Bar. 6:7). God is the builder, but the messiah 'would be a perfect fit for this picture' (75). Cho concludes part one by emphasizing that none of the documents claim that the royal messiah would be the high priest or make the temple redundant and that the 'consistent pattern' is 'whenever awaiting the coming of the eschatological king, the literature also anticipates the restoration of the Israelite worship system' (p. 76).

In chapter three, Cho looks at the messiahship of Jesus in Markan Christology to establish the 'importance of royal messianism to Mark' (p. 78). Cho asserts that 'Son of God' in Mark refers to Israel's eschatological king, based on the use of Psalm 2 in Mark 1:11 (also 9:7) and the close association of the kingdom of God with 'Son of God' (1:1, 15). While the phrase 'son of David' or similar occurs three times in Mark (10:46–52; 11:9–10; 12:35–37), Cho asserts that these passages confirm the identification of Jesus as the son of David.

> **'Son of God' refers to Israel's eschatological king.**

In chapter four, Cho examines Mark 1–10. He argues, despite few references to the temple or priesthood, that Mark does not repudiate the temple establishment; instead, Mark's narrative hopes that the priests will repent and acknowledge Jesus. In Mark 1:1–8, the ministries of John and Jesus are placed within the context of Jewish hopes for the restoration of Zion through the quotations of Malachi 3 and Isaiah 40. In Mark 1:40–44, Jesus sends a cleansed leper to offer sacrifices. Thus, Jesus does not reject the temple establishment, and Jesus calls the priests to repentance ('as a witness to them,' 1:44). In Mark 2:22–23, the recollection of Abiathar/Ahimelech shows the authority of the chosen king of Israel. As Ahimelech was deferential to David, so the priests should be towards Jesus.

In chapter five, Cho explores the interactions between Jesus and the priests in Mark 11–16. He notes the lack of welcome given to Jesus upon his entrance to the temple (Mark 11:11) in light of the expectation of priests giving a benediction to the messiah at the temple (Ps. 117:25–26 LXX). Cho views the overturning of tables as symbolic of God's impending judgment (see Jeremiah 7:11), but not because of immoral (financial) practices. The priests constitute a 'cave of bandits' conspiring to kill the messiah. In Mark 11:27–33, Jesus rebukes the priests for the lack of belief in John's baptism, and, consequently, in himself. Mark 12:1–9 draws on language from Isaiah 5:1–7, a proclamation of judgment for infidelity. In the context of Mark 11:27–12:9, these leaders are the Jerusalem establishment, and they are rejected for despising the heir to the vineyard. Cho argues that the points of the charge of blasphemy by the high priest is its illegitimacy. The high priest still convicts Jesus even though to claim to be the messiah was not blasphemy. Jesus does not reject the temple. Instead, 'the priests' negative response to Jesus as the royal messiah is…what lies at the centre of Jesus's criticism of the temple' (p. 205).

Mark is well known for how messiahship is redefined in the relation to the cross. Jesus' interaction with the temple and priests is similar, Cho argues. How can Jesus be the messiah if the temple is not restored and about to be destroyed? Mark the Jewish authorities' rejection of Jesus.

Cho's book is well-researched and well-written. The work is clear, and the argument is easy to follow. A major strength of Cho's work is in his attention to how Mark draws from the same passages from the Jewish Scriptures throughout the gospel. The Second Temple texts considered have some gaps. For example, the argument would be improved by including the relationship between the messiahs of Judah and Levi in the Testaments of the Twelve Patriarchs. Furthermore, if the reader holds that one cannot read the larger context of a citation from the Jewish Scriptures, then many of Cho's arguments will fall flat. In total, however, the book makes a cogent argument and is worth study for anyone interested in messianism in Mark.

Devlin R. McGuire
Princeton Theological Seminary

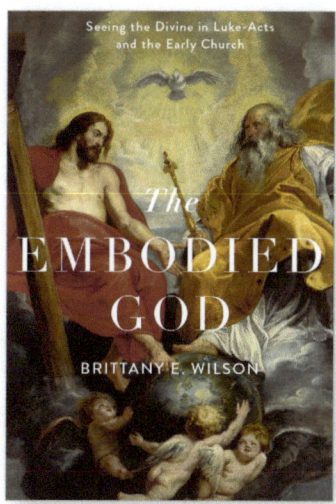

Brittany E. Wilson. *The Embodied God: Seeing the Divine in Luke-Acts and the Early Church.* New York: Oxford University Press, 2022. 360pp. ISBN: 9780190080822. £64.00.

Brittany E. Wilson's *The Embodied God* explores the various ways God is seen in Luke-Acts, arguing that God in Luke-Acts is visually experienced, fluid and diverse in manifestation, and seen most fully in the person of Jesus. Drawing upon the recent studies of God's embodiment in the Old Testament, Wilson argues that God in Luke-Acts becomes manifest in various theophanies, attributes (e.g. Wisdom, Word, Glory, Name, Power, and Spirit), angels and exalted humans (e.g. Jesus). This understanding of God's embodiment is in contrast to the influence of Platonism on Christian thought, which understands God as invisible and deemphasises the physicality of Jesus. The book is divided into two parts, both parts being three chapters long, with the visibility of God and Jesus being addressed, respectively.

After the introduction, which outlines the various historical and academic positions on God's visibility, chapter one explores the connection between the invisibility of God and idolatry. Wilson convincingly argues that Acts does not associate idolatry with the invisibility of God, rather the key issue at stake with idolatry is that humans create idols, which violates the idea that God is the creator. The Lystran episode (Acts 14:8–18) is also addressed, where Wilson argues that the Lystrans' idolatry derives from their identification of Paul and Barnabas with gods, and not in the Lystran's general openness to divine epiphanies.

Next, in chapter two, Wilson focuses on six key theophanic moments in Luke-Acts, where God becomes visible in different forms. Wilson outlines how Luke crafts the narratives of Jesus' birth, baptism and transfiguration, to highlight the revelation gained through seeing God. Likewise, a similar emphasis on seeing is found in the single theophany in Acts, Stephen's speech before the Jerusalem council, which is bookended and filled with the language of seeing God.

In chapter three, Wilson wades into the contested area of divine fluidity and intermediary figures in Second Temple Judaism and in Luke-Acts. Wilson argues that there was a significant stream of Second Temple Judaism that had a form of inclusive monotheism, where God's divinity was fluid, finding expressions in the divine attributes, angels, and exalted humans. This understanding of inclusive monotheism and divine fluidity is applied to Luke-Acts, where Wilson argues that God often takes on many forms through intermediary figures in Luke-Acts, most particularly through Jesus as an exalted human who embodies the divine attributes of God.

Chapter four more fully addresses the implications of chapters one through three for Luke's presentation of Jesus' divinity. Wilson explores the epiphanic glimpses of Jesus' divinity (e.g. the transfiguration) before his resurrection, arguing that the Lukan Jesus manifests something of the God of Israel from his conception, and so, is more than a human figure that is exalted at the end of their life.

The resurrection scenes in Luke 24 are then addressed, where Wilson notes that Jesus' divinity is more explicit and at the same time, harder for characters in the Gospel to find and discern. As Wilson states, 'Jesus's body remains hidden yet also revealed, a revelation in hiddenness' (p. 190).

In tension with chapter four's emphasis on the divinity of Jesus, chapter five addresses Jesus' human body, where Wilson argues that Luke does not have a clear docetic tendency. Focusing on the body of Jesus in the Gospel of Luke, Wilson argues that Luke highlights the humanity of Jesus in his birth, the visible spectacle of Jesus' crucifixion and the fleshiness of Jesus' resurrection. In light of chapters four and five, Wilson argues that both 'Jesus's body is more human than God's body' (p. 229) and that 'it is difficult to distinguish completely between God's body and Jesus's body' (p. 230). Jesus is both the fullest expression of God in Luke-Acts, but also, by taking on flesh, becomes more embodied than God.

While chapters four and five focused on the divinity and humanity of Jesus respectively in the Gospel of Luke, chapter six follows these arguments by exploring the Christophanies in Acts. Here, Wilson argues that these Christophanies are both very similar to Luke-Acts' theophanies, which draw attention to Jesus' divinity, and also dissimilar, in that Jesus still has a human form. That is, Jesus' flesh and bones remain even in his exalted position at the right hand of the Father.

Wilson's main argument, that God in Luke-Acts is not invisible, but rather, that God is embodied, is convincing. Moreover, the fluidity and fragmentation of God opens the door for further research into the interaction between God's various fragmentations and the followers of Jesus in Acts. Wilson argues that Wisdom and the Spirit can all be understood as manifestations of God, and yet, Wilson focuses mainly on how these manifestations are found in Jesus. Further research could explore the implications of, for example, Stephen being full of the Spirit and Wisdom (Acts 6:3) and having a face like an angel (Acts 6:15), for God's fluidity in the followers of Jesus. Overall, Wilson's book is clearly written and engagingly brings the current research on God's body to Luke-Acts.

John D. Griffiths
Alphacrucis University College

BOOK REVIEWS

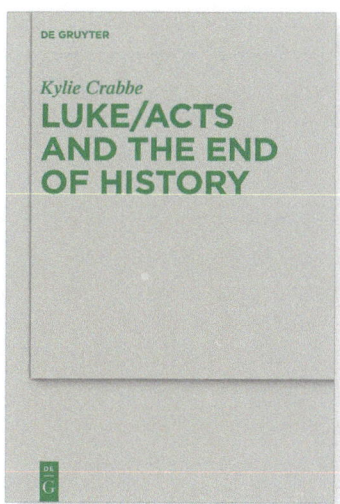

Kylie Crabbe. *Luke/Acts and the End of History*. BZNW 238. Berlin/Boston: Walter de Gruyter, 2019. xvii + 418 pp. ISBN 978-3-11-061455-8 (hardcover). 89.95 €.

Kylie Crabbe's *Luke/Acts and the End of History*, a revised version of her 2017 Oxford doctoral thesis, aims to shed light on Luke's eschatology by focusing on the Lukan notion of history in comparison with ten roughly contemporaneous texts. The ten texts—five non-Jewish and five Jewish—with which Crabbe compares Luke/Acts are these: the *Histories* of Polybius (second century BCE), *The Library of History* by Diodorus Siculus (first century BCE), Virgil's *Aeneid* (late first century BCE), *Memorable Deeds and Sayings* compiled by Valerius Maximus (circa 30 CE), the *Histories* of Tacitus (105–109 CE), 2 Maccabees (late second century to early first century BCE), the Qumran War Scroll or 1QM (circa mid-first century BCE), Josephus' *Jewish War* (late-70s CE), 4 Ezra (circa 100 CE), and 2 Baruch (early second century CE). Scanning this selection of texts, one notes their generic diversity. This is a deliberate feature of Crabbe's cross-genre methodological approach, which she adopts to take account of various conceptions of history evident in Luke's socio-cultural milieu. Hers is also a case-study approach, limiting attention to ten non-Lukan texts that enable her to discuss each text in relative detail, thereby facilitating closer comparison between the case-study texts themselves as well as between them and Luke/Acts.

Crabbe opens her study by drawing attention to two scholarly trends that in her view have contributed either to misconstruing Lukan eschatology or to displacing its significance for understanding Luke/Acts. The first of these takes its bearings from Hans Conzelmann's influential thesis that Luke/Acts reflects a response to evident postponement of the imminently anticipated *parousia* by downplaying this expectation, thereby emphasizing the salvation-historical role of the church. The second trend is the more recent focus on the genre of Luke/Acts, especially in comparison with Graeco-Roman historical texts, with minimal attention given to eschatological themes. On both trends, Crabbe has valuable things to say. Concerning Conzelmann and the reception of his thesis regarding Luke/Acts, she shows how the socio-political context of post-WW2 Europe shaped scholarly perspectives during a defining period in Lukan studies. Moreover, her contention that more recent attention to the genre of Luke/Acts has effectively reinforced Conzelmann's depiction of an "eschatology-lite" Luke warrants careful consideration. At times, however, Crabbe inclines to overstatement, for example, when she characterizes the effect of Conzelmann's conception of Lukan eschatology as a "separation of history from eschatology" (p. 3), or when she refers to 'the basic premise [of Conzelmann] that Luke divorces history from eschatology' (p. 9). In Conzelmann's construal of Lukan eschatology, history still points toward the *parousia*, even though history takes centre stage because the *parousia* is perceived to be postponed. Perhaps in Conzelmann's view on Luke, as Crabbe claims late in her book, 'the end has become so distant as to be irrelevant' (p. 339). Even here, however, one wonders whether Crabbe correctly captures Conzelmann's conception of the third stage in Luke's story of salvation history, clearly identified in the introduction to *Die Mitte der Zeit* (1954) as the evidently extended interval between the ascension of Jesus and his *parousia*.

Crabbe appreciates the importance of genre for responsible interpretation, especially of texts from antiquity. She recognizes that generic conventions of literary form and content evoke readers' expectations and thereby circumscribe, to some extent, how a text will be received and understood. Her concern, however, is that considerations regarding genre tend toward literary classification either as an end in itself or as an overly rigid interpretive constraint, especially with respect to content. While certain themes may predominate in texts of a particular genre, identification of a text's genre does not—or should not—prescribe what themes one will find expressed therein. As Crabbe contends, 'numerous elements of a text transcend genre' (p. 28). Hence her attention to a cross-generic selection of texts to compare with Luke/Acts. Her argument is shaped by a determination not to permit genre considerations to delimit either the themes she considers or the types of texts she compares with Luke/Acts. In this connection, however, it is curious that *none* of the texts chosen by Crabbe for comparison with Luke/Acts is an ancient *bios*. Her own description of the range of texts selected from the Graeco-Roman period is as follows: 'Greek and Latin historiography, popular exempla, Latin epic, Jewish Hellenistic historiography, Dead Sea Scrolls, and Jewish apocalypses' (p. 19).

> **Aims to shed light on Luke's eschatology.**

From Crabbe's title, one immediately notices her departure from the close to century-long convention since Cadbury of referring to the Gospel according to Luke and the Acts of the Apostles as Luke–Acts. Regarding the relationship between Luke and Acts, Crabbe considers them a compositional unity, two integrally related parts of a historiographical whole. Since the earliest extant manuscript evidence does not indicate that Luke's Gospel and Acts were received as a literary unity, however, she refers to this two-part work as Luke/Acts. She dates both volumes to the final three decades of the first century CE and presumes Luke's dependence on Mark's Gospel, although she does not rely heavily on argumentation based on redaction-critical inferences. Rather, she reads Luke/Acts in narrative terms and treats the two-part work in its entirety as historiography. In this connection, one cannot help but wonder whether this generic consideration explains the absence of a single *bios* among Crabbe's case-study texts or whether this judgment is partly the consequence of choosing not to compare Luke/Acts with any ancient *bioi*.

Chapters 3–6 compose the body of Crabbe's book. In each of these chapters she compares Luke/Acts with her selected case-study texts on one of the four following themes: the direction and shape of history; determinism and divine guidance of history; human responsibility within history or, put differently, the interaction within history of divine and human agency; and finally, the relationship between the present and the end of history. In broad structural terms, chapter 3 on discerning a sense of direction in history finds its natural complement in chapter 6 on the relationship between the present and the end of history, whereas chapters 4 and 5 focus, respectively, on divine and human agency within history. All four of these chapters follow a similar, albeit not uniform, pattern in which introductory matters relating to the relevant theme are initially outlined, the case-study texts are then discussed in various combinations, depending on how they illustrate the particular theme under consideration, which leads into a culminating section on the theme of the chapter as it features in Luke/Acts. Throughout, Crabbe's discussions of the ten non-Lukan texts are intrinsically interesting and invariably informative, even though her principal concern is the insight one gains from comparing Luke/Acts to these other texts.

What emerges from Crabbe's comparative evaluation is that, although the Lukan literature has its own distinctives, with respect to history and eschatology Luke/Acts aligns more closely with Jewish than with non-Jewish texts. Engagement with her ten case-study texts also comes at a cost, which is that her discussion of key Lukan texts is somewhat limited. Especially evident is her rather sketchy treatment of major eschatological texts in Luke/Acts, especially Luke 12:35–48 (not discussed, though occasionally referenced); 17:20–18:8 (six paragraphs); 19:11–27 (three paragraphs); 21:5–36 (five or six paragraphs); and Acts 2:14–21 (not discussed, though occasionally referenced). To be fair, the primary focus of Crabbe's discussion of Lukan texts relating to the return of the Son of Man is timing, that is, indications of imminent or postponed eschatological expectation. Furthermore, her discussions of these passages, brief though they are, evince astute exegetical insight and balanced interpretive judgment. Even so, across these texts several exegetical and interpretive cruxes are either ignored or treated in cursory fashion. In view of Crabbe's clear conception of Luke's eschatological convictions, one hopes that she returns to some of these texts to address them in more depth and detail.

Insofar as Lukan scholars continue to take their interpretive bearings from Conzelmann, Crabbe is correct: Luke's interest in history is not at odds with imminent eschatological expectation but is rather inextricable from it. The end of history—the goal to which history is oriented due to divine agency in the Christ-event—bestows upon human agency within history direction, meaning, and purpose. Moreover, eschatology is a central, not peripheral, Lukan concern. In consequence, Luke's attitudes toward Roman imperialism, human suffering, morality, and other topics pertaining to life between the resurrection of Jesus and his return warrant more circumspect and nuanced attention, especially in light of Luke's indeterminate but imminent, and hence 'utopian,' eschatological outlook.

In a brief concluding chapter, Crabbe recapitulates her argument regarding Luke's eschatology and its far-reaching moral and socio-political effects, reappraises and reaffirms her comparative cross-genre method of analysis, and reflects on how post-WW2 concerns about 'salvation history' continue to influence Lukan studies. Her monograph closes with five appendices surveying key temporal terminology in the Gospels and Acts, a fairly extensive bibliography, and three standard indices (ancient sources, modern authors, and subjects). Though lengthy and intricate, this substantial volume is clearly composed and contains but a few typographical errors. With this book Crabbe joins a select number of Australian scholars to have written landmark works on Luke/Acts, and regarding Luke's conception of the relation between history and eschatology her study should be added to the list of must-read titles.

David Neville
St Mark's National Theological Centre
Charles Sturt University, Canberra

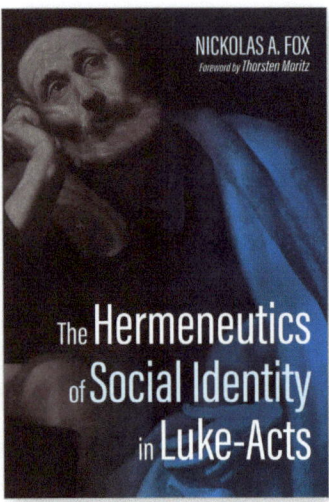

Nickolas A. Fox. *The Hermeneutics of Social Identity in Luke-Acts.* Eugene, OR: Pickwick Publications, 2021. 289pp. ISBN 978-1-7252-7863-9. $36.00. £27.00.

In this book, Nickolas A. Fox engages readers from two perspectives: scholarship and devotion (p. xv). The book, divided into five chapters as well as a detailed introduction and a conclusion, establishes that 'Luke-Acts was written primarily for the purposes of creating identity for a God-fearing audience within the New Christian Movement of the first century CE' (p. 1). This masterpiece employs Social Identity Theory (SIT) and offers a fresh perspective for understanding the purpose of Luke-Acts.

Chapter one lays the foundation for Fox's application of SIT in this study and why it matters for identity formation in Acts. Building on Assmann's argument on communicative memory (sharing memoirs from the proximate past with contemporaries), and cultural memory (sharing memories/stories from group origins), Fox insists that the latter makes it possible for the God-fearers (who did not know Jesus during his earthly ministry, and who did not share in Jewish customs), to share in the identity-forming experiences through group narratives. As he indicates, 'this is key for social identity formation and allows for ongoing group membership generations after the foundational events took place' (p. 15). The chapter also explores four categories of group beliefs (norms, values, goals, and ideology) through which Fox elucidates the assertion that 'as individuals begin to adopt the claims of the group and live in new ways that are consistent with the behaviours practiced and prescribed by the group, they identify socially with the group, and social identity is formed' (p. 34). By implication, when new members participate in the cultural memory of a group the new members are able to share in the group's history and so benefit from the social identity the group affords its members (p. 52).

Having laid a solid foundation in chapter one, the second chapter focuses on God-fearers as the ideal audience of Luke-Acts. God-fearers are a subgroup who are attracted to Judaism and the synagogue but have not become converts. As such 'they presented a great opportunity for Christian evangelists' (p. 53). This chapter also offers insight into the decentralisation of the Jewish establishment, thus allowing for the inclusion of the marginalised (p. 63). Here, Fox affirms that, 'To the degree that it can be shown that Luke-Acts focuses on the decentralisation of the Jewish power structures and creates space for outsiders, specifically God-fearers, Luke is involved in identity formation for the God-fearing reader' (p. 64). He also makes the point that minor characters in Luke's narrative who are marginal people themselves (children, women, the poor) serve Luke's identity-forming purpose for his God-fearing audience, who are marginalised themselves. As minor characters take a lead role in the narrative, the audience sees itself in these characters and is invited into the story of Jesus and the early church (p. 65).

The question may be asked: Why is Luke-Acts so concerned with connections to Israel and the Hebrew Scriptures, if God-fearers are his focus? This is the focal point of chapter three where Fox contends that, 'to the degree that Luke utilises the framing stories of Israel and her scriptures for his audience, he is utilising cultural memory and creating social identity' (p. 89). He further examines Luke's gospel, with particular focus on the canticles and infancy narrative and strongly asserts that, 'To the degree that we see Luke rooting his story of all humanity in Jewish salvation history, he is educating his readers on the narrative trajectory that will include outsiders and lead to the climax of human history' (p. 91). As he argues, God-fearers are thus invited to join with the community of the early church and have their social identity formed, becoming full members of the body of Christ (p. 141).

In chapter four, Fox draws attention to Luke's use of prototypical characters and exemplars to create social identity for God-fearers. Cornelius is the primary prototype for God-fearers; Peter and Paul are prototypical and serve for the inclusion of both Jews and Gentiles in the early church (p. 144); Jesus is also a prototypical figure in the narrative (p. 145). As Fox argues, this strategy helps to 'form social identity in the readers by drawing on their empathy with key characters in the story, even and especially where those characters are almost inevitably "minor" in status' (p. 142). Chapter five then explores how and to what extent Luke emulates the rhetorical convention of the literary world of the first century. Examining speeches in Acts, particularly Acts 7:2–53 (Stephen), and Acts 13:16b–41 (Paul), Fox asserts that these speeches 'tell the story of Jewish salvation history through the lens of the New Christian Movement for the creation of social identity in the God-fearing readers' (p. 3). He demonstrates that Luke utilises the tools of Graeco-Roman rhetoric to his advantage, which strongly supports his argument for God-fearers as the intentional audience of Luke-Acts.

This is an excellent contribution to the current scholarly trend of employing social scientific principles and theories in the study of the New Testament. Fox rightly observes that the presence of different subgroups constituted division and resistance within the community. This challenge (as Luke shows) ensued with the admission of 'outsiders' into the larger community. From my reading, a more detailed consideration of this challenge would have rendered more plausible such assertions as 'outsiders do not become Jewish, but rather, Jews and Gentiles (including God-fearers) are subsumed under the superordinate group of the Way' (p. 64). This also applies to the obvious role of the Spirit especially for the creation of identity in Luke-Acts which is absent in Fox's work. Notwithstanding, this insightful work provides a strong and convincing argument for God-fearers as the focus-audience of Luke-Acts. This study is as rigorous in its scholarship as it is devotionally inspiring. Fox has undoubtedly stirred up grounds for further study of the themes of 'God-fearers' and 'purpose' in Luke-Acts.

Francis Otobo
Yarra Theological Union, University of Divinity, Melbourne

J. D. Atkins. *The Doubt of the Apostles and the Resurrection Faith of the Early Church: The Post-Resurrection Appearance Stories of the Gospels in Ancient Reception and Modern Debate.* WUNT 2.495. Tübingen: Mohr Siebeck, 2019. 569pp. ISBN 978-3-16-158165-6. 109.00 €

In this revised 2017 thesis from Marquette, Atkins tackles the themes of doubt and faith in the resurrection accounts of the Gospels. The primary focus of this book is whether the post-resurrection stories of Luke and John were shaped to counter docetic views. Both accounts feature doubts that are met with physical actions: either eating or the invitation to touch Jesus' wounds. Commentators have surmised that the physicality of these proofs was a direct response to docetic views that denied a physical bodily resurrection. In addition, many have asserted that the doubts of the apostles serve to enhance the believability of these accounts. Atkins sets out to test these hypotheses through a study of reception history. He compares these Gospel accounts with both pro- and anti-docetic texts from the early history of the church, with his conclusion being that an anti-docetic agenda does not fit with the way that Luke and John tell their stories.

Atkins begins by outlining early docetic views and gnostic views that similarly reject a bodily resurrection. The same chapter also covers early Christian perspectives on doubt. Here the conclusion is that early Christian attitudes to doubt were always negative. Thus, he argues that the idea that the resurrection accounts are made more convincing through presenting those who were sceptical but became convinced is incompatible with the attitudes of early Christians. Indeed, the doubts of the apostles could be exploited by docetic writers to argue their views.

The main section of the book (Part II) is a reception history of these resurrection stories in the context of early docetic and gnostic debates. This is an extensive and wide-ranging study, covering many early texts with substantial references, such that this volume is twice the length of many in this series. The first chapter presents two readings of the resurrection appearances, one docetic and the other anti-docetic. The former comes in the description of gnostic views in Irenaeus *Haer.* 1.30, where Atkins argues the views represented entail a rewriting of Luke that accepts the witness of the Apostles but rejects their interpretation of the resurrection. The anti-docetic text is Ignatius *Smyrn.* 3–5. Ignatius uses Luke 24, but with redaction that seems aimed at countering docetic ideas as well as omitting apostolic doubt. Atkins argues these texts point to Luke 24 as not ideal for anti-docetic use, requiring modification, while also being open to docetic interpretations.

The next chapter broadens the range of texts explored to other proto-orthodox writers that have some anti-docetic elements. These include 1 Clement, The Preaching of Peter, Justin Martyr, Theophilus of Antioch, (Ps-)Athenagoras of Athens, Irenaeus, and 3 Corinthians. Atkins examines how the resurrection stories are used, noting that they are often absent from defences against docetic views. He points as well to a consistent removal of apostolic doubt in apologetic contexts, and a greater focus on the idea of OT fulfilment rather than physical proofs of the resurrection. This is contrasted in the following chapter with gnostic reception of the resurrection accounts which use the doubt motif as a means to expand gnostic ideas, characterising doubt as an opportunity. This is demonstrated from texts including: *The Apocryphon of John*, the *Gospel of Mary*, *Letter of Peter to Philip*, *Treatise on the Resurrection*, Heracleon's *Commentary on John*, and the *Tripartite Tractate*.

Chapters continue to alternate between pro- and anti-docetic views, with chapter 6 examining readings of Luke 24 in Tertullian, *Against Marcion*, and (Ps-)Justin, *On the Resurrection*. Both of these texts seek to counter docetic readings of Luke 24 as depicting *phantasma/phantasia*. Atkins highlights the way that these debates are an 'exegetical battle over Luke 24' (p. 235), showing that both sides could appeal to the canonical resurrection accounts. Chapter 7 deals with the *Acts of John*. The *Acts of John* uses the idea of non-recognition in John 21 to introduce a polymorphic Jesus, as well as adding a docetising reading whereby when John touches Jesus, it is not a solid body. The final chapter of the section addresses Mark's longer ending and the *Epistula Apostolorum*. Atkins argues that the longer ending emphasises doubt more than other texts do, yet it still presents it as a problem that needs to be resolved. Similarly, the *Epistula Apostolorum* gives space to doubt as a problem or a liability. There are attempts to mitigate the doubt of the apostles in comparison to the Markan longer ending.

Part III seeks to bring the evidence together to make a final argument. In chapter 9, Atkins strongly counters the view that Luke 24 and/or John 20 are constructed to deliberately counter docetic views. The comparisons with other texts that have that explicit aim show significant differences. Later texts remove the element of Jesus' abrupt appearance, add more references to *sarx*, as well as including explicitly touching Jesus' body and confirming that the body is real flesh. Doubt is never seen as positive in any pre-250 Christian texts, and thus its inclusion cannot have an apologetic motivation, as does its omission in many later texts. The risen Jesus eating food, which perhaps has the best case for being an anti-docetic element, is not an issue for the docetists in the texts examined. As Atkins argues, the reality of anti-docetic discourse does not always align with modern assumptions. He concludes that neither Luke nor John modifies tradition in an anti-docetic direction, and indeed they sometimes make it susceptible to such an interpretation.

Chapter 10 offers a new reading of Luke and John that does not begin from assumptions of anti-docetic apologetics. For Luke, Atkins points to the central role of fulfilment, setting this in the context of a general early Christian attitude of the "epistemic priority of prophecy over physical proofs" (413). Even while the eating proof has a role, it requires the support of Scripture. In John, meanwhile, Jesus' humanity is assumed, rather than being something to believe. In the scene with Thomas there is no need to narrate the touching because it is seeing Jesus pierced that reveals his divinity, following Zech 12:10. The primary thrust of the resurrection appearances, according to Atkins, is fulfilment rather than the physicality of the resurrection.

Overall, Atkins' argument against an anti-docetic reading of the resurrection accounts is compelling. He demonstrates persuasively that the way the way these texts were used by ancient authors within their arguments over docetic views does not align with modern assumptions upon which the anti-docetic reading rests.

One flaw in the book is that it assumes a cognitive perspective on belief. The short section which provides context on belief in early Christianity has little reference to ongoing discussions of belief terminology. Most striking is the absence of Teresa Morgan's work on faith, and the concomitant highlighting of active and relational dimensions of faith.[1]

---

1   Teresa Morgan, *Roman Faith and Christian Faith: Pistis and Fides in the Early Roman Empire and Early Churches* (Oxford: Oxford University Press, 2015).

Now this does not undermine the entire project, in part because the author concludes that the aim of these resurrection stories is not to argue against Docetism. However, the framing of belief in purely cognitive terms is evident throughout the book, and influences how questions are asked, as well as shaping the reading of these passages that the author proposes. This is not to deny the significance of the idea of fulfillment that the author identifies in the resurrection accounts, but it does raise the possibility that the reading Atkins argues for is only one aspect of the faith that these passages depict or seek to evoke in their audiences.

As a technical monograph, this book will primarily be of interest for scholars and doctoral researchers. As well as biblical scholars, especially those with an interest in reception history, the argument of the book is relevant for those who are concerned with the apologetic or homiletical uses of these passages.

Christopher Seglenieks
Bible College of South Australia

BOOK REVIEWS

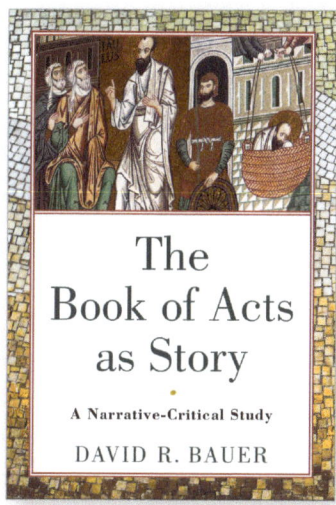

David R. Bauer. *The Book of Acts as Story: A Narrative-Critical Study.* Grand Rapids: Baker Academic, 2021. 284pp.
ISBN 978-0-8010-9832-1. €30.64. $32.99.

Narrative criticism on the book of Acts has been conducted for years, but David Bauer claims to be the first to study the entire book from the point of view of narrative criticism.[1] Bauer intends his book to be a narrative-critical commentary on the book of Acts and succeeds in doing so in a concise way with many helpful insights.

After a short introduction, the book opens with a chapter dealing with some preliminaries regarding Acts: its relation to the Gospel of Luke and its genre. Date and authorship are not covered, presumably because they are not considered relevant to a narrative-critical reading – although Bauer does seek to acquire 'the level of knowledge and the kind of perspective that the author assumed his intended readers would have' (p. 5), and one might argue that this level and perspective would not be entirely the same if these readers were situated in the early sixties or in the mid-second century. Bauer suggests that Acts is the second volume of a two-volume work, with a distinct message but not fully understandable without knowledge of the Gospel. It is historiography (and not, like the gospel, biography), although in a footnote Bauer rightly notes that these genres are not clearly delineated and the two-volume work should be considered as a blending of the historical and biographical.

The second chapter introduces narrative criticism as a method, with helpful discussions of plot, characterization and setting. Interestingly, Bauer notes that Luke employs settings ironically, such as when he makes a prison the setting for God's deliverance or meals the setting for division or murder. Commenting on the narrator (who is identical to the implied author in Acts, according to Bauer), Bauer notes that the we-passages suggest 'real but limited association' (p. 36) of the narrator with Paul; through the first-person speech, he 'assumes the role of an eyewitness' (p. 37). He discusses various forms of point of view and the rhetorical devices employed in the narrative, and observes that Luke imitates both the classical Greek writers, suggesting the relevance of the narrative for the Greek world, and the Semitic style of the Old Testament, suggesting that it is the full realization of the salvation-historical narrative of the Old Testament.

> **A narrative-critical commentary.**

The third chapter discusses the literary structure of Acts. Bauer proceeds from Acts 1:8 and divides the book in three units, Acts 1 as introduction, followed by 2-12 (witness in Jerusalem, Judea and Samaria) and 13-28 (the Gospel on its way to the end of the earth,

---

1. He notes R.C. Tannehill, *The Narrative Unity of Luke-Acts: A Literary Interpretation* (2 vols; Philadelphia: Fortress, 1986–90) and F. Scott Spencer, *Journeying through Acts: A Literary-Cultural Reading* (Peabody, MA: Hendrickson, 2004) as related works. Also related but absent from Bauer's book are U.E. Eisen, *Die Poetik der Apostelgeschichte: eine narratologische Studie* (NTOA 58; Fribourg: Academic Press; Göttingen: Vandenhoeck & Ruprecht: 2006) and Jean-Noël Aletti, *Quand Luc raconte: le récit comme théologie* (Lire la Bible 115; Paris: Cerf, 1998).

which as such lies beyond Rome). A good case has also been made for Acts 15 as concluding the first half of the book, but Bauer does not discuss this interpretation.

In the subsequent chapters, Bauer provides running commentary on the narrative of Acts 1, Acts 2-7, Acts 8-12, and Acts 13-28. The commentary contains many good insights. One such insight is that conflicts, both internal and external to the Church, time and again result in missional advancement. Another is that the church in (Syrian) Antioch 'functions almost like a character in Acts', with 'well-defined features' and actions that 'significantly move the plot along' (p. 162). A main argument throughout the book is that the focus of Acts is on the actions of the exalted Lord, Jesus (and not on the actions of God). On page 16, Bauer includes a list of activities of Christ that propel the plot of Acts. However, this list includes Acts 3:26, that Jesus 'has been sent to Israel to bless Israel' (p. 16). That seems to be an action of God rather than of Jesus. In spite of Bauer's claim that 'God is not actually a character in the book' (p. 15), Christine Aarflot has recently published a fine book on the characterization of God in Acts.[2] It may be true that God does not act in the narrative itself, but Bauer underappreciates the extent to which actions are ascribed to God in the lengthy speeches of Acts.

The book demonstrates the added value of narrative criticism as supplement to historical-critical approaches. For example, it is helpful to think about the conflicts with Jews in Acts in terms of how conflicts contribute to the plot, rather than jumping to conclusions about the Christian-Jewish relationships in Luke's own context. The narrative should first be understood on its own terms, and then we can attempt to contextualize it in the context of the late first or beginning of the second century, an attempt that goes beyond what Bauer set out to do.

Apart from the clear and up-to-date introduction in narrative criticism, the book will be most helpful as commentary, to be consulted both for sermon preparation and for academic study of Acts. It is written in a fluent style with concise and cogent argumentation, supported by helpful graphs. I have not spotted any typos. The book is warmly recommended.

Arco den Heijer
Theological University Kampen

---

[2] C.A. Aarflot, *God (in) Acts: The Characterization of God in the Acts of the Apostles* (Eugene, OR: Pickwick, 2020).

BOOK REVIEWS

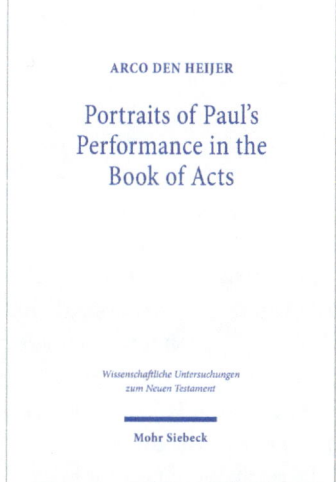

Arco den Heijer. *Portraits of Paul's Performance in the Book of Acts: Luke's Apologetic Strategy in the Depiction of Paul as Messenger of God.* WUNT 2.556. Tübingen: Mohr-Siebeck, 2021. 260 pp. 978-3-16-160859-9. €79.00.

While there have been a variety of studies devoted to the Lukan depiction of Paul asking questions about the relationship between 'the Paul of Acts' and 'the Paul of the Epistles' or examining the broader literary function Paul plays within the larger agenda of the Acts of the Apostles, this is the first study to apply the concept of 'performance' to the Lukan Paul. Den Heijer's research question stated simply is: 'How is Paul's performance portrayed in five episodes of the book of Acts, and what is the function of this depiction?' (p. 10). Den Heijer offers a helpful review of contemporary research on the concept of performance and offers the following summary: 'A performance is an action, or set of actions (including actions of speaking), done in a particular situation, in the presence of others, using cultural codes and conventions to communicate meaning to them' (p. 13). Den Heijer notes that Quintilian's work on rhetoric is a key source for performance in antiquity as he discusses the orator's delivery, setting, or context for the speech, and the use of cultural scripts and moral authority.

Den Heijer looks at five specific episodes where Paul's performance is on display. Paul in Paphos (Acts 13:6–12), Pisidian Antioch (13:14–52), Lystra (14:6–20), Athens (17:16–34), and Caesarea (25:23–26:32). I will set forth his method by looking at two of these episodes: Paphos and Athens.

The first case study, in chapter 2, is 'Performance in Paphos (Acts 13:6–12).' Den Heijer examines Paul's performance through the lens of the following categories (the same basic set of categories used for the following chapters as well): narrative context and structure, setting: place and location, setting: persons, performance, audience response, script, and function of Paul's portrait. Paul's performance on Paphos is structurally significant since this is the first episode where 'Saul' is referred to now as 'Paul' and is the first instance where Paul is depicted as enacting his role as God's messenger. This is related to the significance of the setting as a synagogue in that it highlights Paul's ministry to the Jewish people. Luke draws a contrast between Paul and Bar-Jesus as the latter is a deceiving false prophet. The Roman proconsul of Cyprus, Sergius Paulus, is notable for being one of the most elite persons in the book of Acts and one who rightly responds to Paul's message. Den Heijer notes two significant elements to Paul's performance. First, Luke refers to Paul's 'gaze'—a gesture highlighting his oration—as indicating that his speech will have the power to expose the hearts of both Elymas and Sergius Paulus. Second, the speech emphasizes how the Lord's teaching will successfully stand against those who seek to oppose the ways of the Lord. The response of Sergius Paulus functions to bolster 'the apologetic agenda of Luke that esteemed members of the Roman elite, such as Sergius

> **The first study to apply the concept of 'performance'.**

Paulus, could be believers of the Gospel in the Julio-Claudian age precisely in their capacity as proconsul' (p. 58). Den Heijer also briefly notes how Luke uses prophetic scripts such as the biblical contrast between false and true prophets who speak to rulers. The function of Paul's performance is to demonstrate that Paul is a true prophet and that his teaching, in its success before a wise Roman proconsul, is not a superstitious or foolish message, 'but a teaching that strikes highly distinguished Roman senators as convincing and trustworthy' (p. 60).

In 'Performance in Athens (Acts 17:16–34)', chapter five, den Heijer notes how Athens functions to symbolize Greek culture and Gentile idolatry. The Areopagus functions as an important judicial court and this highlights Paul's depiction of 'God as supreme judge over even the most awe-inspiring human court' (p. 137). This corresponds to the major emphasis of Paul's speech, namely, his 'announcement of judgment on behalf of God, and a command from God to mankind to change their mind and conduct, delivered by Paul as his messenger or herald' (p. 142). The successful response, at least amongst Dionysius the Areopagite and Damaris, shows again how Paul's gospel is accepted even by the noteworthy and elite. Paul's speech 'contrasts the excessive religiosity of the Athenians, which is characterized by ignorance, with the reasonable teaching of Paul, thus countering the Roman elite's labelling of the Christians as adherents of a *superstitio*' (p. 165).

Den Heijer successfully shows how the concept of performance illuminates the Lukan strategy of portraying Paul as a character with high moral authority who is able to persuade his audiences of the truth of his prophetic message. He taps into a scholarly trajectory with long-standing pedigree, namely, the Lukan apologetic attempt to depict the early Christian movement as both faithful to the heritage of Israel and as reasonable and non-superstitious. Most of den Heijer's analysis draws upon well-established and largely non-controversial scholarship on the Book of Acts. While I did not find the book necessarily breaking new ground in terms of innovation, I did find the study to be an excellent piece of scholarship which successfully shows how the concept of performance can show how the various elements of Pauline episodes relate to each other.

Joshua W. Jipp
Trinity Evangelical Divinity School

BOOK REVIEWS

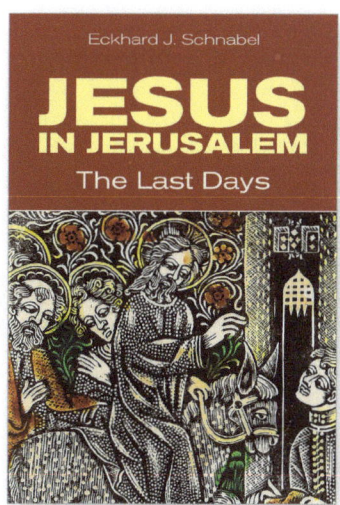

Eckhard J. Schnabel. *Jesus in Jerusalem: The Last Days.* Grand Rapids: Eerdmans, 2018. xxiv+680pp. ISBN 9780802875808 (hardback). $62.99.

The events of the last week of Jesus' earthly life have had a formative influence on the Christian Church. For that reason, they also stand at the centre of New Testament studies. By means of historical enquiry and theological reflection, scholars have mined the New Testament Gospels for information about the content of Jesus' teaching and the circumstances of his death, as well as its wider significance. Keeping abreast of developments in this area of Jesus scholarship is a challenge even for specialists, and threatens to overwhelm pastors and lay readers. That is why Eckhard Schnabel's encyclopaedic study, *Jesus in Jerusalem: The Last Days,* will be welcomed by many. It is a comprehensive, but manageable, survey of the data from the New Testament Gospels relating to the last week of Jesus' life.

Leading into the main body of the work, a brief introductory chapter surveys the methodological landscape of historical Jesus studies. Schnabel notes a waning of confidence in the 'criteria of authenticity' used to ascertain what may be asserted with confidence about the historical Jesus and laments 'the flight from history' in Gospel studies (p.3). He describes the Gospels as biographies of Jesus, which are compiled from eyewitness testimony. Even allowing for the inevitable 'perspectives' of the eyewitnesses and Gospel writers, it is 'neither gullible nor uncritical' to treat the Gospels as 'good historical sources' which document the last week of the life of Jesus (p.7). This confidence in the historical reliability of the Gospels serves a pastoral purpose as 'it will help believers grasp in fresh ways what it means to be a follower of Jesus, who was crucified in Jerusalem in AD 30 and whom God raised from the dead on the third day' (p.9).

The main body of *Jesus in Jerusalem* is composed of five chapters: the first describes seventy-two people who appear in the Gospel narrative; the second provides background information on seventeen places which figure in the Gospel narrative; the third offers a detailed description of what happened in each day of Jesus' final week in Jerusalem; the fourth recounts twenty-four events which took place during Jesus' last days; and the fifth assesses the significance of Jesus' final week by surveying five theological themes.

Of the seventy-two people described in chapter one, forty-three are individual persons, while the rest are groups of people; thirty are mentioned by name, while others are unnamed (such as the disciple from Emmaus, the poor widow, and the relative of Malchus) or larger groupings (such as crowds, tax-collectors, Sadducees and Herodians). Thus, the chapter provides information which would not normally be found in bible dictionaries or encyclopaedias (for example 'the man with sponge at Golgotha', p.101). Naturally, significant biographical information is given about Jesus and his main followers (both male and female), as well as those who played important roles in Jesus' arrest, trial and execution. The discussion of these figures leaves few avenues of enquiry unexplored. For instance, in the section on Nicodemus, there is a lengthy discussion of how he might fit into the large and complex network of the ben Gurion family in Jerusalem (p.35–39). The discussion on Pilate challenges the commonly held view that Pilate was a client of L. Aelius Sejanus and that Sejanus' fall from grace in Rome weakened Pilate's hand in the face of Jewish demands for Jesus' death (p.93). In each case the author's argument is supported by extensive references in endnotes. These provide the reader with many leads for further research and ample opportunity to consider alternative conclusions.

Chapter two gives a valuable compendium of background information about seventeen places which are either named (such as the Mount of Olives, Bethany and Bethphage) or alluded to (Akeldama and the Lithostrotos or stone pavement) in the gospel narratives of Jesus' final week in and around Jerusalem. As the Gospels do not give detailed descriptions of these places (p.102) this section is, understandably, less focused on examination of the text of the Gospels, and more on extra-biblical sources which shed light on the Gospels.

Chapter three, on the timeline of Jesus' last week in Jerusalem, begins with a brief but cogent statement of the arguments supporting an early date for Jesus' crucifixion: AD 30 (April 7th). Thereafter the events of each day as they are narrated in the Gospels are synthesised. Two apparent discrepancies between John and the Synoptic gospels are discussed in some detail: the date of the Last Supper and the time of Jesus' crucifixion. The wide range of explanations of why the Synoptic Gospels present the Last Supper as a Passover meal on the Thursday, while John places the Last Supper before the Passover, are fairly summarised and examined. The explanation which Schnabel adopts is that the marker for the beginning of the month of Nisan that year was 'a questionable new moon' which resulted in the Priests and Pharisees observing the 14th of Nisan on different days (p.146). The other matter of disputed chronology is the discrepancy between Mark 15:25 and John 19:14 concerning time of Jesus' crucifixion. Not every reader will be convinced by the explanation that John gives an approximate time, and that the crucifixion began at around 11 am, but the analysis is worthy of serious consideration.

Chapter 4 analyses twenty-four events from Jesus' last week. These proceed in sequence from the anointing in Bethany to the resurrection appearances of Jesus. Each section provides 'a synthetic account' of the events as reported in the four canonical gospels, so as to give a canonical overview, yet without losing sight of the distinctive perspective of each evangelist. John in particular embeds in his narrative the theological reasons for Jesus' death (notably Caiaphas' proposal in John 11:51–52), while at the same time recording '"a straightforwardly historical explanation" of the causes of Jesus arrest, trial and death' (p.153).

Although it is not one of the twenty-four events specifically addressed, Schnabel describes the raising of Lazarus as the first of three events which lead to the decision of the Jewish leaders to seek the execution of Jesus (p.152–53). The two others are the anointing of Jesus at Bethany (which was a turning point for Judas, p.165) and 'Jesus' prophetic action on the Temple Mount' (p.159–65).

Interestingly, Schnabel finds the common explanation of 'the cleansing of the Temple'—that Jesus was protesting against the corruption of the Temple by its priestly guardians—to be wanting (p.161). Instead, basing his reading on the Old Testament passages quoted by Jesus, he argues that Jesus was announcing 'the beginning of the messianic era when gentiles will worship Israel's God and the coming destruction of the temple' (p.164).

Schnabel's comments on the cursing of the fig tree critique another popular interpretation of the gospel narrative. He rejects the explanation of Mark 11:12–25 as a rhetorical 'sandwich' which surrounds the cleansing of

Confidence in the historical reliability of the Gospels.

the temple with accounts of the cursing and subsequent withering of the fig tree, in order to suggest that Jesus was actually cursing the Temple (p.167). Instead, focusing on Jesus' teaching in Mark 11:22, Schnabel argues that the fig-tree passages teach Jesus' disciples how to pray humbly but hopefully (p.168). Even if the reader prefers other explanations of these events, Schnabel's alternative perspective is provocative and refreshing.

Although Schnabel has reflected on the theological significance of the people, places, timelines and events in his first four chapters, chapter five places the focus squarely on the abiding significance of the events of Jesus final week in Jerusalem. He draws together the threads of theological reflection under five headings: Jesus the Messiah; Jesus and the Temple; Jesus' death; Jesus' resurrection; and Jesus' mission and the mission of his followers. This section is more than a concluding summary; it seeks to explain how the teaching of Jesus and the events of his last days in Jerusalem—especially his death and resurrection—shaped the worship, teaching and mission of early Christianity. The implications of Jesus' death and resurrection which Schnabel examines are many and varied. The following are just a sample: the prominence and implications of the title χριστός in the New Testament letters and Christian liturgy (p.379–81); Jürgen Moltmann's thesis that a 'death within God' took place when Jesus died on the cross (p.386); and the influence of Christian resurrection narratives upon Roman fictional literature (p.392). Most importantly, Schnabel emphasises, if Jesus had not died and risen in the course of that momentous week in Jerusalem it is most unlikely that his life would have been recorded at all, or that five and a half million congregations of Christians would exist today (p.397).

In conclusion, this reviewer has to pay tribute to Schnabel's encyclopaedic work of scholarship on the last days of Jesus. The voluminous endnotes are a testimony to the research which underpins the sometimes brief and often illuminating articles on specific people, places and events. The use of endnotes rather than footnotes means that these articles are not overshadowed by references to secondary sources. Thus, they provide an excellent resource for pastors and general readers in their study of the Gospels. St. Augustine stated that the Gospel of John was 'deep enough for an elephant to swim and shallow enough for a child not to drown.' *Jesus in Jerusalem* contains abundant material into which specialists may dive and swim to their hearts' content. Yet it also contains helpful summaries which disciples of Jesus may consult in order to discover afresh the person of their Lord and Saviour.

Andrew Stewart
Reformed Theological College

Centre for Gospels and Acts Research Volumes

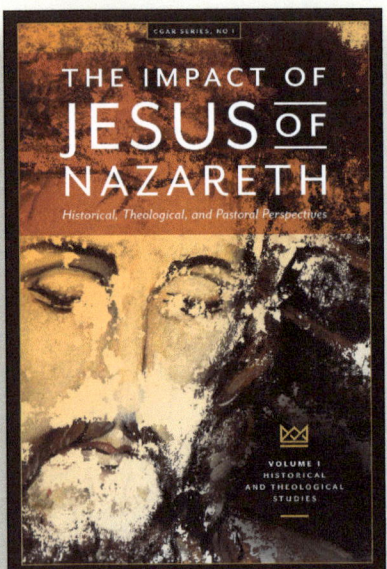
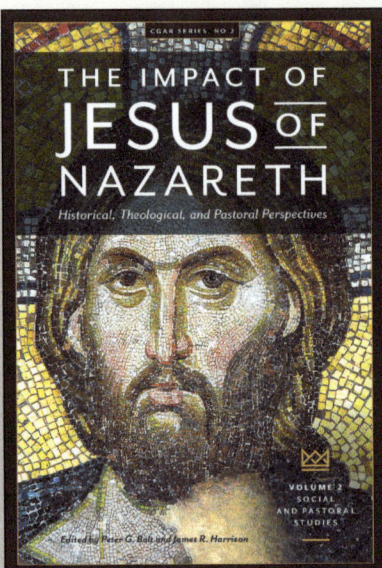
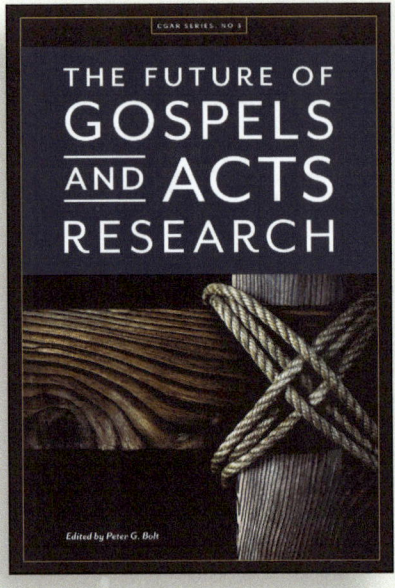

The Impact of Jesus of Nazareth: Historical, Theological, and Pastoral Perspectives
CGAR Series, No 1

Despite his relatively short life and his tragic death, Jesus of Nazareth made a profound impact upon the first-century Graeco-Roman world. Wherever his heritage is celebrated and remembered, Jesus of Nazareth continues to make an impact. The greatness of Jesus of Nazareth was supremely displayed in his moment of greatest weakness on the cross. Those who felt his immediate impact either chafed under his teaching, or embraced it, but rarely did anyone remain untouched by him. The mystery of his salvific death inspires; the power of his resurrection hope sustains; and his impact continues to work its way outwards in manifold implications as his gospel finds a hearing, wherever and whenever that might be.

The Impact of Jesus of Nazareth: Historical, Theological, and Pastoral Perspectives
CGAR Series, No 2

Writing from a variety of perspectives, the essays in these two volumes, explore the impact of Jesus of Nazareth on his own and subsequent times. After Volume 1 collects historical and theological essays, volume 2 moves from the historical and theological, towards the wider impact of Jesus on pastoral practice in our contemporary world.

The Future of Gospels and Acts Research
CGAR Series, No 3

This volume of essays represents a selection of eleven of the papers from the Centre for Gospels and Acts Research 2019 conference, 'Discerning the Trends'. This collection provides a sounding of current Gospels and Acts research. Each essay builds on current research and opens up new questions charting a direction for research in the future.

Purchase via the SCD Press Shop
scd.edu.au/shop/
or email scdpress@scd.edu.au.

Centre for Gospels and Acts Research Volume 4

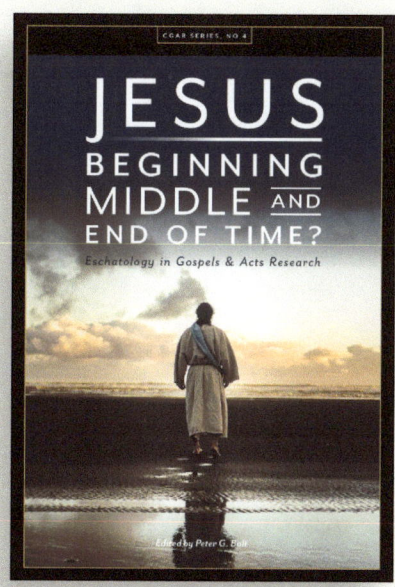

**Peter G. Bolt (ed.), *Jesus: Beginning, Middle, & End of Time? Eschatology in Gospels & Acts Research*
(CGAR Series, No 4; Macquarie Park, NSW: SCD Press, 2022)**

Table of Contents

Craig A. Evans	Kingdoms in Conflict I: The Four-Kingdoms Schema In The East And The West
Craig A. Evans	Kingdoms in Conflict II: The Jesus Movement And The Roman Empire
David J. Neville	Ethics and Eschatology in the Synoptic Tradition: A Theological-Moral Response to N. T. Wright's Gifford Lectures
Mary J. Marshall	The 'New Covenant' Debate Revisited
Jonathan Thambyrajah	Wicked Wizards of the East: The μάγοι in Historical Context and Ambiguity as Narrative Technique in Matthew 2
Daniel W. McManigal	The Function of John's Baptism in Matthew's Gospel: A Dramatised Declaration of the Coming Judgement
Tim Bradford	'Like the angels'?: Embodiment and Eschatology in Matthew's Gospel
Steven Groom	The Use of Verbal Aspect for Differentiating between the Events associated with Christ's παρουσία and Christ's ἔρχομαι Comings in Matthew 24:42-44.
Michael Modini	The Markan Alphabet Theory: Eschatological Origins of Mark's Gospel
Peter G. Bolt	The Eschatological Coherence of Mark 11:20-25
Anthony Petterson	The Apocalyptic Attack of Jerusalem by Non-Israelite Nations In Zechariah 9-14 and the Death of Jesus In Mark 13
Michele Connolly	Mark 13: Literary Impetus to the Passion Narrative and Christian Faith for All Generations
Denise Powell	The View from the Ditch: Reading the Good Samaritan Parable as Wisdom not Virtue
James R. Harrison	From Petitionary Rhetoric to Eschatological Vindication: Comparing the Widow Aurelia Artemis from Theadelphia with Jesus' Persistent Widow (Luke 18:1-8)
Debra Snoddy	Realising the Now and the Not Yet of the Realised Eschatology in the Gospel of John: John's Focus and Purpose and Why it Still Matters to All Christians.
John D. Griffiths	In The Last Days: Alteration, Eschatology, and the Spirit
Francis Otobo	'In the last days...' (Acts 2:17): Eschatology, Cultural Diversity, and the Challenge of Inclusivity in Acts
C. Bruce Riding	Contrary to Popular Tradition, Saul/Paul was not Converted to Christianity on the Road to Damascus